FOCUS
ON
GRAMMAR

AN INTEGRATED SKILLS APPROACH

SECOND EDITION

IRENE E. SCHOENBERG
JAY MAURER

PEARSON
Longman

FOCUS ON GRAMMAR 1: **An Integrated Skills Approach**

Pearson Education, 10 Bank Street, White Plains, NY 10606

Vice president, multimedia and skills: Sherry Preiss
Executive editor: Laura Le Dréan
Development editor: John Barnes
Associate managing editor: Jane Townsend
Production supervisor: Christine Edmonds
Art director: Ann France
Marketing director: Oliva Fernández
Senior manufacturing buyer: Nancy Flaggman
Photo research: Aerin Csigay
Cover design: Rhea Banker
Cover images: background: Comstock Images; background shell and center shell: Nick Koudis
Text design: Quorum Creative Services, Rhea Banker
Text composition: ElectraGraphics, Inc.
Text font: 11/13 New Aster, 11/13 Myriad Roman

Photo credits: see p. x.

Illustrators: Steve Attoe: pp. 1, 2, 9, 10 (top), 11, 13, 18, 25, 30, 32, 49, 53, 56, 65, 70, 74, 82, 85, 87, 89, 90 (middle), 96, 100, 101, 105, 109, 110, 111, 114, 115, 122, 123 (bottom), 129, 130, 131, 135, 139, 143, 146, 150, 151, 153, 156, 157, 161, 167, 170, 171, 177, 187, 191, 193, 200, 204, 208, 218, 222, 225, 229, 232, 235, 242, 247, 248, 255, 258, 260, 262; Ronald Chironna: pp. 39, 132 (top), 147; Paul McCusker: pp. 47, 188, 215, 249 (top), 256 (top); Tom Newsom: pp. 10 (bottom), 31, 33 (top), 75 (top), 83, 106, 121, 138, 152 (bottom), 164, 176, 211 (bottom), 233 (top), 253; Dusan Petricic: pp. 5 (bottom), 6 (top), 17, 33 (bottom), 38, 50, 55, 57, 94, 159, 211 (top), 243, 246, 254, 256 (bottom); Steve Schulman: pp. 6 (bottom), 40 (top), 66, 97 (top), 116, 123 (top), 145, 154, 214, 226, A-5; Susan Scott: pp. 19 (bottom), 75 (bottom), 90 (top); Tom Sperling: pp. 19 (top), 27, 90 (bottom), 97 (bottom), 113, 140, 141, 249 (bottom); Gary Torrisi: pp. 3, 5 (top), 8, 26, 40 (bottom), 41, 43, 48, 78, 152 (top), 178, 194, 201, 219, FG-1, FG-2.

Library of Congress Cataloging-in-Publication Data

Focus on grammar. An integrated skills approach — 3rd ed. [Level 1: 2d ed.]
    p. cm.
   ISBN 0-13-147466-9 (v. 1 : student book : alk. paper) — ISBN 0-13-189971-6 (v. 2 : student book : alk. paper) — ISBN 0-13-189984-8 (v. 3 : student book : alk. paper) — ISBN 0-13-190008-0 (v. 4 : student book : alk. paper) — ISBN 0-13-191273-9 (v. 5 : student book : alk. paper)
   1. English language—Textbooks for foreign speakers. 2. English language—Grammar—Problems, exercises, etc.
PE1128.F555 2005
428.2'4—dc22

2005007655

ISBNs: 0-13-147466-9 (Student Book)
         0-13-147480-4 (Student Book with Audio CD)

LONGMAN ON THE **WEB**

Longman.com offers online resources for teachers and students. Access our Companion Websites, our online catalog, and our local offices around the world.

Visit us at **longman.com**.

Printed in the United States of America
      5 6 7 8 9 10—WC—12 11 10 09 08   (Student Book)
      6 7 8 9 10—WC—12 11 10 09 08   (Student Book with Audio CD)

CONTENTS

FROM GRAMMAR TO WRITING

APPENDICES

GLOSSARY OF GRAMMAR TERMS

INFORMATION GAPS

PUZZLES, GAMES, AND INFORMATION GAPS ANSWER KEY

REVIEW TESTS ANSWER KEY

INDEX

ABOUT THE AUTHORS

Irene E. Schoenberg has taught ESL for more than two decades at Hunter College's International English Language Institute and at Columbia University's American Language Program. Ms. Schoenberg holds a master's degree in TESOL from Columbia University. She has trained ESL and EFL teachers at Columbia University's Teachers College and at the New School University. She has given workshops and academic presentations at conferences, English language schools, and universities in Brazil, Chile, Dubai, El Salvador, Guatemala, Japan, Mexico, Nicaragua, Peru, Taiwan, Thailand, and throughout the United States.

Ms. Schoenberg is the author of *Talk about Trivia*; *Talk about Values*; *Speaking of Values 1: Conversation and Listening*; *Topics from A to Z*, Books 1 and 2; and *Focus on Grammar 2: An Integrated Skills Approach*. She is the co-author with Jay Maurer of the *True Colors* series and *Focus on Grammar 1: An Integrated Skills Approach*.

Jay Maurer has taught English in binational centers, colleges, and universities in Portugal, Spain, Mexico, the Somali Republic, and the United States; and intensive English at Columbia University's American Language Program. In addition, he has been a teacher of college composition and literature at Santa Fe Community College and Northern New Mexico Community College. Mr. Maurer holds M.A. and M.Ed. degrees in Applied Linguistics and a Ph.D. degree in The Teaching of English, all from Columbia University.

Mr. Maurer is the co-author of the three-level *Structure Practice in Context* series; co-author of the *True Voices* video series; co-author of *Teen Zone II*; and author of *Focus on Grammar 5: An Integrated Skills Approach*. He is the co-author with Irene Schoenberg of the five-level *True Colors* series and of *Focus on Grammar 1: An Integrated Skills Approach*. Currently he writes and teaches in Seattle, Washington.

CREDITS

Grateful acknowledgment is given to the following for providing photographs:

p. 14 Mike Finn-Kelcey/Reuters/Corbis; **p. 18** Royalty-Free/Corbis;
p. 25 *(top left)* age fotostock/George White, *(right)* Chuck Pefley/Alamy,
(bottom left) Douglas Peebles/Corbis; **p. 29** *(top)* Stockdisc/Getty Images,
(bottom) DesignPics Inc./Index Stock Imagery; **p. 56** Hubert Stadler/Corbis;
p. 57 Francis G. Mayer/Corbis; **p. 63** Woods Wheatcroft/Outdoor Collection/
Aurora; **p. 66** *(left)* Reuters/Corbis, *(right)* Adrian Dennis/AFP/Getty Images;
p. 73 *(top)* Bohemian Nomad Picturemakers/Corbis, *(bottom)* E. Hummel/zefa/
Corbis; **p. 93** *(left)* ArenaPal/Topham/The Images Works, *(right)* William
Coupon/Corbis; **pp. 116, 120** DENNIS THE MENACE®, used by permission
of Hank Ketcham and © by North America Syndicate; **p. 127** *(left)* Joseph
Sohm/ChromoSohm Inc./Corbis, *(middle)* Torleif Svensson/Corbis, *(right)* age
fotostock/SuperStock; **p. 132** Patrick Sheandell O'Carroll/Getty Images;
p. 180 Robert Galbraith/Reuters/Corbis; **p. 193** *(left)* Jack Stein Grove/
PhotoEdit, *(right)* Jeremy Horner/Getty Images; **p. 196** Richard Nowitz
Photography; **p. 197** Dave L. Ryan/Index Stock Imagery; **p. 205** Alan Becker/
Getty Images; **p. 217** Richard Olsenius/Getty Images; **p. 225** Hugh Sitton/Getty
Images; **p. 230** John Morrison/Getty Images; **p. 238** Angelo Cavalli/Index Stock
Imagery; **p. 243** AP/Wide World Photos; **p. FG-1** Bananastock/Jupiterimages;
p. FG-3 i2i Images/Photis/Jupiterimages; **p. FG-5** David Stoecklein/Corbis;
p. FG-6 age fotostock/Roberto Benzi; **p. FG-7** *(left)* Warner Bros./ZUMA/Corbis,
(right) Miramax/Imagine/Parkway Productions/The Kobal Collection/Kraychyk,
George; **p. FG-9** Richard Hamilton Smith/Corbis; **p. FG-11** Robert Landau/
Corbis; **p. IG-3** *(left)* age fotostock/J. D. Heaton, *(middle)* Steve Allen/Getty
Images, *(right)* Royalty-Free/Corbis.

INTRODUCTION

The *Focus on Grammar* Series

Written by ESL/EFL professionals, *Focus on Grammar: An Integrated Skills Approach* helps students to understand and practice English grammar. The primary aim of the course is for students to gain confidence in their ability to speak and write English accurately and fluently.

The **new edition** retains this popular series' focus on English grammar through lively listening, speaking, reading, and writing activities. The new *Focus on Grammar* also maintains the same five-level progression as the previous edition:

- Level 1 (Beginning, formerly Introductory)
- Level 2 (High-Beginning, formerly Basic)
- Level 3 (Intermediate)
- Level 4 (High-Intermediate)
- Level 5 (Advanced)

What is the *Focus on Grammar* methodology?

Both controlled and communicative practice

While students expect and need to learn the formal rules of a language, it is crucial that they also practice new structures in a variety of contexts in order to internalize and master them. To this end, *Focus on Grammar* provides an abundance of both controlled and communicative exercises so that students can bridge the gap between knowing grammatical structures and using them. The many communicative activities in each Student Book unit provide opportunity for critical thinking while enabling students to personalize what they have learned in order to talk to one another with ease about hundreds of everyday issues.

A unique four-step approach

The series follows a four-step approach:

Step 1: Grammar in Context shows the new structures in natural contexts, such as conversations, e-mail messages, and personal ads.

Step 2: Grammar Presentation presents the structures in clear and accessible grammar charts, notes, and examples.

Step 3: Focused Practice of both form and meaning of new structures is provided in numerous and varied controlled exercises.

Step 4: Communication Practice allows students to use the new structures freely and creatively in motivating, open-ended activities.

Thorough recycling

Underpinning the scope and sequence of the *Focus on Grammar* series is the belief that students need to use target structures many times, in different contexts, and at increasing levels of difficulty. For this reason, new grammar is constantly recycled throughout the book so that students have maximum exposure to the target forms and become comfortable using them in speech and in writing.

A complete classroom text and reference guide

A major goal in the development of *Focus on Grammar* has been to provide students with books that serve not only as vehicles for classroom instruction but also as resources for reference and self-study. In each Student Book, the combination of grammar charts, grammar notes, a glossary of grammar terms, and extensive appendices provides a complete and invaluable reference guide for students.

Ongoing Assessment

Review Tests at the end of each part of the Student Book allow for continual self-assessment. In addition, the tests in the new *Focus on Grammar* Assessment Package provide teachers with a valid, reliable, and practical means of determining students' appropriate levels of placement in the course and of assessing students' achievement throughout the course. At Levels 4 (High-Intermediate) and 5 (Advanced), proficiency tests are also available to give teachers an overview of their students' general grammar knowledge.

What are the components of each level of *Focus on Grammar*?

Student Book

The Student Book is divided into eight or more parts, depending on the level. Each part contains grammatically related units, with each unit focusing on specific grammatical structures; where appropriate, units present contrasting forms. The exercises in each unit are thematically related to one another, and all units have the same clear, easy-to-follow format.

Teacher's Manual

The Teacher's Manual contains a variety of suggestions and information to enrich the material in the Student Book. It includes general teaching suggestions for each section of a typical unit, answers to frequently asked questions, unit-by-unit teaching tips with ideas for further communicative practice, and a supplementary activity section. Answers to the Student Book exercises and audioscripts of the listening activities are found at the back of the Teacher's Manual. Also included in the Teacher's Manual is a CD-ROM of teaching tools, including PowerPoint® Presentations that offer alternative ways of presenting selected grammar structures.

Workbook

The Workbook accompanying each level of *Focus on Grammar* provides additional exercises appropriate for self-study of the target grammar of each Student Book unit. Tests included in each Workbook provide students with additional opportunities for self-assessment.

Audio Program

All of the listening exercises from the Student Book, as well as the Grammar in Context passages and other appropriate exercises, are included on the program's CDs. In the book, the symbol ∩ appears next to the listening exercises. Another symbol, ∩, indicating that listening is optional, appears next to the Grammar in Context passages and some exercises. Scripts for all of the listening exercises appear in the Teacher's Manual and may be used as an alternative way of presenting the activities.

Some Student Books are packaged with a Student Audio CD. This CD includes the listening exercise from each unit and any other exercises that have an essential listening component.

CD-ROM

The *Focus on Grammar* CD-ROM provides students with individualized practice and immediate feedback. Fully contextualized and interactive, the activities broaden and extend practice of the grammatical structures in the reading, writing, speaking, and listening skills areas. The CD-ROM includes grammar review, review tests, score-based remedial practice, games, and all relevant reference material from the Student Book. It can also be used in conjunction with the *Longman Interactive American Dictionary* CD-ROM.

Assessment Package (NEW)

An extensive, comprehensive Assessment Package has been developed for each level of the third edition of *Focus on Grammar*. The components of the Assessment Package are:

1. Placement, Diagnostic, and Achievement Tests

- Placement Test, to screen students and place them into the correct level
- Diagnostic Tests for each part of the Student Book
- Unit Achievement Tests for each unit of the Student Book
- Part Achievement Tests for each part of the Student Book

2. Audio CD

The listening portions of the Placement, Diagnostic, and Achievement Tests are recorded on CDs. The scripts appear in the Assessment Package.

3. Test-Generating Software

The test-bank software provides thousands of questions from which teachers can create class-appropriate tests. All items are labeled according to the grammar structure they are testing, so teachers can easily select relevant items; they can also design their own items to add to their tests.

Transparencies (NEW)

Transparencies of all the grammar charts in the student book are also available. These transparencies are a classroom visual aid that will help instructors point out important patterns and structures of grammar.

Companion Website

The companion website contains a wealth of information and activities for both teachers and students. In addition to general information about the course pedagogy, the website provides extensive practice exercises for the classroom, a language lab, or at home.

What's new in this edition of the Student Book?

In response to users' requests, this edition has:

- a new four-color design
- easy-to-read color coding for the four steps
- new and updated texts for Grammar in Context
- more exercise items
- an editing (error analysis) exercise in each unit
- From Grammar to Writing exercises for each part
- a Glossary of Grammar Terms
- expanded Appendices

References

Alexander, L. G. (1988). *Longman English Grammar.* White Plains, NY: Longman.

Biber, D., S. Conrad, E. Finegan, S. Johansson, and G. Leech (1999). *Longman Grammar of Spoken and Written English.* White Plains, NY: Longman.

Celce-Murcia, M., and D. Freeman (1999). *The Grammar Book.* Boston: Heinle and Heinle.

Celce-Murcia, M., and S. Hilles (1988). *Techniques and Resources in Teaching Grammar.* New York: Oxford University Press.

Firsten, R. (2002). *The ELT Grammar Book.* Burlingame, CA: Alta Book Center Publishers.

Garner, B. (2003). *Garner's Modern American Usage.* New York: Oxford University Press.

Greenbaum, S. (1996). *The Oxford English Grammar.* New York: Oxford University Press.

Leech, G. (2004). *Meaning and the English Verb.* Harlow, UK: Pearson.

Lewis, M. (1997). *Implementing the Lexical Approach.* Hove, East Sussex, UK: Language Teaching Publications.

Longman Dictionary of English Language and Culture. (2002). Harlow, UK: Longman.

Willis, D. (2003). *Rules, Patterns, and Words.* New York: Cambridge University Press.

TOUR OF A UNIT

Each unit in the *Focus on Grammar* series presents a specific grammar structure or structures and develops a major theme, which is set by the opening text. All units follow the same unique **four-step approach**.

Step 1: Grammar in Context

The **conversation** or other text in this section shows the grammar structure in a natural context. The high-interest text presents authentic language in a variety of real-life formats. Students can listen to the text on an audio CD to get accustomed to the sound of the grammar structure in a natural context.

Lively text *that presents the grammar structure in a realistic context.*

Words *section presents graphic definitions to help students enrich their vocabulary.*

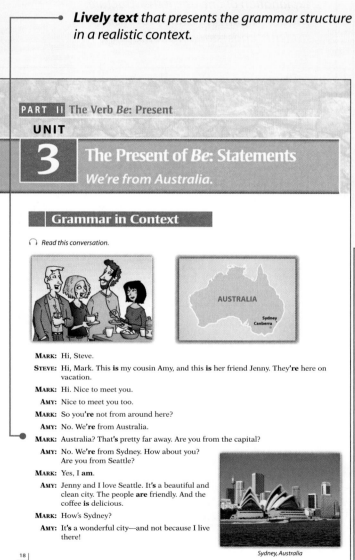

PART II The Verb *Be*: Present

UNIT 3
The Present of *Be*: Statements
We're from Australia.

Grammar in Context

∩ *Read this conversation.*

AUSTRALIA
Sydney
Canberra

MARK: Hi, Steve.
STEVE: Hi, Mark. This **is** my cousin Amy, and this **is** her friend Jenny. They**'re** here on vacation.
MARK: Hi. Nice to meet you.
AMY: Nice to meet you too.
MARK: So you**'re** not from around here?
AMY: No. We**'re** from Australia.
MARK: Australia? That**'s** pretty far away. Are you from the capital?
AMY: No. We**'re** from Sydney. How about you? Are you from Seattle?
MARK: Yes, I **am**.
AMY: Jenny and I love Seattle. It**'s** a beautiful and clean city. The people **are** friendly. And the coffee **is** delicious.
MARK: How's Sydney?
AMY: It**'s** a wonderful city—and not because I live there!

Sydney, Australia

18

Words

∩ *Do you know these words? Read the words. Write new words in your notebook.*

Mmm . . . good.   Ugh.

clean   dirty   delicious   awful

Expressions

∩ *Do you know these expressions? Read the conversations. Write new expressions in your notebook.*

1. A: Are you *from around here*?
   B: No, I'm from Australia.

2. A: Are you here *on business*?
   B: No, we're here *on vacation*.

Working Together

A *Practice the conversation in the opening reading with two partners.*

B *Work with a partner. Take turns. Ask and answer the question.*

Are you here on business?   Yes, I am.

Other Possible Answers
No, I'm not. I live here.
No, I'm not. I'm here on vacation.
No, I'm not. I'm a student here.

C *What do you think about the city you are in? Talk to your partner.*
• The people are friendly here.
• The city is clean.
• The coffee is delicious.

Expressions *section presents idiomatic expressions and common phrases in conversations*

*A **post-reading activity** helps students understand the text and focus on the grammar structure.*

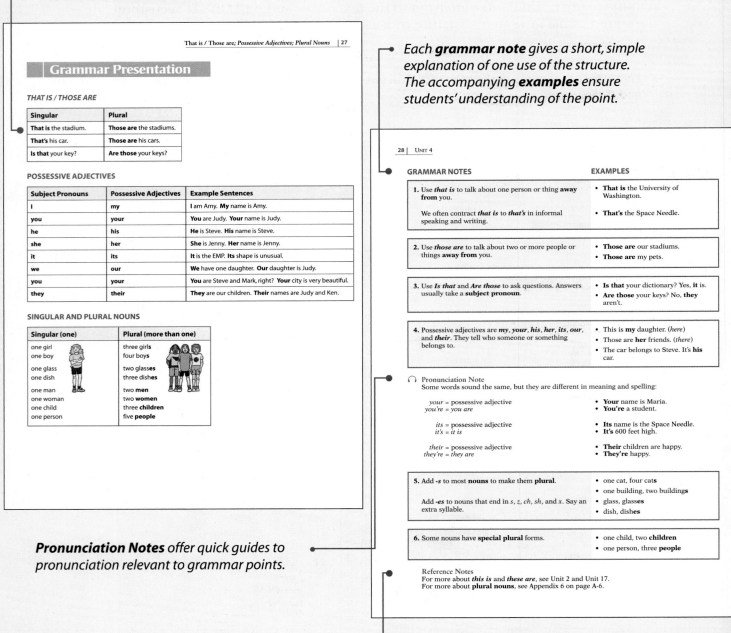

Step 2: Grammar Presentation

This section is made up of grammar charts, notes, and examples. The **grammar charts** focus on the forms of the grammar structure. The **grammar notes** and **examples** focus on the meanings and uses of the structure.

Clear and easy-to-read **grammar charts** present the grammar structure in all its forms and combinations.

Each **grammar note** gives a short, simple explanation of one use of the structure. The accompanying **examples** ensure students' understanding of the point.

Pronunciation Notes offer quick guides to pronunciation relevant to grammar points.

Reference notes direct students to additional information and examples.

That is / Those are; Possessive Adjectives; Plural Nouns | 27

Grammar Presentation

THAT IS / THOSE ARE

Singular	Plural
That is the stadium.	**Those are** the stadiums.
That's his car.	**Those are** his cars.
Is that your key?	**Are those** your keys?

POSSESSIVE ADJECTIVES

Subject Pronouns	Possessive Adjectives	Example Sentences
I	my	I am Amy. **My** name is Amy.
you	your	**You** are Judy. **Your** name is Judy.
he	his	**He** is Steve. **His** name is Steve.
she	her	**She** is Jenny. **Her** name is Jenny.
it	its	**It** is the EMP. **Its** shape is unusual.
we	our	**We** have one daughter. **Our** daughter is Judy.
you	your	**You** are Steve and Mark, right? **Your** city is very beautiful.
they	their	**They** are our children. **Their** names are Judy and Ken.

SINGULAR AND PLURAL NOUNS

Singular (one)	Plural (more than one)
one girl one boy	three girls four boys
one glass one dish	two glasses three dishes
one man one woman one child one person	two men two women three children five people

---

28 | UNIT 4

GRAMMAR NOTES	EXAMPLES
1. Use *that is* to talk about one person or thing **away from** you. We often contract *that is* to *that's* in informal speaking and writing.	• **That is** the University of Washington. • **That's** the Space Needle.
2. Use *those are* to talk about two or more people or things **away from** you.	• **Those are** our stadiums. • **Those are** my pets.
3. Use *Is that* and *Are those* to ask questions. Answers usually take a **subject pronoun**.	• **Is that** your dictionary? Yes, **it** is. • **Are those** your keys? No, **they** aren't.
4. Possessive adjectives are *my*, *your*, *his*, *her*, *its*, *our*, and *their*. They tell who someone or something belongs to.	• This is **my** daughter. (*here*) • Those are **her** friends. (*there*) • The car belongs to Steve. It's **his** car.

🎧 Pronunciation Note
Some words sound the same, but they are different in meaning and spelling:

your = possessive adjective *you're = you are*	• **Your** name is Maria. • **You're** a student.
its = possessive adjective *it's = it is*	• **Its** name is the Space Needle. • **It's** 600 feet high.
their = possessive adjective *they're = they are*	• **Their** children are happy. • **They're** happy.

5. Add *-s* to most **nouns** to make them **plural**. Add *-es* to nouns that end in *s, z, ch, sh,* and *x*. Say an extra syllable.	• one cat, four cat**s** • one building, two building**s** • glass, glass**es** • dish, dish**es**
6. Some nouns have **special plural** forms.	• one child, two **children** • one person, three **people**

Reference Notes
For more about *this is* and *these are*, see Unit 2 and Unit 17.
For more about **plural nouns**, see Appendix 6 on page A-6.

Step 3: Focused Practice

This section provides students with a variety of contextualized **controlled exercises** to practice both the forms and the uses of the grammar structure.

● Focused Practice *always begins with a "for recognition only" exercise called* **Discover the Grammar**.

The Past of Be: Wh- Questions | 59

Focused Practice

1 DISCOVER THE GRAMMAR

Circle the question word. Underline the verb **be**. *Then match these questions and answers.*

_b_ **1.** (Where) were you last night?   **a.** It was warm.

____ **2.** Who was with you?   **b.** I was at a soccer game.

____ **3.** How was the game?   **c.** Two hours.

____ **4.** How long was the game?   **d.** Exciting.

____ **5.** How was the weather?   **e.** My sister.

2 CONVERSATIONS   *Grammar Notes 1–5*

Put these words in the right order. Make conversations.

1. A: How / your weekend / was / ?   **A:** _How was your weekend?_

   B: was / It / great / .   **B:** _____

2. A: you / were / Where / ?   **A:** _____

   B: a jazz concert / At / .   **B:** _____

3. A: was / When / the concert / ?   **A:** _____

   B: last night / was / It / .   **B:** _____

4. A: the musician / Who / was / ?   **A:** _____

   B: was / Wynton Marsalis / It / .   **B:** _____

5. A: the concert / long / was / How / ?   **A:** _____

   B: two hours / It / was / .   **B:** _____

3 WHAT'S THE QUESTION?   *Grammar Notes 1–6*

Write questions about the <u>underlined</u> words.

1. A: _How was the weather_ ?   **3. A:** _____ Pierre on

   B: It was <u>sunny</u>.   Monday?

2. A: _____ at the   **B:** He was <u>in Paris</u>.

   movies?   **4. A:** _____ ?

   B: <u>Mark</u> was.   **B:** The party was <u>yesterday</u>.

                              (continued)

● Exercises are **cross-referenced** to the appropriate grammar notes to provide a quick review.

● A **variety of exercise types** *guide students from recognition to accurate production of the grammar structure.*

44 | UNIT 6

4 WHERE'S THE POST OFFICE?   *Grammar Notes 1–3*

A *Complete this conversation. Use the sentences in the box.*

| Is it on Main Street? | Where's First Avenue? |
| Turn right at the corner. | Is this Main Street? |

   MAN: Excuse me. _Is this Main Street?_

WOMAN: Yes, it is. We're on Main Street near Second Avenue.

   MAN: I'm looking for the post office. _____

WOMAN: No, it's not. It's on First Avenue.

   MAN: Oh. _____

WOMAN: Walk to the corner of this street. _____

        The post office is next to the bank. It's on the corner of First and Washington.

🎧 **B** *Listen and check your work.*

C *Look at the map in Exercise 3. Where are the man and woman now? Put an* **X** *on the street.*

5 EDITING

Correct these conversations. There are eight mistakes. The first mistake is already corrected.

1. A: _Where_ ~~Where's~~ are you from?

   B: I'm from Bogotá.

   A: Where Bogotá?

   B: It's on Colombia.

2. A: Is your apartment in this floor?

   B: No, it's on the eight floor.

3. A: Where's the bookstore?

   B: It's First Avenue.

   A: Is it next the museum?

   B: Yes, it is.

4. A: Is the supermarket on First in Main and Washington?

   B: No, it's between Main and Jackson.

● Focused Practice *always ends with an* **editing** *exercise to teach students to quickly find and correct typical mistakes.*

Step 4: Communication Practice

This section provides open-ended **communicative activities** giving students the opportunity to use the grammar structure appropriately and fluently.

A **listening** activity gives students the opportunity to check their aural comprehension.

4 | EDITING

Correct this letter to advice columnist Dahlia. There are seven mistakes. The first mistake is already corrected.

> Dear Dahlia,
>
> My boyfriend, Joe, is wonderful. He's a kind, honest, and intelligent. He has an job good and a heart kind. There's only one problem. He doesn't like to spend money. We always watch TV at his house, and he doesn't even have TV cable. Sometimes we go to frees concerts and picnics. I have fun with Joe, but I want to do differents things. Do you have any suggestions?
>
> Sincerely,
>
> Rosa

Communication Practice

5 | A DESCRIPTION OF MIA

🎧 Listen to the conversation between Ken and his friend Brian. Listen again and find Brian's friend Mia. Put a circle around Mia.

Many exercises and activities are **art-based** to provide visual cues and an interesting context and springboard for meaningful conversations.

Information gaps encourage students to ask and answer questions using target structures.

7 | INFORMATION GAP: WHEN IN THE WORLD?

Work in pairs.

Student B, look at the Information Gap on page IG-4. Follow the instructions there.

Student A, get information from Student B. Ask questions with **when** or **what time**. Then answer Student B's questions. Use the phrases in the box. Use **in, on,** or **at** in each answer.

Example: **A:** When do Americans vote?
B: Americans usually vote on a Tuesday. When do the French vote?
A: The French usually vote on a Sunday.

Student A's questions

1. Americans / vote / ?
2. summer normally begin / in the Southern Hemisphere / ?
3. afternoon / begin / ?
4. Brazilians / celebrate / Carnaval / ?
5. fall normally begin / in the Southern Hemisphere / ?

Carnaval in Brazil

Student A's answers

12:00 midnight	July 1	December 21	September	a Sunday

▶ To check your answers, go to the Answer Key on page P-2.

8 | GAME: IN, ON, AT

Write down the date and time of a big event in your life.

Examples: My sister got married on June 3, 2003, in the evening.
I graduated from college on May 15, 2000, in the afternoon.

Then tell the class about the event. Do not tell them the date or time. Your classmates ask a maximum of 10 yes / no questions to guess the date and the time of the event.

Example: **A:** I got married.
B: Did you get married in July?
A: No, I didn't.
C: Did you get married in June?
A: Yes, I did.

Exciting **games** give students the opportunity to expand on the content of the unit and interact with their classmates creatively and fluently.

TOUR BEYOND THE UNIT

In the *Focus on Grammar* Series, the grammatically related units are grouped into parts, and each part concludes with a **Review Test**.

Review Test

This review section, covering all the grammar structures presented in the part, can be used as a test. A **Review Tests Answer Key** is provided at the back of the book.

The Review Tests *include **multiple-choice questions** in standardized test formats, giving students practice in test taking.*

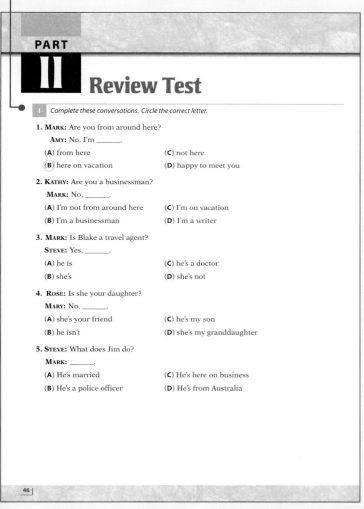

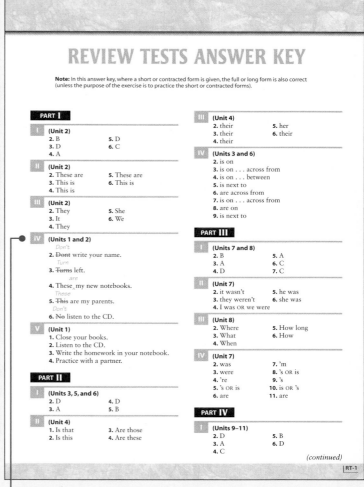

The Review Tests Answer Key *provides **cross-references** to the appropriate unit(s) for easy review.*

From Grammar to Writing

This section at the back of the book contains writing activities for each part. Each activity presents a grammar point which applies specifically to writing, for example, using *can* and *can't* in a written response to an invitation. Students are guided to practice the point in a **piece of extended writing**.

● A *pre-writing activity* focuses attention on details.

PART IV Using the Simple Present

You and a good friend are in different cities. Answer your friend's letter. Follow the model.

Dear _____,
    I often think about you. How is everything in _____? Are you busy? What are your days like? What do you usually do on weekends? Do you ever ski?
        Please write.
                                        _____

Model

Dear Marta,
    I was so happy to hear from you.
    My life here is different. Sometimes it's busy and exciting. Sometimes it's lonely. It's hard to speak a second language all the time.
    I enjoy my job. I'm a graphic artist for a small publisher. I love to design CD and book covers, but I don't love to work on very long books.
    I start work at 9:00 and finish at 5:00. I get to work by train. My co-workers are friendly and helpful, but I don't have any good friends yet.
    In the evening I usually watch videos. On weekends I go to the movies. I still love movies. I never ski. It's too expensive here.
    I miss our trips to the museum and the stores. I also miss our skiing trips.
    Please tell me about yourself. Perhaps you can visit me this summer.
Best wishes,
Alfredo

FG-5

Writing formats include personal letters, notes, e-mail messages, and short compositions.

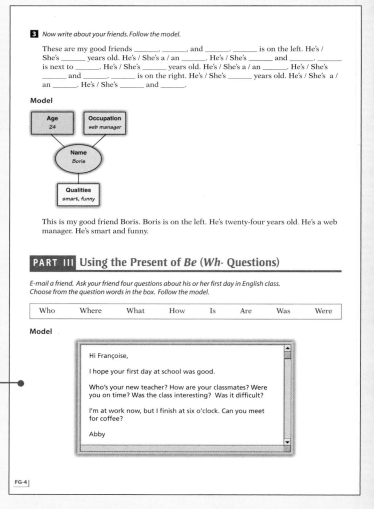

3 *Now write about your friends. Follow the model.*

These are my good friends _____, _____, and _____. _____ is on the left. He's / She's _____ years old. He's / She's a / an _____. He's / She's _____ and _____. _____ is next to _____. He's / She's _____ years old. He's / She's a / an _____. He's / She's _____ and _____. _____ is on the right. He's / She's _____ years old. He's / She's a / an _____. He's / She's _____ and _____.

Model

Age
24

Occupation
web manager

Name
Boris

Qualities
smart, funny

This is my good friend Boris. Boris is on the left. He's twenty-four years old. He's a web manager. He's smart and funny.

PART III Using the Present of *Be* (*Wh-* Questions)

E-mail a friend. Ask your friend four questions about his or her first day in English class. Choose from the question words in the box. Follow the model.

| Who | Where | What | How | Is | Are | Was | Were |

Model

Hi Françoise,

I hope your first day at school was good.

Who's your new teacher? How are your classmates? Were you on time? Was the class interesting? Was it difficult?

I'm at work now, but I finish at six o'clock. Can you meet for coffee?

Abby

FG-4

ACKNOWLEDGMENTS

The principal challenge of writing a new edition of *Focus on Grammar 1* was keeping the materials that were the most simple, natural, and interesting. It was a task we could not do alone. We extend our thanks to our students who helped us realize what made their eyes light up. We are especially grateful to **Hsiao-Chuan Huang,** who worked energetically and faithfully through the entire first edition.

We offer our gratitude to the following reviewers for their many helpful comments:

Luz Inés Barceló, Instituto Cumbre del Noroeste, Ciudad Obregón, Sonora; **Jaime Bolaños,** Colegio Ker Liber Guadalajara, Jalisco; **Jessie Castañeda,** Colegio Ker Liber Guadalajara, Jalisco; **Elena Lattarulo,** Cuesta College, San Luis Obispo, CA; **Jennifer Lebedev,** Approach International, Allston, MA; **Gabriella Morvay,** Bronx Community College, NY; **Rachel Robbins,** Red River College, Winnipeg, Manitoba; **Jackie Saindon,** University of Georgia, Athens, GA; **Jacqueline Torres Ramírez,** Instituto Horland Johnson, Guadalajara, Jalisco.

We are also grateful to the wonderful people at Pearson Longman for their unflagging support and devotion to this project. In particular we wish to thank:

- The people in production who helped carry the project through: Jane Townsend, Linda Moser, and Rhea Banker.

- Aerin Csigay, who researched and found great photos to make the pages come alive.

- Joan Poole for her excellent suggestions in the early stages of this project.

- John Barnes, who took over the project and, with his keen eye for what works best, offered many thoughtful and perceptive comments and suggestions.

- Laura Le Dréan, the series director, who in addition to managing the entire series, took the time to look at individual units of this text and offer invaluable comments.

Once again we'd like to acknowledge those who had a role in the first edition: Marjorie Fuchs, Louisa Hellegers, Sandra Heyer, Françoise Leffler, Alison Rice, Ellen Shaw, and Marietta Urban.

Finally, we wish to thank Joanne Dresner, whose support and encouragement of our work has never wavered. We also thank her for her foresight in developing and supporting the *Focus on Grammar* series.

As always, our thanks to our families for their love and support: Harris, Dan, Dahlia, Jonathan; Priscilla.

I.E.S. and J.K.M.

Getting Started
Classroom Instructions

1 | IN CLASS

🎧 *Listen and read. Listen again and repeat.*

Look at page 1.

Listen to the CD.

Read the sentence.

Write the word *English*.

Circle the word *English*.

Underline the word *English*.

Ask a question.

Answer the question.

2 | WORKING TOGETHER

Student A, read a sentence from Exercise 1.

Student B, point to the sentence.

Take turns.

UNIT

1 Imperatives

Drive to the corner. Then turn left.

Grammar in Context

Read this conversation.

MARK: Is the restaurant close? I'm hungry.

STEVE: Yes, it is.

MARK: Is it good?

STEVE: **Don't worry.** It's very good. It's Indian.

MARK: Great.

STEVE: Now **drive** to the corner, and **turn** left at Jackson Street.

MARK: At the gas station?

STEVE: Yes. Then **go** two blocks on Jackson.

MARK: Got it.

STEVE: OK. **Turn** right at the next corner.

MARK: At Third Avenue?

STEVE: Yes. The restaurant is on the corner on your right.

MARK: Is that it?

STEVE: Yes, it is. **Don't park** here. It's a bus stop. **Park** behind the truck.

MARK: OK . . . Uh, Steve? The restaurant is empty.

STEVE: Really? It's usually full.

MARK: Is that a sign on the door?

STEVE: Uh-huh . . . Closed for vacation.

Words

🎧 *Do you know these words? Read the words. Write new words in your notebook.*

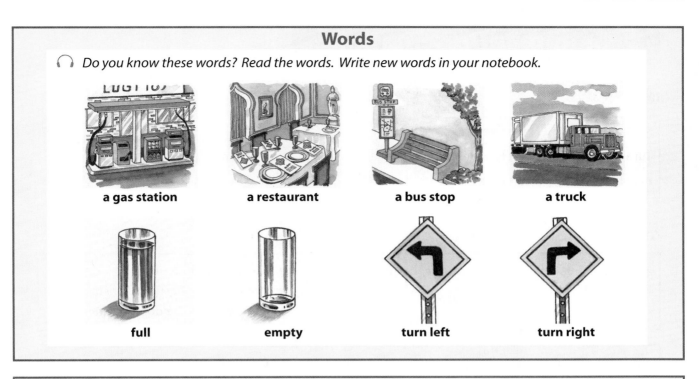

a gas station **a restaurant** **a bus stop** **a truck**

full **empty** **turn left** **turn right**

Expressions

🎧 *Do you know these expressions? Read the conversation. Write new expressions in your notebook.*

A: Turn left. It's on the corner of Jackson and Third. ***OK?***
B: ***Got it.***

Working Together

A *Practice the conversation in the opening reading with a partner.*

B *Work with a partner. Look at this map. Read the conversation in the opening reading. Draw Mark's route. Write an **X** at the restaurant.*

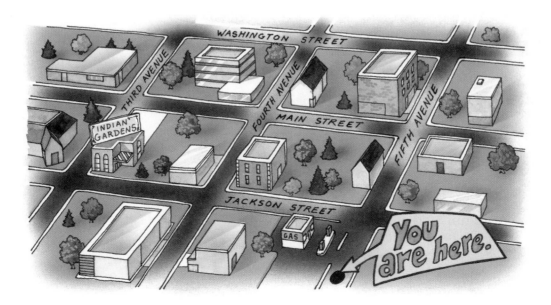

Grammar Presentation

IMPERATIVES

Affirmative	Negative
Turn left.	**Don't turn** right.
Park here.	**Don't park** there.

GRAMMAR NOTES

EXAMPLES

1. Use the imperative for **directions**, **instructions**, and **requests**.	• **Turn left.** (direction) • **Answer** the questions. (instruction) • **Please open** the door. (request)
2. Use the **base form** of the verb for the imperative.	• **Open** the door.
3. Use *do not* + the **base form** for the negative form of the imperative. *Don't* is the short form (**contraction**) of *do not*.	• **Do not park** here. • **Don't park** here.
4. *Please* makes a request more **polite**. *Please* comes at the beginning or at the end of the sentence.	• **Please** help me. OR • Help me, **please**.

Focused Practice

1 | DISCOVER THE GRAMMAR

Read these sentences. Underline the negative imperatives. Then match the sentences.

__c__ **1.** <u>Don't walk.</u>　　　　**a.** Please open the door.

_____ **2.** Don't park there.　　　**b.** Turn right.

_____ **3.** My hands are full.　　　**c.** Take a bus.

_____ **4.** Don't turn left.　　　　**d.** It's a bus stop.

2 | DIRECTIONS

Grammar Notes 1–3

Look at the pictures and write the sentences.

| Turn left. | Turn right. | Make a U-turn. | Don't park here. |

1. _____*Turn left.*_____ **2.** _____ **3.** _____ **4.** _____

3 | WHAT ARE THE PEOPLE SAYING?

Grammar Notes 1–4

Look at the pictures. What are the people saying? Choose a sentence in the box.
Write the sentence.

| Please don't smoke. | ~~Please sit down.~~ | Close the window, please. |
| Don't read this book. | Listen to this CD. | Please turn to page 6. |

1. _____*Please sit down.*_____   **2.** _____

3. _____   **4.** _____

(continued)

5. _____

6. _____

4 | FOLLOW INSTRUCTIONS
Grammar Notes 1–4

A *Look at sentence A. Then follow the instructions.*

- Circle the word *open*.
- Underline the word *not*.
- Change the word *window* to *door*.
- Change *do not* to the short form.
- Write the new sentence on the line.

A. Do not (open) the window.

_____

B *Look at sentence B. Then follow the instructions.*

- Add *please* to the sentence.
- Change *do not* to the short form.
- Change *driveway* to *garage*.
- Write the new sentence on the line.

B. Do not park in the driveway.

_____

5 | REQUESTS AND SUGGESTIONS
Grammar Notes 1–4

Complete these sentences. Use the words in the box.

~~close~~	Don't park	don't sit	listen	open

1. It's cold. Please _____*close*_____ the window.

2. Please _____ in the chair. It's broken.

3. It's a bus stop. _____ there.

4. It's hot in here. Please _____ the window.

5. I love his music. Let's _____ to his CD.

6 | EDITING

Correct these sentences. There are six mistakes. The first mistake is already corrected.

1. Please ~~not to~~ ^{don't} open your book.

2. You no sit here.

3. Study please page 3.

4. Completes the sentences.

5. Don't please worry.

6. No close the window.

Communication Practice

7 | WHAT'S THE HOMEWORK?

🎧 **A** *Listen and repeat the numbers.*

1 = one	2 = two	3 = three	4 = four	5 = five
6 = six	7 = seven	8 = eight	9 = nine	10 = ten

🎧 **B** *Now listen to the teacher. Then listen again. What's the homework?*

Read pages 1 to _____.

Study _____ on page _____.

_____ questions on page _____.

_____ question _____.

8 | MAKE REQUESTS

Work with a partner. Take turns. Make requests. Use the words in the box.

Verbs						
answer	ask	close	move	open	read	write

Nouns

your name	your e-mail address	your arms	a question	your book
your address	your phone number	your eyes	a sentence	your dictionary

Examples: Please close your eyes.
Please write your e-mail address.

9 | GAME: FIND THE PLACE

A *Work with a partner. Look at the map. Read the directions. Your partner listens and checks (✓) the place.*

Directions: *You are at Union Street and 3rd Avenue. Walk two blocks on Third Avenue to Pine Street. Turn right. Then go one block. Where are you?*

_____ **a.** Westlake Park

_____ **b.** Victor Steinbrueck Park

_____ **c.** Regrade Park

B *Switch roles. Start at the same place. Give directions to the other parks. Your partner names the park.*

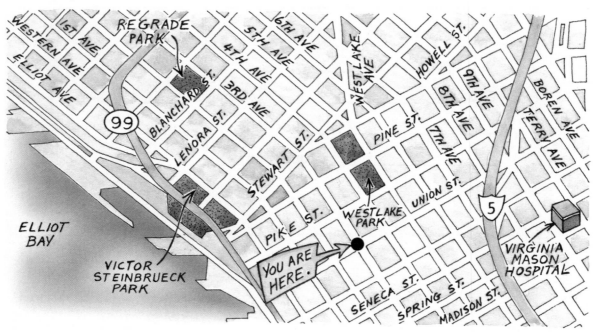

This is / These are; Subject Pronouns

This is my apartment.

Grammar in Context

🎧 *Read about Steve Beck.*

Hi. **I'm** Steve Beck. **This is** my apartment in Seattle. **It's** small but comfortable.

These are my CDs. **They're** classical and jazz. **This is** my guitar.

These are my pets, Pam and Kip. **They're** wonderful. Pam is eight years old and can talk. Kip is two years old.

We like our apartment. **We're** happy here.

I have a great family. **These are** my parents on the left. **This is** my sister Jessica in the middle, with her husband and children.

Words

🎧 *Do you know these words? Read the words. Write new words in your notebook.*

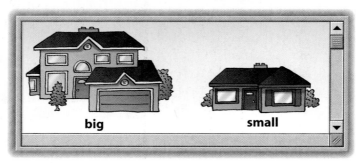

Expressions

🎧 *Do you know these expressions? Read the conversations. Write new expressions in your notebook.*

1. A: Hi, I'm Steve Beck.
   This is my sister Jessica.
B: *Nice to meet you.*
   I'm Sun Hee Kim.

2. A: Luis, this is my brother Victor.
   B: Nice to meet you, Victor.
   C: *Nice to meet you too.*

3. A: *Have a nice day.*
   B: *You too.*

Working Together

A *Practice the opening reading with a partner.*

B *Walk around the classroom. Meet three classmates.
Make introductions.*

Grammar Presentation

THIS IS / THESE ARE

Singular	Plural
This is my friend Pedro.	**These are** my friends Maria and Pedro.
This is my seat.	**These are** our seats.
Is this your seat?	**Are these** your seats?

SUBJECT PRONOUNS

Subject Pronouns	Example Sentences
I	**I**'m Steve Beck.
you	Hi, Maria. How are **you**?
he	**He**'s a teacher.
she	**She**'s a reporter.
it	This is my apartment. **It**'s in Seattle.
we	The apartment is small, but **we**'re happy here.
you	Hi, Mom and Dad. How are **you**?
they	**They**'re a nice family.

GRAMMAR NOTES

EXAMPLES

1. Use *this is* to introduce or talk about **one** person or thing **near** you.	• **This is** my friend Pedro. • **This is** my seat.
2. Use *these are* to introduce or talk about **two or more** people or things **near** you.	• **These are** my friends Maria and Pedro. • **These are** our seats.
3. Use *Is this* and *Are these* to ask questions.	**A: Is this** your cat? Yes, it is. **B: Are these** your books? No, they aren't.

---

4. *Singular* means "one." *Plural* means "more than one." Most **plural nouns** end in *-s* or *-es*.

   NOTE: **Nouns** are the names of people, animals, places, things, and ideas.

- This is my **friend**. (*one friend*)
- These are my **friends**. (*more than one friend*)
- This is my **class**. (*one class*)
- These are my **classes**. (*more than one class*)

---

5. *I*, *you*, *he*, *she*, *it*, *we*, *you*, and *they* are **subject pronouns**. They replace a subject noun.

   Use **contractions** (short forms) with pronouns in speaking and informal writing.

I am = **I'm**	he is = **he's**	she is = **she's**
you are = **you're**	we are = **we're**	
they are = **they're**		

   NOTE: Use *it* or *he* or *she* to talk about an animal.

- **Pam and Kip** are my pets. **They**'re wonderful.
- **Kip** is my cat. **He**'s active.

- **It**'s a big cat! OR **He**'s a big cat! OR **She**'s a big cat!

Pronunciation Note
Some plural nouns that end in *-es* have an extra syllable: class   class**es**
(1   1   2)

Reference Notes
For more about **plural nouns**, see Unit 4.
For more about the **spelling and pronunciation of plural nouns**, see Appendix 6 on page A-6.

Focused Practice

1 | DISCOVER THE GRAMMAR

Match these sentences.

__b__ 1. This is Montreal.

_____ 2. These are my pets.

_____ 3. This is my apartment.

_____ 4. This is Jessica.

_____ 5. This is Kip.

_____ 6. These are my CDs.

a. He's my cat.

b. It's in Canada.

c. She's my sister.

d. They're active and wonderful.

e. They're classical and jazz.

f. It's in Seattle.

2 | MY PHOTOS
Grammar Notes 1–3

*Complete these sentences. Use **this** or **these**.*

1. ___*These*___ are my photos.

2. _____ is my mother.

3. _____ are my sisters.

4. _____ is my father.

5. _____ is my apartment.

6. _____ are my friends.

7. Is _____ your cat?

8. Are _____ your keys?

3 | TALK ABOUT PEOPLE
Grammar Note 5

*Complete these sentences with **I**, **you**, **he**, **she**, **it**, **we**, or **they**.*

This is Judy Johnson. ___*She*___ 's a student at the
                              1.
University of Washington. Judy and her roommate

Helen live in an apartment. _____ like it. _____ 's
                                    2.   3.
small but nice.

Judy's parents telephone her sometimes: "Are

_____ OK?"
  4.

"Yes, _____ am."
        5.

"How are your classes?"

"_____ 're good, and _____ like Seattle a lot."
   6.   7.

Judy is in Steve Beck's journalism class at the university. Everyone likes Steve.

"_____ all think _____ 's a very good teacher," Judy says.
    8.   9.

4 | EDITING

Correct these conversations. There are five mistakes. The first mistake is already corrected.

1. **A:** ~~These~~ *This* is my friend Pedro.

   B: Nice to meet you, Pedro.

2. **A:** This are my brothers.

   B: Hello. Nice to meet you both.

3. **A:** This my partner, Ahmed.

   B: Hi, Ahmed.

4. **A:** Is these your books?

   B: No, they not.

Communication Practice

5 | THIS OR THESE?

🎧 **A** *Listen to these conversations. Then listen again and check (✓) **This** or **These**.*

	This	These			This	These			This	These
1.	☐	☐		3.	☐	☐		5.	☐	☐
2.	☐	☐		4.	☐	☐				

B *Work with a partner. Say a sentence, **a** or **b**. Your partner points to the correct sentence.*

1. **a.** This is my friend. **b.** These are my friends.
2. **a.** These are my photos. **b.** This is my photo.
3. **a.** These are our tickets. **b.** This is our ticket.
4. **a.** This is my sister. **b.** These are my sisters.
5. **a.** Is this your key? **b.** Are these your keys?

6 | MY FAMILY AND FRIENDS

Bring photos of your family or friends to class. Work in small groups. Talk about the photos.

Examples: **A:** Is this your mother?
 B: Yes. She's in Lima right now.
 C: This is my boyfriend. He's in Tokyo.
 D: These are my friends Emiko and Yuri.

7 | GAME: DON'T REPEAT

Work in small groups. Don't use a dictionary.

*Student A, touch something in the classroom and say, **This is a / an _____** OR **These are _____**.*

Student B, touch and name a different thing or different things. Continue. The last person to name a different thing wins.

8 | PEOPLE IN THE NEWS

Bring a newspaper with photos to class. Work with a partner. Look at the pictures.

*Student A says, **This is _____** OR **These are _____**. Student B says another thing, using a pronoun.*

Example: **A:** **This is** Nicole Kidman.
 B: **She**'s a movie star.

Nicole Kidman

Review Test

I *Complete these conversations. Circle the correct letter.*

1. STUDENT: What's the homework?

   TEACHER: _____

   (A) Answer questions 1 to 4 on page 10.

   (C) I'm Steve Beck.

   (B) Thank you.

   (D) This is my homework.

2. STEVE: _____

   MARK: Yes, it is.

   (A) These are the restaurants.

   (C) Are you hungry?

   (B) Is this the restaurant?

   (D) Are these the signs?

3. PEDRO: _____

   MARIA: Nice to meet you, Steve.

   (A) This is the University of Washington.

   (C) They live in a big house.

   (B) I live in Seattle.

   (D) This is my friend Steve.

4. STEVE: _____

   PEDRO: It's a good photo. They look happy.

   (A) These are my parents.

   (C) These are our seats.

   (B) Is this your parrot?

   (D) Are these your keys?

5. STEVE: _____

   MARK: OK.

   (A) Are these your pets?

   (C) Is the restaurant close?

   (B) Is this a bus stop?

   (D) Don't park there.

6. MARK: Is this your guitar?

   STEVE: _____

   (A) These are.

   (C) No, it's not.

   (B) Yes, she is.

   (D) No, they're not.

II *Complete these sentences.* Use **This is** *or* **These are**.

1. _____*This is*_____ my daughter.

2. _____ my sons.

3. _____ my classmate.

4. _____ my apartment.

5. _____ good photos.

6. _____ Steve Beck.

III *Complete these sentences.* Use **He**, **She**, **It**, **We**, *or* **They**.

1. My daughter is a student. ____*She*____ is at the library.

2. My sons are in Seattle. _____ are reporters.

3. My apartment is small. _____ is near the university.

4. My photos are in my book. _____ are family photos.

5. My mother is fine. _____ is in Florida.

6. My father and I are in Seattle. _____ are at the theater.

IV *Correct these sentences.*

Answer
1. ~~Answers~~ the questions.

2. Dont write your name.

3. Turns left.

4. These my new notebooks.

5. This are my parents.

6. No listen to the CD.

V *Look at the pictures. What is the teacher saying? Write the answer. Choose sentences from the box.*

Write the homework in your notebook.	Close your books.
Listen to the CD.	Practice with a partner.

1. _____

2. _____

3. _____

4. _____

▶ *To check your answers, go to the Answer Key on page RT-1.*

UNIT

3 The Present of *Be*: Statements
We're from Australia.

Grammar in Context

🎧 *Read this conversation.*

MARK: Hi, Steve.

STEVE: Hi, Mark. This **is** my cousin Amy, and this **is** her friend Jenny. They**'re** here on vacation.

MARK: Hi. Nice to meet you.

AMY: Nice to meet you too.

MARK: So you**'re** not from around here?

AMY: No. We**'re** from Australia.

MARK: Australia? That**'s** pretty far away. Are you from the capital?

AMY: No. We**'re** from Sydney. How about you? Are you from Seattle?

MARK: Yes, I **am**.

AMY: Jenny and I love Seattle. It**'s** a beautiful and clean city. The people **are** friendly. And the coffee **is** delicious.

MARK: How's Sydney?

AMY: It**'s** a wonderful city—and not because I live there!

Sydney, Australia

Words

🎧 *Do you know these words? Read the words. Write new words in your notebook.*

| **clean** | **dirty** | **delicious** | **awful** |

Expressions

🎧 *Do you know these expressions? Read the conversations. Write new expressions in your notebook.*

1. A: Are you *from around here*?
   B: No, I'm from Australia.

2. A: Are you here *on business*?
   B: No, we're here *on vacation*.

Working Together

A *Practice the conversation in the opening reading with two partners.*

B *Work with a partner. Take turns. Ask and answer the question.*

Other Possible Answers

No, I'm not. I live here.
No, I'm not. I'm here on vacation.
No, I'm not. I'm a student here.

C *What do you think about the city you are in? Talk to your partner.*

- The people are friendly here.
- The city is clean.
- The coffee is delicious.

Grammar Presentation

THE PRESENT OF *BE*

Affirmative Statements		
am	*is*	*are*
I **am** from Seattle.	He **is** from Seattle. She **is** from Sydney. It **is** clean. Seattle **is** clean.	We **are** from Sydney. You **are** cousins. They **are** friends. Jenny and I **are** from Sydney. Jenny and Amy **are** friends.
Contractions		
I am = I**'m**	he is = he**'s** she is = she**'s** it is = it**'s**	we are = we**'re** you are = you**'re** they are = they**'re**

Negative Statements		
am not	*is not*	*are not*
I **am not** from Sydney.	He **is not** from Sydney. She **is not** from Seattle. It **is not** dirty.	We **are not** from Seattle. You **are not** from here. They **are not** from here.
Contractions		
I am not = I**'m not**	he is not = he**'s not** OR he **isn't** she is not = she**'s not** OR she **isn't** it is not = it**'s not** OR it **isn't**	we are not = we**'re not** OR we **aren't** you are not = you**'re not** OR you **aren't** they are not = they**'re not** OR they **aren't**

GRAMMAR NOTES

EXAMPLES

1. The **present** of *be* has three forms: *am*, *is*, *are*.	• I **am** from Seattle. • It **is** clean. • They **are** friendly.

2. Use the correct form of *be* + *not* to make a **negative statement**.	• I **am not** from Sydney. • It **is not** dirty. • We **are not** cold.

3. Sentences have a subject and a verb. The **subject** is a noun or a pronoun.	subject noun verb • **Amy** **is** my cousin. subject pronoun verb • **She** **is** from Australia.

4. Use **contractions** (short forms) in speaking and informal writing.

NOTE: There are **two** negative contractions for *is not* and *are not*. We often use *isn't* or *aren't* after **subject nouns**. We often use *'s not* or *'re not* after **subject pronouns**.

- **I'm** from Seattle. **I'm not** from Sydney.

- Sydney **isn't** cold. OR It**'s not** cold.

- Jenny and Amy **aren't** cousins. OR They**'re not** cousins.

Focused Practice

1 | DISCOVER THE GRAMMAR

*Read the sentences. Write **A** for affirmative or **N** for negative.*

__N__ **1.** She's not from around here.

_____ **2.** She's here with a friend.

_____ **3.** They're here on vacation.

_____ **4.** They aren't here on business.

_____ **5.** I'm not from the capital.

2 | PEOPLE AND PLACES   *Grammar Note 1*

A *Write **She is**, **He is**, **It is**, **We are**, or **They are**.*

1. Amy is a student. ___She___ ___is___ from Australia.

2. Amy and Jenny are students. _____ _____ in Seattle on vacation.

3. Sydney is a beautiful city. _____ _____ in Australia.

4. My friends and I are in school. _____ _____ in room 2.

5. Mark is a student. _____ _____ in Seattle.

B *Now say each sentence aloud. Use contractions.*

3 | WHAT'S TRUE?

A *Check (✓) true sentences. Change false sentences to the negative. Write the full form.*

_____ **1.** I am a teacher.   _____*I am not a teacher.*_____

_____ **2.** I am a new student.   _____

_____ **3.** My parents are in Australia.   _____

_____ **4.** The Sydney Opera House is in Canberra.   _____

_____ **5.** We are in room 2.   _____

_____ **6.** Mexico is the capital of Mexico City.   _____

_____ **7.** Mexico City is the capital of Mexico.   _____

_____ **8.** My parents are from around here.   _____

_____ **9.** It is hot here.   _____

B *Now read each negative sentence. Use contractions.*

4 | A LETTER

Complete the letter. Choose from the words in parentheses.

Dear Mum and Dad,   Sept. 15

    Amy and I ____*are*____ in Seattle. We _____ at the Western Hotel now.
          1. (am / are)   2. (not / 're not)

It was expensive and far from everything. We _____ at a youth hostel on
                       3. ('re / be)

Second Avenue. It _____ clean. It _____ expensive. And all the
          4. ('s / 're)   5. (no is / 's not)

people here _____ friendly.
        6. (are / aren't)

    We love Seattle! It _____ a beautiful city, and the food _____
            7. ('s / 's not)   8. (is / are)

delicious, especially the Asian dishes. It _____ cool at night, and you
                   9. (be / 's)

often need an umbrella. But we _____ happy to be here.
           10. ('s / 're)

    I hope you _____ fine. Send my love to Aunt Kitty.
          11. (is / are)

                Love,

                Jenny

5 | NO, SHE'S NOT

Grammar Notes 1–4

Complete these sentences. Use the affirmative or negative form of **be**. *Use contractions.*

1. A: She's here on business.

    B: No. She *'s not* _____ here on business. She's here on vacation.

2. A: You're a student.

    B: No, I _____ a student. I'm a writer.

3. A: You're cold.

    B: Cold? We're not cold. We _____ fine.

4. A: They're from Austria.

    B: No, they're not. They _____ from Australia.

5. A: It's cool today.

    B: Cool? It _____ cool. It's warm.

6. A: Egypt is the capital of Cairo.

    B: No, it _____. Cairo is the capital of Egypt.

    A: Oh, you're right.

6 | EDITING

Correct these conversations. Use contractions. There are seven mistakes. The first mistake is already corrected.

1. A: Please close the window. ~~It~~ *It's* cold here.

    B: It's no cold. It's hot.

2. A: Please open the window. I be hot.

    B: Hot? It's not hot. Is cold.

3. A: My cousin from Tokyo. She's a student.

    B: My cousin from New York. She's a student too.

4. A: Seattle is the capital of Washington.

    B: No, it's isn't. Olympia is the capital.

Communication Practice

7 | TRUE OR FALSE?

🎧 *Listen to the conversation. Then listen again and check (✓)* **True***,* **False***, or* **No Information***.*

	True	False	No Information
1. The woman is from Australia.	_____	_____	_____
2. The woman's parents are from Australia.	_____	_____	_____
3. The man is from Italy.	_____	_____	_____
4. They are at a hotel.	_____	_____	_____
5. The woman thinks Italian food is delicious.	_____	_____	_____

8 | I'M NOT HERE ON BUSINESS

A *Write true sentences. Read your sentences to your partner. Check (✓) sentences that are the same for you and your partner. The first sentence is written for you.*

Same

1. I / here on business. *I'm not here on business.* ☐

2. I / here on vacation. _____ ☐

3. It / hot in class. _____ ☐

4. I / from Italy. _____ ☐

5. My teacher / from Australia. _____ ☐

6. I / happy to be here. _____ ☐

7. I / cold. _____ ☐

8. My parents / from Seattle. _____ ☐

9. It / noisy in class. _____ ☐

10. It / crowded. _____ ☐

B *Now write two true sentences and one false sentence. Read your sentences to the class. The class says* **True** *or* **False** *after each sentence.*

Example: **MASAE:** My teacher is from Australia.
    CLASS: False.

1. _____

2. _____

3. _____

That is / Those are; Possessive Adjectives; Plural Nouns

That's the Space Needle.

Grammar in Context

🎧 *Read this conversation.*

AMY: So **is that** it?

STEVE: Yes. **That's** the Space Needle. How about a picture?

AMY: Sure. It's too bad Jenny isn't here, but I have **her** camera.

STEVE: Come on. Let's go up.

* * * * *

AMY: Wow! What **are those** big **buildings**?

STEVE: They're the **stadiums**. Here, look through **my binoculars**.

AMY: They're huge! And **those are people** next to them. They look so tiny.

STEVE: Yes. Now look that way. **That's** the University of Washington.

AMY: **That's your** university, right?

STEVE: Yes, it is. OK, now look down. Look at that colored building.

AMY: What is it? The **colors** are beautiful, but **its** shape is really unusual.

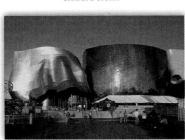

STEVE: **That's** the EMP. It's a music museum. It belongs to Paul Allen. It's **his** "baby."

AMY: Let's go see it.

STEVE: **That's** a great idea.

Words

🎧 *Do you know these words? Read the words. Write new words in your notebook.*

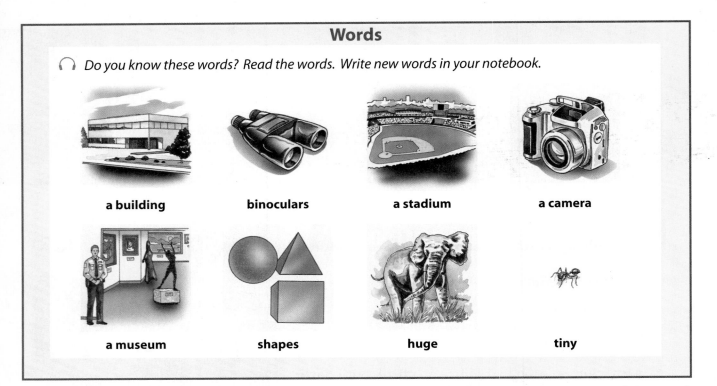

a building	binoculars	a stadium	a camera

a museum	shapes	huge	tiny

Expressions

🎧 *Do you know these expressions? Read the conversations. Write new expressions in your notebook.*

1. **A:** *How about* a picture?
   B: That's *a great idea*.

2. **A:** It's *too bad* Jenny isn't here.
   B: Yeah.

3. **A:** That's your university, *right*?
   B: Yes, it is.

Working Together

A *Practice the conversation in the opening reading with a partner.*

B *Read this story with a partner and answer the question. Then check your answer on page P-1.*

What Am I?

I am famous in Seattle and in the world. I am very tall—my height is about 600 feet, or 200 meters. My top has a restaurant. I have elevators. My initials are S.N. What's my name?

Grammar Presentation

THAT IS / THOSE ARE

Singular	Plural
That is the stadium.	**Those are** the stadiums.
That's his car.	**Those are** his cars.
Is that your key?	**Are those** your keys?

POSSESSIVE ADJECTIVES

Subject Pronouns	Possessive Adjectives	Example Sentences
I	**my**	**I** am Amy. **My** name is Amy.
you	**your**	**You** are Judy. **Your** name is Judy.
he	**his**	**He** is Steve. **His** name is Steve.
she	**her**	**She** is Jenny. **Her** name is Jenny.
it	**its**	**It** is the EMP. **Its** shape is unusual.
we	**our**	**We** have one daughter. **Our** daughter is Judy.
you	**your**	**You** are Steve and Mark, right? **Your** city is very beautiful.
they	**their**	**They** are our children. **Their** names are Judy and Ken.

SINGULAR AND PLURAL NOUNS

Singular (one)	Plural (more than one)
one girl	three girl**s**
one boy	four boy**s**
one glass	two glass**es**
one dish	three dish**es**
one man	two **men**
one woman	two **women**
one child	three **children**
one person	five **people**

GRAMMAR NOTES	EXAMPLES
1. Use *that is* to talk about one person or thing **away from** you. We often contract *that is* to *that's* in informal speaking and writing.	• **That is** the University of Washington. • **That's** the Space Needle.
2. Use *those are* to talk about two or more people or things **away from** you.	• **Those are** our stadiums. • **Those are** my pets.
3. Use *Is that* and *Are those* to ask questions. Answers usually take a **subject pronoun**.	• **Is that** your dictionary? Yes, **it** is. • **Are those** your keys? No, **they** aren't.
4. Possessive adjectives are *my*, *your*, *his*, *her*, *its*, *our*, and *their*. They tell who someone or something belongs to.	• This is **my** daughter. (*here*) • Those are **her** friends. (*there*) • The car belongs to Steve. It's **his** car.

⌒ **Pronunciation Note**
Some words sound the same, but they are different in meaning and spelling:

your = possessive adjective *you're* = you are	• **Your** name is Maria. • **You're** a student.
its = possessive adjective *it's* = it is	• **Its** name is the Space Needle. • **It's** 600 feet high.
their = possessive adjective *they're* = they are	• **Their** children are happy. • **They're** happy.

5. Add *-s* to most **nouns** to make them **plural**. Add *-es* to nouns that end in *s*, *z*, *ch*, *sh*, and *x*. Say an extra syllable.	• one cat, four cat**s** • one building, two building**s** • glass, glass**es** • dish, dish**es**
6. Some nouns have **special plural** forms.	• one child, two **children** • one person, three **people**

Reference Notes
For more about *this is* and *these are*, see Unit 2 and Unit 17.
For more about **plural nouns**, see Appendix 6 on page A-6.

Focused Practice

1 | DISCOVER THE GRAMMAR

Read these questions and answers. Underline the possessive adjectives. Circle the nouns that follow. Then match the questions and statements.

___d___ **1.** Are those <u>your</u> (books)?

_____ **2.** Is that his school?

_____ **3.** Are those your children?

_____ **4.** Is that the EMP?

_____ **5.** Is that your college?

_____ **6.** Are those your stadiums?

a. Yes. One is for football. The other is for baseball.

b. Yes. Their names are Judy and Ken.

c. Yes. Its shape is unusual, right?

d. No, they're her books.

e. No, it's my school.

f. No, I go to Boston College.

2 | THAT OR THOSE?   Grammar Notes 1–3

*Complete these sentences with **that** or **those**.*

1. _____ *That* _____ 's my new car.

2. Are _____ your children?

3. Is _____ Jenny's camera?

4. _____ are my friends.

5. Is _____ your wallet on the table?

6. Are _____ your binoculars?

3 | HOME VIDEO

*Judy is showing a DVD about her visit home. Complete her sentences with **my**, **his**, **her**, **its**, or **our**.*

That's me and ___my___ brother, Ken, with _____ parents in front of _____
                1.   **2.**   **3.**
house. See those cars? The old one belongs to Ken—it's _____ first car. _____
                                          4.   **5.**
battery is dead, so it doesn't run. But he loves it. The new car belongs to Dad. It's _____
                                                                6.
favorite thing. And the garden belongs to Mom. It's _____ favorite place.
                                                      7.

4 | SINGULAR OR PLURAL?

🎧 **A** *Listen to the conversations. Then listen again and circle the word you hear.*

1. (woman)   women

2. man   men

3. parent   parents

4. purse   purses

5. dish   dishes

6. key   keys

B *Work with a partner. Say one of the words in each item. Your partner points to the word you say.*

5 | EDITING

Correct these conversations. There are seven mistakes. The first mistake is already corrected.

1. **A:** Are those your ~~key~~ ^{keys}?

   B: No, they her keys.

2. **A:** That is my daughters.

   B: She's a beautiful women.

3. **A:** Are that your childs?

   B: Yes. That's our son, and that's our daughter.

4. **A:** Are it tires flat?

   B: Yes, they are.

Communication Practice

6 | ARE THOSE YOUR CHILDREN?

🎧 *Listen to the conversation. Then listen again and complete these sentences.*

A: Are those _____ _____?
                    1.   2.

B: Yes. They're _____ _____, Jeremy and Ben. And that's
                       3.   4.

_____ _____, Annie.
      5.   6.

A: And is that _____ dog?
                       7.

B: Yes. _____ name _____ Bozo.
                8.   9.

A: Who are _____ other kids?
                     10.

B: Those are _____ friends.
                      11.

7 | THE POSSESSIVE GAME

A *Play this game with the class. Each student puts an item on the teacher's table. For example:*

a notebook	a jacket	keys
a CD player	an earring	sunglasses
a backpack	a watch	

B *The teacher picks up one thing. Who does it belong to? A student points to the owner and says:*

That's his / her _____.

That's her backpack.

No, that's his backpack.

Who does it belong to?

Example: **TEACHER:** Who does it belong to?
    STUDENT A: [*pointing to Student B*] That's her backpack.
    STUDENT B: No [*pointing to Student C*], that's his backpack.
        OR
        Right. It's my backpack.

Grammar in Context

🎧 *Mark, Steve, and Kathy are at a wedding reception for Amanda and Josh. Read these three conversations.*

STEVE: Mark?

MARK: Steve! **Are you** here for the wedding?

STEVE: **Yes, I am.** Amanda is my cousin. What about you?

MARK: Josh and I are friends from school. Boy, this is a great wedding.

STEVE: Yes, it is.

KATHY: **Who's** that man with Steve?

AMANDA: His name is Mark. He and Josh are friends.

KATHY: Hmm. **Is he** single?

AMANDA: **Yes, he is.**

KATHY: What does he do?

AMANDA: He's a student and a writer.

KATHY: What kind of writer?

AMANDA: He writes travel books.

MARK: **Who's** that woman with Amanda?

STEVE: Her name is Kathy.

MARK: **Is she** married?

STEVE: **No, she's not.**

MARK: Hmm . . . What does she do?

STEVE: She's a travel agent.

Words

🎧 *Do you know these words? Read the words. Write new words in your notebook.*

married

single

a writer

a travel agent

Expressions

🎧 *Do you know these expressions? Read the conversations. Write new expressions in your notebook.*

1. **A:** I'm here for the wedding. ***What about you?***
   B: I'm here for the wedding too.

2. **A:** ***What do you do?***
   B: I'm a writer.

3. **A:** ***Boy,**** this is a nice wedding.
   B: Yes, it is.

   *Informal word used when you are excited about something

Working Together

A *Practice the conversations in the opening reading with a partner.*

B *Work with a partner. Match the words and the pictures. Use your dictionary.*

| a cashier | a mechanic | a nurse | ~~a police officer~~ |

      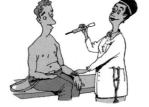   

1.  *a police officer*   2. _____   3. _____   4. _____

C *Talk with a partner about other people in the class. Follow the example.*

Example: **A:** Who's that man / woman near _____?
B: That's _____.
A: Is he / she single?

B: _____.
A: What does he / she do?
B: He's / She's _____.

Grammar Presentation

THE PRESENT OF *BE*: *YES / NO* QUESTIONS

Yes / No Questions
Singular
Am I right?
Are you a writer?
Is he a student?
Is she single?
Is your car new?

Short Answers	
Affirmative	**Negative**
Yes, **you are.**	No, **you're not.** OR No, **you aren't.**
Yes, **I am.**	No, **I'm not.**
Yes, **he is.**	No, **he's not.** OR No, **he isn't.**
Yes, **she is.**	No, **she's not.** OR No, **she isn't.**
Yes, **it is.**	No, **it's not.** OR No, **it isn't.**

Plural
Are you happy?
Are we late?
Are they brothers?

Affirmative	Negative
Yes, **we are.**	No, **we're not.** OR No, **we aren't.**
Yes, **you are.**	No, **you're not.** OR No, **you aren't.**
Yes, **they are.**	No, **they're not.** OR No, **they aren't.**

THE PRESENT OF *BE*: QUESTIONS WITH *WHO* AND *WHAT*

Questions with *Who / What*	Short Answers	Long Answers
Who is that woman? **What's** her name?	Kathy. Kathy.	That's Kathy. It's Kathy.

GRAMMAR NOTES

1. In a *yes / no* question with *be*, put *am*, *is*, or *are* before the subject.

2. We often use contractions in **negative short answers**.

Don't use contractions in **affirmative short answers**.

EXAMPLES

- Statement: I ^{subject} **am** right.

  Statement: I **am** right.
- Question: **Am** I right?

A: Is she married?
B: No, she**'s not.** OR No, she **isn't.**

A: Are they brothers?
B: No, they**'re not.** OR No, they **aren't.**

A: Am I right?
B: Yes, **you are.** NOT Yes, ~~you're.~~

A: Is she single?
B: Yes, **she is.** NOT Yes, ~~she's.~~

3. Use *who* to ask for information about **people**. Use *what* to ask for information about **things** or **ideas**.

We often use the contractions *who's* and *what's* in speaking and informal writing.

- **Who** is that woman with Amanda?
- **What** is her name?
- **Who's** that woman?
- **What's** her name?

Focused Practice

1 | DISCOVER THE GRAMMAR

Read these conversations. Circle the questions with **be**. *Underline the short answers.*

1. **MARK:** She looks interesting. (Is she married?)

   STEVE: No, she's not.

2. **MARK:** Are you here for the wedding?

   STEVE: Yes, I am. Amanda is my cousin.

3. **KATHY:** Is Mark single?

   AMANDA: Yes, he is. And he's a nice guy.

4. **STEVE:** Are you and Josh friends?

   MARK: Yes, we are. Actually, we're friends from school.

2 | QUESTIONS   *Grammar Notes 1–2*

Match these questions and answers.

  c   **1.** Is Amanda your sister?

_____ **2.** Are Mark and Helen teachers?

_____ **3.** Am I right?

_____ **4.** Are you and Josh friends?

_____ **5.** Is Mark married?

_____ **6.** Are you and Tim from Seattle?

a. No, he isn't.

b. No, we're from Redmond.

c. No, she isn't. She's my cousin.

d. No, they aren't. They're writers.

e. Yes, you are.

f. Yes, we are.

3 | WHO OR WHAT?

Grammar Note 3

Complete these conversations with **who** or **what**.

1. A: ___Who___ 's that woman with Mark?

   B: That's my mother.

2. A: _____'s her name?

   B: Mary.

3. A: _____'s that man with Judy?

   B: That's Mark.

4. A: _____'s the teacher in this class?

   B: Professor Beck. Steve Beck.

5. A: _____'s the capital of Australia?

   B: Canberra.

6. A: _____'s the capital of Brazil?

   B: Brasília.

4 | CONVERSATIONS

Grammar Notes 1–3

Change the order of the words. Make conversations.

1. A: Steve / Portland / Is / from / ?

   A: _Is Steve from Portland?_____

   B: not / No, / he's / .

   B: _No, he's not._____

2. A: today / the game / Is / ?

   A: _____

   B: Yes, / is / it / .

   B: _____

3. A: cousins / Are / they / ?

   A: _____

   B: aren't / No, / they / . / brothers / They're / .

   B: _____

4. A: man / that / Who / is / ?

   A: _____

   B: my / 's / teacher / He / .

   B: _____

5. A: Seattle / hot / Is / ?

   A: _____

   B: isn't / No, / it / .

   B: _____

5 | WHO'S THAT WOMAN?

Grammar Notes 1–3

🎧 *Listen to the conversations. Then listen again and complete these sentences.*

1. A: _____Who's_____ that ____woman____ with Amanda?

   B: Her name is Kathy.

   A: _____ _____ married?

   B: _____, _____ _____.

2. A: _____ _____ your brother?

   B: _____, he _____.

   A: Is he _____ _____?

   B: _____, he's _____. _____ _____ _____.

6 | EDITING

Correct these conversations. There are 10 mistakes. The first mistake is already corrected.

1. A: ~~Is~~ *Are* you a singer?

   B: Yes, I'm.

2. A: Is she single?

   B: No, she not.

3. A: They students?

   B: No, they are.

4. A: Is he your father?

   B: No, he's.

5. A: Are your car new?

   B: No, it old.

6. A: Is he an engineer?

   B: No, he not. He a writer.

Communication Practice

7 | NICE WEDDING, RIGHT?

🎧 *Listen to the conversation. Then listen again and answer each question with a short answer.*

1. Is Susan a doctor? _____

2. Is she married? _____

3. Are Bobby and Mike brothers? _____

4. Is Laura single? _____

8 | GAME: TEN QUESTIONS

A *Your classmates choose the name of a famous person. They write it on a piece of paper and put it on your back. You don't see the name.*

B *Ask your classmates 10 yes / no questions about the person. Your classmates answer with short answers.*

Examples: **A:** Am I a man?
                 B: No, you aren't.

                 A: Am I a writer?
                 B: No, you aren't.

C *Guess who you are.*

Example: **A:** Am I Salma Hayek?
               B: Yes, you are. OR No, you aren't.

The Present of *Be*: Questions with *Where*; Prepositions of Place

It's on First between Jackson and Main.

Grammar in Context

🎧 *Read these e-mail messages.*

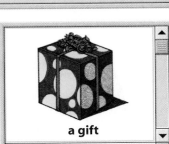

a birthday cake

Subj: Yuko's birthday
Date: Wednesday, November 3
From: JudyJohnson@UW.edu
To: MM@UW.edu

Hi Mark,

I want to go to Yuko's party, but I don't have her address. **Where's** her new apartment?

Judy

---

a gift

Subj: Yuko's birthday
Date: Wednesday, November 3
From: MM@UW.edu
To: JudyJohnson@UW.edu

Hi Judy,

Her apartment is **on** First Avenue **between** Jackson and Main. (I think it's **at** 10 First Avenue, but I'm not sure.) It's **across from** a library and **next to** a gym. She's **on** the second floor, Apartment 2A. Take the number 4 bus. It stops **on the corner of** First and Jackson. (Her phone number is 206-555-2343.)

See you Saturday.

Mark

By the way, any gift ideas?

Words

⌒ *Do you know these words? Read the words. Write new words in your notebook.*

a supermarket

a gym

a library

an apartment building

ORDINAL NUMBERS

1st = first	2nd = second	3rd = third	4th = fourth	5th = fifth
6th = sixth	7th = seventh	8th = eighth	9th = ninth	10th = tenth

Expressions

⌒ *Do you know these expressions? Read the conversations. Write new expressions in your notebook.*

1. A: ***See you*** tomorrow.
   B: ***See you.***

2. A: ***By the way***, any gift ideas?
   B: How about flowers?

Working Together

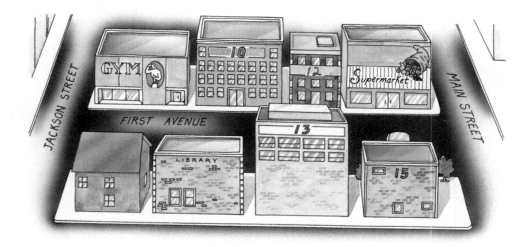

Read the e-mail messages again. Look at the map. What's Yuko's address?

She lives at _____.

Grammar Presentation

QUESTIONS WITH *WHERE*

Questions with *Where*	Short Answers	Long Answers
Where is the art museum?	On First Avenue.	It's on First Avenue.
Where are Yuko and Keiko from?	Japan.	They're from Japan.

PREPOSITIONS OF PLACE

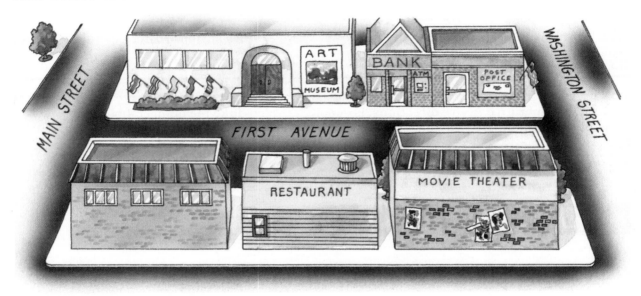

The art museum is **on** First Avenue. It's **across from** an apartment building and a restaurant. The bank is **between** the art museum and the post office. The restaurant is **next to** the movie theater.

GRAMMAR NOTES

1. Use *where* to ask questions about location.

Where's is the short form for *where is*.

2. *In*, *on*, *at*, *next to*, *between*, and *across from* are prepositions of place. They tell the location of places and things.

EXAMPLES

A: **Where** is the restaurant?
B: It's on First Avenue.

A: **Where's** the bank?
B: It's next to the museum.

• My school is **in** Seattle.
• It's **on** Main Street.
• It's **next to** a bank.

3. Use:

at + street address	• My school is **at** 15 Main Street.
on + street name	• It is **on** Main Street.
on the + floor	• My English class is **on the** second floor.
in + city, state, country, or continent	• It is **in** Seattle.
NOTE: We don't always say "street" or "avenue" in informal speaking or writing.	**A:** Where's your school? **B:** It's on **Main**. OR It's on **Main Street**.

4. Use ordinal numbers for streets and floors.

• It's on **Tenth** Street.
• She's on the **second** floor.

5. Use the **imperative** to give **directions**. For more about the **imperative**, see Unit 1.

• **Take** the number 4 bus to the museum.

Focused Practice

1 | DISCOVER THE GRAMMAR

Look at the map on page 41. Write the letter of the place next to its location.

        a. ~~the post office~~   **b.** the movie theater   **c.** the restaurant

a **1.** It's on the corner of First Avenue and Washington Street. It's next to a bank.

_____ **2.** It's on First Avenue between Washington and Main. It's between a movie theater and an apartment building.

_____ **3.** It's on the corner of First and Washington. It's next to a restaurant.

2 | A BUSINESS CARD
Grammar Note 3

Look at Yuko's business card. Complete the sentences.

Yuko Shinohara
10 First Avenue, Apt. 2A
Seattle, Washington 98104

1. Yuko lives (city, state) _____*in Seattle, Washington*_____ .

2. She lives _____ Avenue.

3. Her building is at _____ .

4. Her apartment is _____ floor.

3 | LOCATIONS
Grammar Notes 1–2

Look at the map. Match the questions and answers.

___*b*___ **1.** Where's the art museum?

_____ **2.** Where's the hospital?

_____ **3.** Where's the bank?

_____ **4.** Where's the park?

a. It's across from the hospital.

b. It's next to the bank.

c. It's between the art museum and the post office.

d. It's on the northeast corner of Second and Washington.

4 | WHERE'S THE POST OFFICE?

Grammar Notes 1–3

A *Complete this conversation. Use the sentences in the box.*

Is it on Main Street?	Where's First Avenue?
Turn right at the corner.	~~Is this Main Street?~~

MAN: Excuse me. *Is this Main Street?* _____

WOMAN: Yes, it is. We're on Main Street near Second Avenue.

MAN: I'm looking for the post office. _____

WOMAN: No, it's not. It's on First Avenue.

MAN: Oh. _____

WOMAN: Walk to the corner of this street. _____

The post office is next to the bank. It's on the corner of First and Washington.

B *Listen and check your work.*

C *Look at the map in Exercise 3. Where are the man and woman now? Put an **X** on the street.*

5 | EDITING

Correct these conversations. There are eight mistakes. The first mistake is already corrected.

1. A: ~~Where's~~ *Where* are you from?

   B: I'm from Bogotá.

   A: Where Bogotá?

   B: It's on Colombia.

2. A: Is your apartment in this floor?

   B: No, it's on the eight floor.

3. A: Where's the bookstore?

   B: It's First Avenue.

   A: Is it next the museum?

   B: Yes, it is.

4. A: Is the supermarket on First in Main and Washington?

   B: No, it's between Main and Jackson.

Communication Practice

6 | WHERE IS THE SUPERMARKET?

🎧 *Look at the map in Exercise 3. Listen to the conversation. Then listen again and write* **supermarket** *and* **flower shop** *on the correct buildings.*

7 | INFORMATION GAP: WHAT'S THE ADDRESS?

Work in pairs.

Student B, look at the Information Gap on page IG-0. Follow the instructions there.

Student A, look at business cards 1 and 2 on this page. Ask your partner questions and complete the cards. Then answer your partner's questions about cards 3 and 4.

1.
China Palace
_____ Main Street
_____, ____ 48104
U.S.A.

2.
Turkish Delights
213 East _____ Street
_____, New York 10021
U.S.A.

3.
The Fitness Club
80 West Street
Ottawa, Ontario
Canada

4.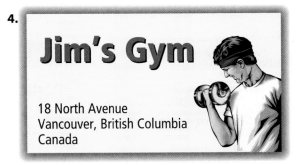
Jim's Gym
18 North Avenue
Vancouver, British Columbia
Canada

Example: **A:** Where's China Palace?
B: In Ann Arbor, Michigan.
A: What's the address?
B: 30 Main Street.

PART II

Review Test

I *Complete these conversations. Circle the correct letter.*

1. MARK: Are you from around here?

    AMY: No, I'm _____.

  (**A**) from here   (**C**) not here

  (**B**) here on vacation   (**D**) happy to meet you

2. KATHY: Are you a businessman?

    MARK: No, _____.

  (**A**) I'm not from around here   (**C**) I'm on vacation

  (**B**) I'm a businessman   (**D**) I'm a writer

3. MARK: Is Blake a travel agent?

    STEVE: Yes, _____.

  (**A**) he is   (**C**) he's a doctor

  (**B**) she's   (**D**) she's not

4. ROSE: Is she your daughter?

    MARY: No, _____.

  (**A**) she's your friend   (**C**) he's my son

  (**B**) he isn't   (**D**) she's my granddaughter

5. STEVE: What does Jim do?

    MARK: _____.

  (**A**) He's married   (**C**) He's here on business

  (**B**) He's a police officer   (**D**) He's from Australia

II *Look at the pictures. Complete each question with* **Is this**, **Is that**, **Are these**, *or* **Are those**. *Use each phrase once.*

1. _____ your daughter?

2. _____ your snowboard?

3. _____ your children?

4. _____ your books, Kevin?

III *Complete these sentences. Use* **his**, **her**, *or* **their**.

You know the Becks and the Olsons. Bill Beck is married to Mary (Meyers) Beck. Mary

is ___*his*___ second wife. Steve Beck and Jessica (Beck) Olson are _____ children. Steve
　　1.　　　　　　　　　　　　　　　　　　　　　　　　　　　2.

Beck is _____ son. Jessica Olson is _____ daughter. Jessica is married. Tim Olson is
　　　　3.　　　　　　　　　　　4.

_____ husband. Jeremy, Annie, and Ben Olson are _____ children.
　5.　　　　　　　　　　　　　　　　　　　　　　6.

IV *Look at the map. Complete these sentences. Use* **is** *or* **are** *and* **on**, **next to**, **between**, *or* **across from**.

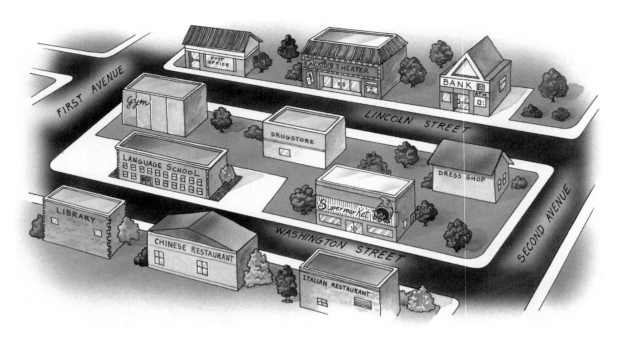

1. Lincoln Street _____*is between*_____ First Avenue and Second Avenue.

2. The library _____ Washington Street.

3. The gym _____ Lincoln Street _____ the post office.

4. The movie theater _____ Lincoln Street _____ the post office and the bank.

5. The drugstore _____ the dress shop.

6. The dress shop and the drugstore _____ the bank and the movie theater.

7. The language school _____ Washington Street _____ the library.

8. The Italian restaurant and the Chinese restaurant _____ Washington Street.

9. The Chinese restaurant _____ the Italian restaurant.

▶ *To check your answers, go to the Answer Key on page RT-1.*

UNIT

The Past of *Be*: Statements, Yes / No Questions

7

Were you alone?

Grammar in Context

🎧 *Read this conversation.*

KATHY: Hello?

AMANDA: Hi, Kathy. This is Amanda.

KATHY: Hi, Amanda. How's it going?

AMANDA: Fine. Hey, Josh and I **were** at your house last night, but you **weren't** there. Or **were you** asleep?

KATHY: Actually, I **wasn't** at home last night. I **was** at the movies.

AMANDA: **Were you** alone?

KATHY: Uh, no. I **was** with . . . someone. The movie **was** great. Really exciting. And funny too.

AMANDA: Really! What movie **was** it?

KATHY: *Frankenstein's Uncle.*

Words

🎧 *Do you know these words? Read the words. Write new words in your notebook.*

alone

asleep

funny

exciting

Expressions

🎧 *Do you know these expressions? Read the conversations. Write new expressions in your notebook.*

1. A: Hi, Kathy. This is Amanda.
   B: Hi, Amanda. *How's it going?*
   A: Fine.

2. A: We were at your house last night, but you weren't there.
   B: Actually, I wasn't at home last night. I was *at the movies*.

Working Together

A *Practice the conversation in the opening reading with a partner.*

B *Practice asking and answering these questions. Ask a partner. Then your partner asks you.*

A: Were you at _____ (school / work / home) (yesterday / yesterday afternoon / last night)?
B: No, I wasn't. I was at _____ (the movies / a concert / a game).

A: What _____ (movie / concert / game)?
B: _____.

A: How was it?
B: It was _____ (great / pretty good / pretty bad / awful).

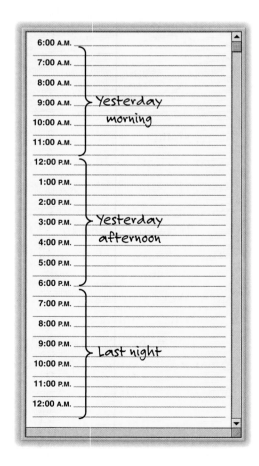

Grammar Presentation

THE PAST OF *BE*: AFFIRMATIVE STATEMENTS

Affirmative Statements	
was	*were*
I **was** at a movie last night. He **was** at home. She **was** at the gym. It **was** hot.	We **were** at a birthday party yesterday. You **were** wonderful in the play. You and Ryan **were** both wonderful. They **were** at the soccer game.

THE PAST OF *BE*: NEGATIVE STATEMENTS

Negative Statements	
was not	*were not*
I **was not** at home last night. He **wasn't** at a movie. She **wasn't** at the library. It **wasn't** cold yesterday.	We **were not** at home last night. You **weren't** in class yesterday. Why not? They **weren't** at the library yesterday.

YES / NO QUESTIONS

Yes / No Questions
was / were
Was I right?
Was he at home?
Was she at the game?
Was it cold yesterday?
Were we right?
Were you at home?

Short Answers	
Affirmative	Negative
Yes, you **were**.	No, you **weren't**.
Yes, he **was**.	No, he **wasn't**.
Yes, she **was**.	No, she **wasn't**.
Yes, it **was**.	No, it **wasn't**.
Yes, you **were**.	No, you **weren't**.
Yes, I **was**.	No, I **wasn't**.

GRAMMAR NOTES

EXAMPLES

1. The past of **be** has two forms: **was** and **were**. Use *was* with these subject pronouns: *I*, *he*, *she*, and *it*. Use *were* with these subject pronouns: *you*, *we*, and *they*.	• I **was** at a movie last night. • The girls **were** at the library yesterday. • They **were** at the library yesterday.

2. Use *was* or *were* + *not* to make negative statements.

We often use the contractions *wasn't* and *weren't* in speaking and informal writing.

- I **was not** alone.
- You **were not** at home.
- I **wasn't** alone.
- You **weren't** at home.

3. To ask a *yes / no question*, put *was* or *were* before the subject.

subject
- **Was** the movie interesting?

subject
- **Were** you alone at the movie?

4. Use a subject pronoun and *was*, *wasn't*, *were*, or *weren't* in short answers.

A: Was Mary at the library yesterday?
B: Yes, **she was**.

A: Were your friends at home last night?
B: No, **they weren't**.

Focused Practice

1 | DISCOVER THE GRAMMAR

A *Circle the subjects and underline the past forms of* **be**. *Then match these questions and answers.*

___d___ **1.** Were (you) at home yesterday?

_____ **2.** Was he in class yesterday?

_____ **3.** Was the concert good?

_____ **4.** Was the movie interesting?

_____ **5.** Was Susan at the library yesterday?

_____ **6.** Were you at the ball game last night?

a. No, it wasn't. The music was pretty bad.

b. Yes, she was. We were both there.

c. Yes, I was. It was a really exciting game.

d. No, I wasn't. I was at a concert.

e. No, he wasn't. He was sick.

f. Yes, it was. Johnny Depp is a great actor.

B *Read this e-mail. Underline the past forms of* **be** *and their subjects.*

Judy,

You didn't call me last night. Where were you? Were you out? I was at home from 6:00 on. I tried you a couple of times. We need to talk. Please call soon.

Ken

2 | **WERE THE KIDS WITH YOU?** *Grammar Notes 1–4*

Complete these questions and answers with **was**, **wasn't**, **were**, *or* **weren't**.

A: ___*Was*___ Joan in class yesterday morning?
      1.

B: Yes, she _____.
                      2.

A: _____ you at home last night?
      3.

B: No, I _____. I _____ at the movies.
               4.   5.

A: _____ the kids with you?
      6.

B: No, they _____. They _____ at a concert.
                    7.   8.

3 | **LAST NIGHT** *Grammar Notes 1–2*

Look at the pictures. Where were these people last night? Complete these sentences. Use **was** *or* **were** *and an expression below.*

at a concert	**at the movies**	**at a play**
at a party	**at a soccer game**	**at home**

1. Last night, Tim and Jessica ___*were at the movies*_____.

2. Mary, Annie, and Ben _____.

3. Jeremy _____.

4. Mark _____.

5. Steve and his father _____.

6. Judy _____.

4 | EDITING

Correct this note from Kathy. There are seven mistakes. The first mistake is already corrected.

Mark,

Sorry I ~~was~~ *wasn't* home last night. I were at a basketball game. Amanda and Josh was

with me. It were really exciting.

Where were you on Tuesday afternoon? Susan and Brent and I are at the soccer

game, but you were there. Too bad. It is really exciting.

I'll talk to you soon. Call me.

Kathy

Communication Practice

5 | WHAT'S THE MESSAGE?

🎧 *Listen to the message on the answering machine. Check (✓) **True**, **False**, or **No Information**.*

	True	False	No Information
1. Mark is at home now.	☐	☐	☐
2. Josh was at the movies last night.	☐	☐	☐
3. Amanda was at home last night.	☐	☐	☐
4. Josh was alone at the movies.	☐	☐	☐
5. The movie was exciting.	☐	☐	☐
6. The theater was too hot.	☐	☐	☐
7. The movie was *Spider-Man 3*.	☐	☐	☐

"Hello, this is Mark . . ."

6 | YESTERDAY

Work with a partner. Answer these questions. Give more information.

1. Were you late to class yesterday morning?
2. Were you at a concert yesterday?
3. Were you at home last night?
4. Were you at the library yesterday afternoon?
5. Were you at the movies last night?
6. Were you at school yesterday?

   Example: **A:** Were you late to class yesterday morning?
   B: Yes, I was. The bus was late.

7 | TALK ABOUT AN EVENT

Tell a partner about a movie, a play, a concert, or a game. How was it? Use the following words.

   Example: **A:** I was at the movies last night. I saw *The Interpreter.*
   B: Was it good?
   A: Yes! It was exciting—and pretty scary.

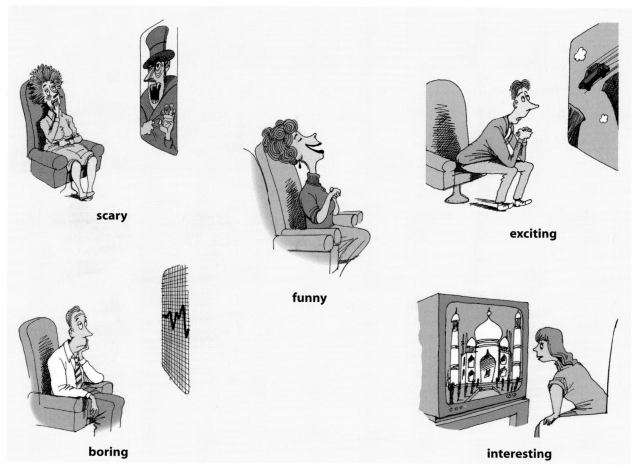

scary

funny

exciting

boring

interesting

The Past of *Be*: *Wh-* Questions

How was your vacation?

Read this conversation.

JASON: Hi, Mark.

MARK: Hey, Jason.

JASON: Welcome back. **How was** your vacation?

MARK: Great.

JASON: You look good. **Where were** you?

MARK: In Spain.

JASON: Nice. **How long were** you there?

MARK: Ten days. Ten wonderful days.

JASON: That's a long vacation. My parents were there last month. It was hot. **How was** the weather?

MARK: Hot and sunny. But it was cool at the beach.

JASON: And the food?

MARK: Delicious.

JASON: So . . . were you on a tour?

MARK: No, but I was with a guide.

JASON: A guide? **Who was** your guide?

MARK: Remember Kathy? At Amanda's wedding? The travel agent?

JASON: Sure.

MARK: Well, she's in Barcelona this month. She was my guide.

JASON: You lucky man!

Words

🎧 *Do you know these words? Read the words. Write new words in your notebook.*

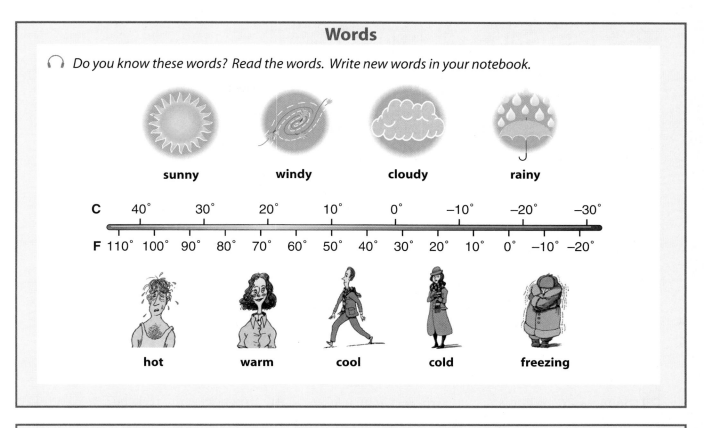

sunny   **windy**   **cloudy**   **rainy**

C	40°	30°	20°	10°	0°	−10°	−20°	−30°
F	110° 100° 90° 80°	70° 60°	50° 40°	30°	20° 10°	0° −10° −20°		

hot   **warm**   **cool**   **cold**   **freezing**

Expressions

🎧 *Do you know these expressions? Read the conversations. Write new expressions in your notebook.*

1. A: *Welcome back.*
   B: Thanks.

2. A: *Remember* Kathy? (*Do you remember* Kathy?)
   B: *Sure.*

Working Together

A *Practice the conversation in the opening reading with a partner.*

B *Read this paragraph with a partner. Then answer the question. Check your answer on page P-1.*

At the Prado

I was in Madrid, the capital city of Spain. I was at the Prado. There were a lot of paintings by Flemish and Italian artists. My favorite paintings were by Velázquez, El Greco, and Goya. There were visitors from all over the world. It was wonderful.

The Prado is _____.

a. a restaurant   **b.** a museum   **c.** an opera house

Grammar Presentation

THE PAST OF *BE*: *WH-* QUESTIONS

Wh- Questions	Short Answers	Long Answers
Where were you?	(In) Spain.	I was in Spain.
Who were you with?	Friends.	I was there with friends.
How was the weather?	Hot.	It was hot.
How long were you there?	Ten days.	I was there for ten days.

Wh- Questions about the Subject	Short Answers	Long Answers
Who was in Spain?	Mark (was).	Mark was in Spain.

GRAMMAR NOTES

EXAMPLES

1. Some *wh-* questions start with **where**, **when**, **who**, **what**, **how**, or **how long**. These words ask for information. In informal conversation, **answers** are usually **short**.	**A:** **How** was your weekend? **B:** Great!
2. Use **where** to ask about a **location**. Use **when** to ask about a **time**.	**A:** **Where** were you? **B:** In Spain. **A:** **When** were you there? **B:** In June.
3. Use **who** to ask about a **person**. (This question asks about the subject.)	**A:** **Who** was in Spain? **B:** Mark. **A:** **Who** were you with? **B:** A friend.
4. Use **how** to ask for a **description**.	**A:** **How** was your vacation? **B:** Wonderful!
5. Use **how long** to ask for a **length of time**.	**A:** **How long** was the game? **B:** Two hours.
6. Use **it** to talk about the weather.	• **It** was hot. • **It** was sunny.

Focused Practice

1 | DISCOVER THE GRAMMAR

Circle the question word. Underline the verb **be**. *Then match these questions and answers.*

_b_ **1.** (Where) were you last night?   **a.** It was warm.

_____ **2.** Who was with you?   **b.** I was at a soccer game.

_____ **3.** How was the game?   **c.** Two hours.

_____ **4.** How long was the game?   **d.** Exciting.

_____ **5.** How was the weather?   **e.** My sister.

2 | CONVERSATIONS   *Grammar Notes 1–5*

Put these words in the right order. Make conversations.

1. A: How / your weekend / was / ?   **A:** _How was your weekend?_____

   B: was / It / great / .   **B:** _____

2. A: you / were / Where / ?   **A:** _____

   B: a jazz concert / At / .   **B:** _____

3. A: was / When / the concert / ?   **A:** _____

   B: last night / was / It / .   **B:** _____

4. A: the musician / Who / was / ?   **A:** _____

   B: was / Wynton Marsalis / It / .   **B:** _____

5. A: the concert / long / was / How / ?   **A:** _____

   B: two hours / It / was / .   **B:** _____

3 | WHAT'S THE QUESTION?   *Grammar Notes 1–6*

Write questions about the underlined *words.*

1. A: _How was the weather_____?   **3. A:** _____ Pierre on

   B: It was sunny.   Monday?

2. A: _____ at the   **B:** He was in Paris.

   movies?   **4. A:** _____?

   B: Mark was.   **B:** The party was yesterday.

(continued)

5. A: _____?   **6. A:** _____ the movie?

   B: Mark and Jason were <u>with Kathy</u>.   **B:** The movie was <u>three hours long</u>.

4 | EDITING

Correct these conversations. There are eight mistakes. The first mistake is already corrected.

1. **A:** How ~~were~~ ^{was} your weekend?

   B: Saturday evening was great.

   A: Where was you?

   B: At a soccer game.

   A: How the game was?

   B: Exciting and long.

   A: How long were it?

   B: Three hours.

2. **A:** How were your vacation?

   B: OK.

   A: Where you were?

   B: Was at the beach.

   A: How were the weather?

   B: Cool and rainy.

   A: That's too bad.

Communication Practice

5 | HOW WAS JASON'S WEEKEND?

🎧 *Listen to the conversation. Answer these questions.*

1. Jason's weekend was _____.

   a. good   **b.** great   **c.** bad

2. He was at _____.

   a. the beach   **b.** the movies   **c.** home

3. The weather was _____.

   a. sunny and cool   **b.** sunny and hot   **c.** sunny and cold

6 | INFORMATION GAP: HOW WAS THE WEATHER ON SUNDAY?

A *Do you know the days of the week? Read them aloud.*

| Sunday | Monday | Tuesday | Wednesday | Thursday | Friday | Saturday |

B *Work with a partner.*

Student B, look at the Information Gap on page IG-1. Follow the instructions there.

Student A, complete this chart. Ask your partner questions about the weather in Tokyo.

Then answer your partner's questions about the weather in Rio.

Example: **A:** How was the weather in Tokyo last Sunday?
B: It was warm and sunny.

	Tokyo	**Rio de Janeiro**
Sunday		warm
Monday		hot
Tuesday		warm

7 | GAME: WHO WAS REALLY THERE?

A *Work in groups of three. Choose a place where only one student was.*

All three students say, "I was in _____."

Example: **STUDENT A:** I was in Kyoto.
STUDENT B: I was in Kyoto.
STUDENT C: I was in Kyoto.

B *The class asks the three students questions.*

Examples: When were you there? / How was the weather? / Who were you with? /
Were you on a tour? / How long were you there?

C *Students A, B, and C answer the questions. The class guesses who was really there.*

I *Complete these conversations. Circle the correct letter.*

1. AMANDA: Where were you last night?

    KATHY: _____

  (**A**) Yes, I was.   (**C**) Were you alone?

  (**B**) At the movies.   (**D**) For two hours.

2. MARK: Was she at the library?

    STEVE: _____

  (**A**) No, she was.   (**C**) Who was at the library?

  (**B**) Yes, she was.   (**D**) No, they weren't.

3. KATHY: _____

    AMANDA: Where were you?

  (**A**) Sorry I wasn't home last night.   (**C**) Are you at the library?

  (**B**) Were you at home?   (**D**) Mark and I are at a soccer game.

4. JASON: How long were you there?

    MARK: _____

  (**A**) Fine, thanks.   (**C**) Yesterday.

  (**B**) By car.   (**D**) Four days.

5. JASON: _____

    MARK: It was cool.

  (**A**) How was the weather?   (**C**) How long was it?

  (**B**) How are you?   (**D**) Where were you?

6. JASON: _____

    MARK: No, I wasn't. I was alone.

  (**A**) How were you?   (**C**) Were you on a tour?

  (**B**) Where were you?   (**D**) What movie was it?

7. AMANDA: _____

    KATHY: It was scary.

  (**A**) How long was the movie?   (**C**) How was the movie?

  (**B**) How is the movie?   (**D**) Who was in the movie?

II   *Complete these conversations. Use* **was**, **were**, **wasn't**, *or* **weren't** *and* **I, you, he, she, it,** *or* **they** *in your answers.*

1. A: Was I right?

  B: Yes, _____*you*_____ _____*were*_____.

2. A: Was it hot in Mexico City?

  B: No, _____ _____. It was cool.

3. A: Were they in Madrid?

  B: No, _____ _____. They were in Barcelona.

4. A: Were you at home?

  B: Yes, _____ _____ at home all day.

5. A: Was John F. Kennedy ever president of the United States?

  B: Yes, _____ _____.

6. A: Was your aunt in Hawaii?

  B: No, _____ _____ in Fiji.

III   *Complete these questions about the photo. Use the words in the box.*

How	How long	What	When	Where	~~Who~~

A: _____*Who*_____'s that woman?
      1.

B: My sister.

A: _____ is she?
     2.

B: In Bryce.

A: _____'s Bryce?
     3.

B: It's a national park in Utah. We were there with her on a family vacation.

A: _____ were you there?
       4.

B: Last year.

A: _____ were you there?
      5.

B: Three days.

A: It looks hot. _____ was the weather?
           6.

B: Really, really hot.

IV *Complete this letter from Judy to her family. Use the present or past of **be**. Use contractions with pronoun subjects.*

Hi Everyone,

    Last week ___was___ terrible. It _____ exam week. My friends and I
              1.   **2.**
_____ at the library every day. But this is an easy week. We _____ free
  3.   **4.**
to read and relax. No homework, no exams.

    How _____ everyone at home? Mom, how _____ your flowers? Beautiful,
        5.   **6.**
I _____ sure. And Ken, how _____ your arm? I hope it _____ OK.
  7.   **8.**   **9.**
Remember! Basketball _____ just a game. Dad, thanks for the check. My
                       10.
classes _____ terrific this year, especially journalism.
        11.

    Well, send my love to Grandma.

                       Love,

                       Judy

▶ *To check your answers, go to the Answer Key on page RT-1.*

UNIT

The Simple Present: Statements

Nick likes computers.

9

Grammar in Context

🎧 *Read this conversation.*

JUDY: I **need** more coffee. Would you like some?

MARK: Yes, please.

JUDY: Here you go.

MARK: Thanks.

JUDY: Oh! New photos?

MARK: Yes . . . Look at this one. This **is** my brother, Nick. He **lives** in Kenya. He **teaches** English there.

JUDY: In Kenya? Wow! . . . You **look** alike.

MARK: I **know**. We both **have** dark brown hair and green eyes.

JUDY: And you**'re** both tall.

MARK: But we**'re** different in a lot of ways.

JUDY: How?

MARK: Well, I **like** people and parties. Nick **likes** computers. I **don't like** computers, and Nick **doesn't like** parties.

JUDY: Anything else?

MARK: Uh-huh. I **speak** Chinese. Nick **speaks** Swahili. I **read** newspapers and magazines. Nick **reads** novels and grammar books. I **call** my friends. I **watch** DVDs almost every night, but Nick **goes** online. He **e-mails** me a lot.

JUDY: Yeah? He **sounds** interesting.

Words

🎧 *Do you know these words? Read the words. Write new words in your notebook.*

| **look alike** | **go online** | **a novel** | **a newspaper** | **a magazine** |

Expressions

🎧 *Do you know these expressions? Read the conversations. Write new expressions in your notebook.*

1. **A:** *Would you like* some coffee?
   B: Yes, please.
   A: *Here you go.*
   B: Thanks.

2. **A:** This is my sister.
   B: You *look alike.*

3. **A:** She *sounds interesting.*
   B: She is.

Working Together

A *Practice the conversation in the opening reading with a partner.*

B *Talk about these people with your partner. Use these words:*

| come from | look alike / don't look alike | sister / brother | speak |

Venus and Serena Williams,
United States, English

Prince Harry and Prince William,
Great Britain, English

Example: Venus and Serena Williams are sisters. They . . .

Grammar Presentation

THE SIMPLE PRESENT: STATEMENTS

Affirmative Statements		
Subject	**Verb**	
I You* We They	**come**	from Brazil.
He She It	**comes**	

Negative Statements			
Subject	*Do not / Does not*	**Base Form of Verb**	
I You* We They	**do not don't**	**come**	from China.
He She It	**does not doesn't**	**come**	from China.

*You is both singular and plural.

GRAMMAR NOTES

EXAMPLES

GRAMMAR NOTES	EXAMPLES
1. Use the **simple present** to talk about **facts** or things that **happen again and again**.	• I **live** in Kenya. (*a fact*) • He **watches** TV every night. (*a thing that happens again and again*)
2. In **affirmative statements**, use the **base form** of the verb with *I*, *you*, *we*, and *they*. Add *-s* or *-es* only with the **third-person singular** (*he*, *she*, *it*). Add *-s* to most verbs. Add *-es* to verbs that end in *ch*, *o*, *s*, *sh*, *x*, or *z*.	• We **live** in Redmond. • They **have** a house in Seattle. • He **reads** travel books. • She **watches** TV at night. • She **does** her homework after class.
3. Use *do not* or *does not* + the **base form** of the verb to make a **negative statement**. We often use the contractions *don't* and *doesn't* in speaking and informal writing.	• They **do not live** in the city. • He **does not speak** Chinese. • They **don't live** in the city. • He **doesn't speak** Chinese.

---

4. *Be* and *have* are **irregular verbs**.

NOTE: Look at Unit 12 for more practice with *be* and *have*.

- I **am** a teacher. Steve **is** a teacher too.
- I **have** a lot of students. Steve **has** a lot of students too.

Reference Note
For more on the **spelling and pronunciation of the third-person singular**, see Appendix 13 on page A-15.

Focused Practice

1 | DISCOVER THE GRAMMAR

A *Check (✓) the sentences in the simple present.*

_____ **1.** Please speak English. Please don't speak Spanish.

__✓__ **2.** Nick and I look alike. We're brothers.

_____ **3.** Jessica speaks Spanish. She doesn't speak Italian.

_____ **4.** I have brown eyes. I don't have blue eyes.

_____ **5.** Drive to the corner and turn left.

_____ **6.** Jeremy has a brother and a sister.

B *Check (✓) the sentences in the third-person singular.*

_____ **1.** Annie and I don't like fish.

_____ **2.** Maryam speaks Arabic.

_____ **3.** It doesn't snow in Brazil.

_____ **4.** She doesn't speak Italian.

_____ **5.** Nick likes computers.

_____ **6.** They come from Hong Kong.

2 | COUNTRIES AND LANGUAGES
Grammar Notes 1–2

Write two sentences about these people.

1.   **Name:** Heng

    Place: Beijing, China _Heng lives in Beijing, China._

    Language: Chinese _She speaks Chinese._

2.   **Name:** Ali

    Place: Amman, Jordan _____

    Language: Arabic _____

3.   **Names:** João and Rosa

    Place: Salvador, Brazil_____

    Language: Portuguese _____

4.   **Name:** Elena

    Place: Santiago, Chile _____

    Language: Spanish_____

5.   **Names:** Maureen and James

    Place: Dublin, Ireland _____

    Language: English _____

3 | AT THE RESTAURANT
Grammar Notes 1–3

Complete this conversation with the correct form of **want.** *Use the affirmative or negative of the simple present.*

WAITER: Can I help you?

TIM: Yes, thanks. The children ___*want*___ ice cream. My son _____ chocolate.
                                                   1.   2.

BEN: No, Dad. I _____ chocolate. I _____ vanilla.
                   3. (not)   4.

    Annie _____ chocolate.
        5.

TIM: OK. My son _____ vanilla. My daughter _____ chocolate.
                    6.   7.

WAITER: And you, sir?

TIM: I _____ ice cream. I just _____ a soda.
        8. (not)   9.

WAITER: Is that all?

TIM: Yes, thanks.

4 | *HAVE, LIKE, NEED, AND WANT*

Look at the pictures. Then complete these sentences with affirmative or negative verbs.

1. Jeremy _____*has*_____ an old car.
(have)

He _____*doesn't have*_____ a new car.

2. Annie _____ pizza.
(like)

She _____ salad.

3. The man _____ water.
(need)

He _____ ice cream.

4. Judy _____ tea.
(want)

She _____ coffee.

5 | EDITING

Correct this letter. There are eight mistakes. The first mistake is already corrected.

> Dear Mary,
>
>   Spain is great. The Spanish people are very friendly, but they ~~speaks~~ *speak* so fast. Jim speak Spanish very well. He don't understand everything, but he understand a lot. I speak a little Spanish. I don't understand much yet.
>
>   It's rainy here! People say it don't usually rain much in the summer here. We're at my cousin's house. He and his wife lives in a beautiful apartment in Madrid. Juan work in an office downtown. His wife Alicia not works. She stays at home with the children.
>
>   See you soon.
>
>   Rose

Communication Practice

6 | EVERYONE SPEAKS THREE LANGUAGES

🎧 *Listen to the conversation between Tim Olson and a man he meets on a train. Then listen again and complete these sentences.*

1. They're going to _____.

   a. Chicago   **b.** Seattle   **c.** Bucharest

2. The man doesn't live in _____.

   a. Romania   **b.** Bucharest   **c.** Chicago

3. The man comes from _____.

   a. Romania   **b.** Russia   **c.** Rwanda

4. A lot of people in the man's country know some _____.

   a. English   **b.** French   **c.** Spanish

5. The man speaks _____ languages.

   a. one   **b.** two   **c.** three

6. Tim doesn't speak any _____.

   a. English   **b.** Romanian   **c.** Spanish

7 | WHAT DO YOU DO?

🎧 *Listen to the next part of the conversation. Then listen again and complete these sentences with simple present verbs.*

TIM: Do you live in Seattle?

MAN: For the moment. My wife has a teaching job at the university this year.

TIM: Oh. What does she teach?

MAN: She _____ European literature. She also writes novels.
1.

TIM: That _____ interesting.
2.

MAN: Yes, it is. But it's also difficult. She _____ American English too well.
3.

What about you? What do you do?

TIM: I'm a graphic artist. I _____ for an advertising agency.
4.

MAN: And do you _____ in Seattle?
5.

TIM: We _____ in the city, but we _____ near it.
6.   7.

8 | TRUE STATEMENTS

A *Write true statements about yourself.*

I live in _____.   I don't like _____.

I work _____.   I need _____.

I don't work _____.   I don't need _____.

I speak _____.   I want _____.

I don't speak _____.   I don't want _____.

I like _____.

B *Now work with a partner. Tell your partner four things about yourself. Your partner tells another classmate about you.*

Example: **A:** [*to B*] I work in a department store. I speak two languages. I like chocolate ice cream. I don't like pizza.

B: [*to C*] She works in a department store. She speaks two languages. She likes chocolate ice cream. She doesn't like pizza.

C: [*to B*] That sounds interesting. What about you?

9 | TRUE OR FALSE?

A *Work with a partner. Take turns. Use the words to make affirmative sentences in the simple present. Three of the statements are true, and four are false. Correct the false statements.*

Example: Most people / in Beijing / speak Spanish
    A: Most people in Beijing speak Spanish.
    B: False. Most people in Beijing speak Chinese.

1. Antonio Banderas / come from / Spain

2. Most people / in Thailand / eat with chopsticks

3. People / in Japan / drive / on the left

4. People / in Great Britain / drive / on the right

5. People / live / at the North Pole

6. Penguins / live / in deserts

7. It / snow / in Chile / in July

B *Check your answers on page P-1.*

Grammar in Context

🎧 *Read this telephone conversation.*

STEVE: Hello.

MARK: Hi, Steve. This is Mark.

STEVE: Hey, Mark. What's up?

MARK: Nothing much. Kathy thinks I need a haircut. I'm not so sure. But **do you know** a good barber?

STEVE: Yes. At least I like him. But he's not a barber. He's a hairstylist. His name is Marcello.

MARK: Oh. **Does he charge** a lot?

STEVE: No, he doesn't. He's very reasonable, but he's pretty busy. You need an appointment.

MARK: Well, then, **do you have** his phone number?

STEVE: I think so. Hold on. I'll get it . . .
It's 306-555-0908. Make an appointment, Mark. I think Kathy's right. You need a haircut.

MARK: **Do you** really **think** so? I kind of like my hair this way. But thanks for the number.

STEVE: No problem. Bye.

MARK: Bye.

Words

🎧 *Do you know these words? Read the words. Write new words in your notebook.*

Thursday	April 5
9:00	
10:00	*haircut with Marcello*
11:30	
12:00	
1:00	
2:00	

a barber   **a hairstylist**   **an appointment**

Expressions

🎧 *Do you know these expressions? Read the conversations. Write new expressions in your notebook.*

1. **A:** Does he **charge a lot**?
   B: Yes, he does. He's expensive.
   OR
   No, he doesn't. He's **reasonable**.

2. **A:** **What's up?**
   B: **Nothing much.**

3. **A:** Do you have his phone number?
   B: Yes, I do. **Hold on.** I'll get it.

Working Together

A *Practice the conversation in the opening reading with a partner.*

B *Work with a partner. Take turns asking your partner for suggestions. Use the words in the box.*

doctor	hairstylist	mechanic	music store	painter	Thai restaurant

Do you know a good _____?

Yes. At least, I like _____.

Sorry, I don't.

think? Discuss with a partner.

picture of Mark on page 74. Does he need a haircut?

artner: Do you cut hair?

Grammar Presentation

THE SIMPLE PRESENT: *YES / NO* QUESTIONS

Yes / No Questions
Do
Do I **need** a haircut?
Do you **want** his phone number?
Do we **have** his new address?
Do they **have** an appointment?

Short Answers	
Affirmative	Negative
Yes, you **do**.	No, you **don't**.
Yes, I **do**.	No, I **don't**.
Yes, we **do**.	No, we **don't**.
Yes, they **do**.	No, they **don't**.

Yes / No Questions
Does
Does she **think** so?
Does he **have** time on Wednesday?
Does it **mean** "yes"?

Short Answers	
Affirmative	Negative
Yes, she **does**.	No, she **doesn't**.
Yes, he **does**.	No, he **doesn't**.
Yes, it **does**.	No, it **doesn't**.

GRAMMAR NOTES

EXAMPLES

1. Use *do* or *does* + a **subject** + the **base form** of the verb to ask *yes / no questions* in the simple present. Use *do* with **I**, *you*, **we**, and *they*. Use *does* with **he**, *she*, and *it*.	• **Do** you **want** his number? • **Does** he **know** Spanish?
2. We usually use **short answers** in conversation. Sometimes we use **long answers**.	A: **Do** you **know** a good doctor? B: **No.** OR **No, I don't.** B: **No. I don't know a good doctor.**

Focused Practice

1 | DISCOVER THE GRAMMAR

Read these sentences. Underline the six yes / no *questions. Then match the sentences on the left and the right.*

_c_ **1.** <u>Do you know a good yoga teacher?</u>

_____ **2.** Do you take yoga lessons with him?

_____ **3.** I think so. Does your cousin have classes for beginners?

_____ **4.** Sure. Do you have a pen? My pen doesn't work.

a. Yes. He gives lessons in the park three times a week. Do you want to learn yoga?

b. No problem.

c. Yes, I do. My cousin teaches yoga. He's excellent.

d. Yes, he does. They're at 6:00 P.M. every Wednesday. Do you want his number?

2 | SHORT CONVERSATIONS   *Grammar Note 1*

Complete these questions with **Do** *or* **Does** *and the correct word from the box.*

cost	have	~~know~~	like	live	mean	need

1. A: _____Do_____ you _____know_____ a good music store?

   B: Yes, I do. I get all my CDs at Power Records.

2. A: _____ that CD _____ a lot?

   B: No, it's not expensive.

3. A: _____ I _____ a haircut?

   B: I think so. Your hair is really long.

4. A: _____ she _____ near you?

   B: Yes, she does. Her home is next door.

5. A: _____ you _____ the music?

   B: Yes. It's beautiful.

6. A: _____ Steve _____ a big apartment?

   B: No. It's small, but comfortable.

7. A: _____ *expensive* _____ the opposite of *cheap*?

   B: Yes, it does.

3 | QUESTIONS

Grammar Note 1

*Write yes / no questions in the simple present. Use the words in parentheses and **Do** or **Does**.*

1. (you / like computer games) _Do you like computer games_ ?

2. (you / know a good Mexican restaurant) _____?

3. (your family / eat dinner together) _____?

4. (your best friend / live near you) _____?

5. (your friends / like to work out) _____?

6. (your friends / spend time at malls) _____?

4 | ANSWERS

Grammar Notes 1–2

*Read these questions. Write short answers and use **do** or **does**.*

1. A: Do you like classical music?

   B: _____Yes, I do_____. I listen to it all the time.

2. A: Does your cousin drive?

   B: _____. He has an international license.

3. A: Do you know a good gym?

   B: _____. Do you want the name of it?

4. A: Does your best friend have a motorcycle?

   B: _____. She has a car.

5. A: Does the car need gas?

   B: _____. The tank is full.

6. A: Do you like Indian food?

   B: _____. It's too spicy for me.

7. A: Does your sister have a pet?

   B: _____. She has a cat.

8. A: Do your parents live in Seattle?

   B: _____. They live in Boston.

5 | AN APPOINTMENT

Complete this conversation. Use the words in parentheses and **do** *or* **does***.*

A: Hello. Fabulous Hair.

B: Hello. I'd like to make an appointment for a haircut this Thursday.

_____*Does Marcello have time*_____?
1. (Marcello / have / time)

A: I'm sorry. He's busy all day Thursday. _____ to try Rob? He's
2. (you / want)

excellent.

B: No. I really want Marcello. _____ next Thursday?
3. (he / have / time)

A: Yes, he does. How about ten o'clock?

B: Great. My name is Mark Mason.

A: _____ Mark with a *k* or a *c* at the end?
4. (you / spell)

B: A *k* . . . By the way, _____ credit cards?
5. (you / take)

A: Yes, we do . . . So, we'll see you Thursday.

B: That's right. See you Thursday at ten.

6 | EDITING

Correct this conversation. There are six mistakes. The first mistake is already corrected.

A: Do you ~~knows~~ *know* a good Thai restaurant?

B: Yes, I do. It's on Main Street.

A: Does it stays open late?

B: Yes, it do.

A: What's the name of the restaurant?

B: Jasmine.

A: Do you spelled it J-A-S-M-I-N?

B: Uh-huh, but it has an *e* at the end.

A: Costs the restaurant a lot?

B: No, it don't. It's very reasonable. And it has a garden.

A: Thanks. It sounds perfect.

Communication Practice

7 | A PERFECT GIFT

Listen to this conversation between Mark and Judy about a birthday gift. Then listen again and complete these sentences.

JUDY: Are you going to the game?

MARK: No. It's my grandmother's birthday and I need to get a gift.

_____?

1.

JUDY: Let's see. _____?

2.

MARK: I don't know.

JUDY: Well, _____?

3.

MARK: I don't really know.

JUDY: _____?

4.

MARK: I think so. But I'm not sure.

JUDY: I've got it. I know the perfect gift.

MARK: You do? What?

JUDY: _____.

5.

MARK: That's not a gift.

JUDY: Yes, it is. _____.

6.

8 | FIND SOMEONE WHO

A *Find someone who does the things in the box. Write five* yes / no *questions. Ask four classmates your questions. Follow the example below.*

Example: **JUAN:**   Anna, do you like chocolate?
           ANNA: Yes, I do.
           JUAN: Pablo, do you like chocolate?
        PABLO: No, I don't.

knows a good joke	likes chocolate	likes the rain
has more than three brothers or sisters	speaks more than three languages	

Yes / No **Questions**	**Student A**	**Student B**	**Student C**	**Student D**
1.				
2.				
3.				
4.				
5.				

B *Tell the class about your classmates.*

Example: **JUAN:** [*to the class*] Anna likes chocolate. Pablo doesn't like chocolate.

Grammar in Context

🎧 *Read this conversation.*

JEREMY: So . . . **how do you like** the United States?

YOSHIO: I like it a lot. But it's really different from Japan.

JEREMY: **What do you mean?**

YOSHIO: Well, for one thing, I think people work longer hours in Japan.

JEREMY: Some people work pretty late here too. **What time do people go** to bed there?

YOSHIO: Well, students study a lot, so they stay up till midnight or later. And my father stays up till 1:00 or 2:00 A.M.

JEREMY: **Why does he stay up** so late? **What does he do?**

YOSHIO: He's a businessman. People in business often meet clients in the evening.

JEREMY: **What time do people get up** in the morning in Japan?

YOSHIO: Oh, maybe seven or seven-thirty. I sleep in on weekends.

JEREMY: Me too. Hmm . . . **What else is** different?

YOSHIO: Hmm . . . Well, people wear their shoes in the house here. In Japan we take our shoes off at the doorway.

JEREMY: Really? Everyone?

YOSHIO: Yes, everyone.

JEREMY: So **what do you like** best about the United States?

YOSHIO: People here are really open. I already have a lot of friends at Redmond High School.

JEREMY: That's great. Hey, we have to go to calculus class.

YOSHIO: **What time does it start?**

JEREMY: Two-thirty.

YOSHIO: OK, let's go.

Words

🎧 *Do you know these words? Read the words. Write new words in your notebook.*

| **go to bed early** | **stay up late** | **get up** | **take off your shoes** |

Expressions

🎧 *Do you know these expressions? Read the conversations. Write new expressions in your notebook.*

1. A: Do you want to see a movie together?
   B: Sure. ***Let's go.***

2. A: How late do you work?
   B: ***Till*** midnight.

3. A: I ***sleep in*** on weekends.
   B: ***Me too.***

Working Together

A *Practice the conversation in the opening reading with a partner.*

B *Ask a partner questions.*

> **Example:** **A:** Do you (stay up late / go to bed early / get up early)?
> **B:** Yes, I do. / No, I don't.
> **A:** What time do you go to bed? / How late do you stay up?
> **B:** Ten-thirty.

C *Read the story and answer the question. Then check your answer on page P-1.*

What Do I Do?

My day begins early. I get up at 5:00 A.M., and I start work at 6:00 A.M. I finish work at 3:00 P.M. For my job, I need a special driver's license. I see a lot of people when I work—young people, adults, and older people. They use cash or a Metrocard to pay. Most of them are nice. Some of them aren't. I am very careful in my work, especially when it rains. Sometimes, when it snows, I don't work. What do I do?

Grammar Presentation

THE SIMPLE PRESENT: *WH-* QUESTIONS

Wh- Questions	Answers
How do I **get** there?	Take the number 3 bus.
Why do you **go** to bed so early?	I start work at 6:00 A.M.
When do we **leave**?	After work.
Where do they **live**?	In Seattle.
What does he **do**?	He's a bus driver.
How late **does** she **stay up**?	At least until midnight.
What time **does** it **start**?	At seven o'clock.

Wh- Questions about the Subject	Answers
Who wakes you **up**? Your mom?	No. My alarm clock does.
What happens on Saturday?	We sleep in.

GRAMMAR NOTES

EXAMPLES

1. ***Wh-* questions** ask for **information**. They often start with ***when***, ***why***, ***how***, ***where***, ***what time***, ***who***, or ***what***.

   - **What time do** you **start** work?
   - **What time does** he **get up**?
   - **Where does** Annie **go** to school?
   - **How does** she **get** to school?

   Use a ***wh-* word** + ***do*** or ***does*** + the subject + the base form of the verb.

   ▶ **BE CAREFUL!** Use ***do*** with ***I***, ***you***, ***we***, and ***they***. Use ***does*** with ***he***, ***she***, and ***it***.

2. To ask a **question about the subject**, use ***who*** or ***what*** + the third-person singular form of the verb. Do not use *do* or *does*.

   - **Who wakes** you **up**? Your mom?
     NOT: Who ~~does wake~~ you up?
   - **What happens** on Sunday?

3. NOTE: To ask about the meaning of a word, say ***"What does . . . mean?"***

   To answer, say, " . . . means . . ."

   To ask about the spelling of a word, say ***"How do you spell . . . ?"***

   A: **What does** *little* **mean**?
   NOT: ~~What means *little*?~~
   NOT: ~~What does mean *little*?~~
   B: *Little* **means** "small."

   A: **How do** you **spell** *shoes*?
   B: S-H-O-E-S.

🎧 Pronunciation Note
Remember: In pronunciation we use falling intonation for *wh-* questions: Where do you live?

Focused Practice

1 | DISCOVER THE GRAMMAR

Read this conversation. Underline the wh- *questions in the simple present.*

MARK: So . . . <u>what do you think of your new job</u>?

JOSH: Great. I love it. But it's really different.

MARK: What do you mean?

JOSH: Well, I have to go to bed early and get up early.

MARK: What time do you go to bed?

JOSH: About 10:30.

MARK: Who wakes you up? Amanda?

JOSH: Amanda? No way! My alarm clock does.

MARK: Hmm. How do you like your boss?

JOSH: She's nice. And I like the other guys in the office. We eat lunch together and have great conversations.

MARK: What do you talk about?

JOSH: Everything. Sports. Travel. Movies.

MARK: That's great.

2 | INTERVIEW

Grammar Note 1

Josh's niece is interviewing him for her school newspaper. Write her wh- *questions in the simple present.*

1. (Where / you / work) *Where do you work* _____ ?

2. (What time / you / start work) _____ ?

3. (What / you do in your job) _____ ?

4. (Who / you / work with) _____ ?

5. (How late / you / stay up at night) _____ ?

6. (What sport / you / really like) _____ ?

7. (Why / you / like it) _____ ?

8. (When / you / play it) _____ ?

3 | WHAT'S THE QUESTION?   *Grammar Notes 1–3*

Write wh- *questions about the underlined words. Use* **how**, **who**, **what**, **where**, **why**, *or* **what time**.

1. A: _Where do they live?_ _____?

   B: They live on <u>40th Street in Redmond</u>.

2. A: Jeremy, _____?

   B: I go to bed <u>at 11:00 or 11:15</u>.

3. A: Annie, _____?

   B: I feel <u>good</u>.

4. A: Ben, _____?

   B: I play soccer <u>because it's very exciting</u>.

5. A: Mom, _____?

   B: *Fascinating* means "<u>very interesting</u>."

6. A: _____?

   B: <u>S-L-E-E-P-Y</u>.

7. A: Yoshio, _____?

   B: <u>My mother</u> wakes my father up in the morning.

4 | EDITING

Correct this conversation. There are four mistakes. The first mistake is already corrected.

A: Hey! I have a new job.

B: Really? Where ^do you work?

A: At a bookstore.

B: What you do?

A: I'm a salesperson.

B: Does you like the work?

A: Yes. It's challenging.

B: *Challenging*? I don't know that word. What means *challenging*?

A: It means "hard but interesting."

Communication Practice

5 | WHAT DO YOU DO, JASON?

🎧 *Listen to this conversation about Jason's first day on the job. Then listen again and answer the questions in complete sentences.*

1. Who is new in the company? _____

2. What does Jason do? _____

3. What does Margaret do? _____

4. Does Jason like his job? _____

5. What does Jason dislike? _____

6. Where do Jason and Margaret live? _____

7. Does Margaret drive to work? _____

8. What time does Margaret catch the bus? _____

6 | ASK YOUR PARTNER

Work with a partner. Ask your partner some of the questions from Exercise 2. Your partner answers the questions.

Example: **A:** Where do you work?
B: I work at a supermarket. Where do you work?
A: I work . . .
OR
I don't work. I go to school full time.

7 | INFORMATION GAP: WHAT DOES *TINY* MEAN?

Work with a partner.

Student B, look at the Information Gap on page IG-2 and follow the instructions there.

Student A, ask Student B about the meaning of a word from your list. Write the answer. Then answer Student B's question. Choose an answer from the box. Take turns.

Example: **A:** What does *tiny* mean?
B: *Tiny* means "very small." What does *large* mean?

Student A's Words

1. tiny: _____ *very small* _____

2. boring: _____

3. noon: _____

4. midnight: _____

5. super: _____

6. unhappy: _____

7. terrible: _____

8. nice: _____

Student A's Answers	
the children of your aunt or uncle	good-looking
your parents, brothers, sisters, grandparents, and so on	intelligent
big	not married
between first and third	totally different

▶ *To check your answers, go to the Answer Key on page P-1.*

The Simple Present: *Be* and *Have*

She has two heads.

Grammar in Context

🎧 *Read this conversation.*

RICK: You**'re** in Music Appreciation 101, aren't you?

JUDY: Uh-huh . . .

RICK: Could you please give these tickets to Sonia Jones? She**'s** in your music appreciation class.

JUDY: Sure. But I don't know her. What does she look like?

RICK: Well, she **has** dark hair and dark eyes.

JUDY: Half the women **have** dark hair and dark eyes. And there **are** 100 students in my class.

RICK: She**'s** tall and thin.

JUDY: OK, but a lot of women **are** tall and thin.

RICK: She**'s** in her early twenties.

JUDY: Rick. That doesn't help. Almost everyone at school **is** 20-something. **Is** there something unusual about her?

RICK: She **has** two heads.

JUDY: Rick!

RICK: Sonia**'s** eight months pregnant. And her cell phone number **is** 917-555-0934.

JUDY: Why didn't you say so right away?

RICK: It**'s** more fun this way.

Words

🎧 *Do you know these words?*
Read the words. Write new
words in your notebook.

tall   short   thin   heavy   pregnant

wavy black hair   curly red hair   straight blond hair   wavy dark-brown hair

Expressions

🎧 *Do you know these expressions? Read the conversations. Write new expressions in your notebook.*

1. **A:** What does he *look like*?
   B: He's short and thin. He has straight brown hair and blue eyes.

2. **A:** How old is he?
   B: He's *20-something*.

3. **A:** Can you do this *right away*?
   B: *No problem.*

Working Together

A *Practice the conversation in the opening reading with a partner.*

B *Read this story with a partner and answer the question. Then check your answer on page P-2.*

Who Am I?

It is 1764. I am eight years old. I am from Austria. I am in England now with my family. My father is a violinist. I have an older sister. She is a violinist too. I play the violin and the harpsichord. I also write music. People say I have a beautiful voice. They say I am a child prodigy. The kings and queens of Europe love my music. My middle name is Amadeus. Who am I?

C *Discuss your musical tastes with a partner.*

1. What's your favorite kind of music? Check (✓) it.

   ☐ jazz   ☐ pop   ☐ hip-hop   ☐ rhythm and blues   ☐ classical   ☐ country

2. Who are your favorite singers?

Grammar Presentation

THE SIMPLE PRESENT: *BE* AND *HAVE*

Be
Affirmative Statements
I **am** short.
He **is** tall.
We **are** late.
Negative Statements
I**'m not** tall.
He**'s not** short. OR He **isn't** short.
We**'re not** early. OR We **aren't** early.
Yes / No **Questions**
Am I late?
Is he 25 years old?
Are we early?
Wh- **Questions**
Where am I?
Who is in your class? OR **Who's** in your class?
What are the tickets for?

Have
Affirmative Statements
I **have** brown eyes.
She **has** blue eyes.
We **have** a problem.
Negative Statements
I **don't have** green eyes.
She **doesn't have** green eyes.
We **don't have** time.
Yes / No **Questions**
Do I **have** any gray hair?
Does he **have** black hair?
Do we **have** time?
Wh- **Questions**
When does he **have** his class?
Who has the tickets?
What do I **have** on the top shelf?

GRAMMAR NOTES

EXAMPLES

1. *Be* and *have* are common irregular verbs. *Be* has three forms in the simple present: *am*, *is*, and *are*.

- I **am** short.
- He **is** tall.
- They **are** tall.

Have has two forms in the simple present: *have* and *has*. Use *have* with *I*, *you*, *we*, and *they*.

- **I have** black hair.
- **You have** blue eyes.
- **We have** blue eyes.
- **They have** brown eyes.

Use *has* with *he*, *she*, and *it*.

- **He has** brown hair.
- **She has** blond hair.
- **It has** green eyes.

2. In **negative statements** with *be*, use *am not*, *is not*, and *are not* or their contractions.

- I**'m not** home.
- She**'s not** tall.
- We **are not** musicians.

In negative statements with *have*, use *do not have* or *does not have* or their contractions.

- I **don't have** blue eyes.
- He **doesn't have** green eyes.

Contractions are more common in speaking and informal writing.

---

3. In a *yes / no* question with *be*, put *am*, *is*, or *are* before the subject.

- **Are you** a student?

In a *yes / no* question with *have*, use *do* or *does* + the subject + *have*.

- **Do you have** blue eyes?
- **Does he have** brown eyes?

---

4. For *wh-* questions with *be*, use the question word + *yes / no* question word order.

- **Where am** I?
- **What is** her name?
- **How are** his parents?

Most *wh-* questions with *have* use the *wh-* question word + *do* or *does* + a subject + the base form of the verb.

- **What does** he **have** for lunch?
- **When do** they **have** dinner?

Questions about the subject use statement word order. They do not use *do* or *does*.

- **Who has** green eyes?
  NOT: Who ~~does have~~ green eyes?

---

5. Use *be* to talk about **age**.

- **A:** How old **are** you?
- **B:** I **am** 21 years old.
  NOT: I ~~have~~ 21 years.

Focused Practice

1 | DISCOVER THE GRAMMAR

*Read each sentence. Write **A** for affirmative statements, **N** for negative statements, and **Q** for questions. Does the sentence use a form of **be** or **have**? Write **be** or **have**.*

_N, be_ **1.** He isn't very tall.

_____ **2.** He has long fingers.

_____ **3.** I am not 10 years old.

_____ **4.** Do you have long hair?

_____ **5.** How old is he?

_____ **6.** Her brother doesn't have a piano.

_____ **7.** Who is 20?

_____ **8.** Who has a violin?

2 | MIDORI   *Grammar Notes 3–4*

Complete these questions about a talented musician. Use the words in parentheses and the correct form of **be** *or* **have**.

A: (Who / Midori) _____*Who is Midori*_____?
                                    1.

B: She's a great violinist. She performs all over the world. She was a child prodigy.

A: (Where / she / from) _____?
                                    2.

B: She's from Osaka, Japan.

A: (she / in Japan / now) _____?
                                    3.

B: No. She lives in New York.

A: (she / any sisters or brothers) _____?
                                    4.

B: She has a brother, Ryu Goto.

A: (he / a violinist) _____?
                                    5.

B: Yes, he is. He's very talented too.

A: (Midori / other interests) _____?
                                    6.

B: Yes, she does. She works for the Midori Foundation. She also has a degree in psychology.

A: (What / the Midori Foundation) _____?
                                    7.

B: It's a group that brings classical music to children in public schools.

3 | EDITING

Correct this conversation. There are six mistakes. The first mistake is already corrected.

JUDY: Who was on the phone?

MARK: My cousin, Francisco.

JUDY: How old ~~has~~ *is* he?

MARK: Twenty-five.

JUDY: Where he from?

MARK: São Paulo.

JUDY: Is he a writer like you?

MARK: No. He a musician. He plays the guitar.

JUDY: He cute?

MARK: Yes, he is. He looks like me.

JUDY: Does he has a girlfriend?

MARK: Yes, he do.

JUDY: That's too bad.

Communication Practice

4 | WHICH MAN ARE THEY TALKING ABOUT?

🎧 *Listen to this conversation about a jazz musician. Look at the pictures. Then listen again. Which man is the woman talking about? Circle the letter of the picture.*

A   B   C   D

5 | WHO'S THE PERSON?

Work with a partner. Describe one of the people in Exercise 4 to your partner. Your partner points to the person. Take turns.

6 | DESCRIBE A FAMOUS PERSON

A *The class makes a list of famous people. Write their names on the board.*

B *Work in groups. A student in each group describes one of the people. Do not tell the name. The others in the group guess the person. Use the vocabulary in the box below.*

Example: **A:** She's from Canada. She's an actor. She's in her 40s. She's average height. She's not thin. She has brown hair. She's the star and writer of the movie *My Big Fat Greek Wedding.*

   B: Is it Nia Vardalo?

   A: Yes, it is.

Personal Information

Country: *See the world map in Appendix 1, page A-0.*

Age: *See numbers in Appendix 3, page A-3.*

Occupation: actor, athlete, political leader, musician, singer, scientist, writer, TV star

Height: tall, average height, short

Eye color: brown, black, blue, green, hazel, gray

Hair color: black, dark brown, light brown, red, blond, gray

Weight: average weight, thin, heavy

Marital status: single, married, divorced

13 Adverbs of Frequency

Do you ever sleep late?

Grammar in Context

Read this conversation.

JOSH: How's it going, Steve? You look kind of tired.

STEVE: Things are fine. I *am* a little tired, though.

JOSH: That's too bad. Any idea why?

STEVE: Well, I don't know . . . Maybe I'm not getting enough sleep.

JOSH: How many hours do you get a night?

STEVE: Oh, about six.

JOSH: What time do you **usually** go to bed?

STEVE: Hmm . . . I **usually** stay up till 12:30 or 1:00. And I get up at 6:30 or 7:00. On weekdays, anyway.

JOSH: Do you **ever** sleep late?

STEVE: **Sometimes**—on the weekend.

JOSH: And you **always** have fast food for lunch. And **sometimes** it's junk food.

STEVE: Well . . . yes . . . and I **sometimes** skip breakfast.

JOSH: So you don't eat three meals a day? Breakfast, lunch, and dinner?

STEVE: Well . . . not really. I'm **usually** in a hurry in the morning. So I skip breakfast.

JOSH: Not good, my friend. What about lunch and dinner?

STEVE: I **always** have a good dinner. But lunch . . . well, I **usually** go to a fast-food place near the university. I'm **always** in a hurry.

JOSH: Hmm. Not enough sleep. No breakfast. Junk food for lunch **sometimes**. You're living dangerously.

STEVE: Maybe. But I have one good habit. I exercise.

JOSH: Great. **How often**?

STEVE: Two or three times a year.

Words

🎧 *Do you know these words? Read the words. Write new words in your notebook.*

fast food

enough / not enough

skip

Expressions

🎧 *Do you know these expressions? Read the conversations. Write new expressions in your notebook.*

1. A: I'm **kind of** tired.
   B: That's too bad. Why?

2. A: Well, I'm always **in a hurry**. And I eat a lot of **junk food**.
   B: You're **living dangerously**.

Working Together

A *Practice the conversation in the opening reading with a partner.*

B *Work with a partner. Look at the pictures. Say what you **never**, **sometimes**, or **often** eat.*

Example: **A:** I never eat carrots.
   B: Really? I often eat carrots. I never eat red meat.

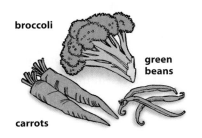
vegetables

fish

rice

doughnuts

red meat

ice cream

Grammar Presentation

ADVERBS OF FREQUENCY

Yes / No Questions	Short Answers		
Do you **ever** stay up late?	Yes, I	always usually often sometimes	do.
	No, I	rarely never	

↑ 100% of the time

↓ 0% of the time

Adverbs of Frequency with *Be*			
	Be	Adverb	
I	am	always usually often rarely	late.
He She It	is		
We You They	are		

Adverbs of Frequency with Other Verbs			
	Adverb	Verb	
I	sometimes	skip	lunch.
He	never	eats	breakfast.

GRAMMAR NOTES

EXAMPLES

1. Adverbs of frequency say **how often** something happens.	• I **often skip** breakfast. • She **sometimes skips** lunch.
2. Adverbs of frequency come **after** the verb *be*.	• I'm **usually** tired in the morning. • The food at that restaurant **is never** very good.
3. Adverbs of frequency usually come **before other verbs**. NOTE: *Usually* and *sometimes* can also come at the beginning or end of a sentence.	• He **usually goes** to a fast-food place near the theater. • It **always rains** on the weekends. • I **usually** get up at eight. OR • **Usually** I get up at eight. / I get up at eight, **usually**. • I **sometimes** skip breakfast. OR • **Sometimes** I skip breakfast. / I skip breakfast, **sometimes**.

<table>
<tr>
<td>

4. Use *ever* in *yes / no* questions. *Ever* means "at any time."

▶ **BE CAREFUL!** Do not use *ever* in affirmative statements.

</td>
<td>

A: Do you **ever sleep** late?
B: **Often.** OR **I often do.**

• I sleep late.
  NOT: I ~~ever~~ sleep late.

</td>
</tr>
<tr>
<td>

5. Use *how often* to ask about frequency.

</td>
<td>

A: **How often** do you exercise?
B: I **usually** exercise three times a week.

</td>
</tr>
</table>

Focused Practice

1 | DISCOVER THE GRAMMAR

Read the paragraph about Josh Wang. Find and circle the 10 adverbs of frequency. The first one is already circled.

Josh Wang has an active life. He (usually) gets up at 6:00 A.M. He always runs 2 or 3 miles with his dog. Sometimes he feels tired, but he still runs. When he gets home from running, he has breakfast. He often has eggs, juice, toast, and coffee, but sometimes he has cereal and fruit. Then Josh goes to work, and he's never late. He works from 9:00 until 5:00. He rarely stays late. In the evenings, Josh sometimes reads. Josh is also an artist, so sometimes he paints. He's always in bed by 10:30.

2 | CONVERSATIONS   *Grammar Notes 1–5*

Put the words in the correct order. Complete the conversation. Write questions and answers.

1. A: *Do you ever stay up late*_____?
          late / ever / Do / up / stay / you

   B: _____.
          do / Yes, / often / I

2. A: _____?
          tired / morning / you / Are / the / in / ever

   B: _____.
          then / always / I'm / tired

3. A: _____?
          often / exercise / How / you / do

   B: _____.
          week / a / five / usually / I / exercise / times

4. A: _____?
          usually / evening / you / do / What / the / in / do

   B: _____.
          piano / the / practice / I / often

3 | JESSICA'S HABITS

Grammar Notes 2–3

*Look at the pictures. Write sentences about Jessica Olson. Use **always**, **usually**, **sometimes**, or **never**.*

S ☑	Th ☑	S ☐	Th ☐	S ☐	Th ☑	S ☐	Th ☐
M ☑	F ☑	M ☐	F ☐	M ☑	F ☑	M ☑	F ☑
T ☑	Sa ☑	T ☐	Sa ☐	T ☑	Sa ☐	T ☐	Sa ☐
W ☑		W ☐		W ☐		W ☑	

1. (take a shower) *Jessica always takes a shower.* _____

2. (drive to work) _____

3. (arrive at work on time) _____

4. (cook dinner) _____

4 | EDITING

Correct Jessica's interview of sports star Domingo Rosario. There are six mistakes. The first mistake is already corrected.

                                                   How often

JESSICA: Domingo, you're a great soccer player. ~~How~~ do you exercise?

DOMINGO: I exercise six or seven days a week.

JESSICA: Do ever you get tired of exercising?

DOMINGO: Sure I do. But always I do it.

JESSICA: OK. How often do you travel?

DOMINGO: I travel a lot—at least three times a month.

JESSICA: Does ever your wife get unhappy because you travel so much?

DOMINGO: No, never she gets unhappy. She travels usually with me.

JESSICA: That's great, Domingo. Now, good luck in your next game.

Communication Practice

5 | A PHONE CALL FROM GRANDMA

🎧 *Listen to this telephone conversation between Ken and his grandmother. Then listen again and complete the statements.*

1. Grandma is calling Ken because tomorrow is _____.

2. Grandma is usually _____.

3. Ken is always _____.

4. Ken usually starts work at _____.

5. He never has time _____.

6. Ken sometimes stays up late _____.

7. Ken usually gets _____ of sleep.

8. Grandma says Ken needs _____ of sleep every night.

6 | TRUE STATEMENTS

A *Write true statements about yourself. Use the words in parentheses and an adverb of frequency.*

1. (be on time to class)_____

2. (read a newspaper in the morning) _____

3. (eat breakfast)_____

4. (eat fast food)_____

5. (sleep till noon on Saturday) _____

6. (go to the movies)_____

7. (play soccer) _____

8. (get enough sleep) _____

B *Change the statements you wrote to* yes / no *questions. Ask your partner the questions. Then tell the class three things about your partner.*

Example: **A:** Are you always on time to class?
B: No, I'm rarely on time to class.
A: Alicia is rarely on time to class.

IV Review Test

I *Complete these conversations. Circle the correct letter.*

1. WOMAN: Do you have his number?

    MAN: _____

(**A**) Yes, you have. It's 870-2278.   (**C**) Yes, I do. It's 870-2278.

(**B**) Yes, I am. It's 870-2278.   (**D**) Yes, you do. It's 870-2278.

2. **BEN:** Does he want chocolate ice cream?

    ANNIE: _____

(**A**) No, he does. He wants vanilla.   (**C**) No, we don't. We want vanilla.

(**B**) Yes, he does. He wants vanilla.   (**D**) No, he doesn't. He wants vanilla.

3. STEVE: _____

    MARK: Yes. Red is her favorite color.

(**A**) Does she like red?   (**C**) Why does she like red?

(**B**) What's her favorite color?   (**D**) Do we like red?

4. PEDRO: _____

    MARIA: "Very small."

(**A**) How do you spell *tiny*?   (**C**) What does *tiny* mean?

(**B**) How do you pronounce *tiny*?   (**D**) Who's tiny?

5. **KATHY:** _____

    AMANDA: At the airport.

(**A**) When does he work?   (**C**) Why does he work?

(**B**) Where does he work?   (**D**) Is he at the airport?

6. **KATHY:** _____

    AMANDA: At 10:30.

(**A**) Does he go to bed?   (**C**) Why does he go to bed at 10:30?

(**B**) Who goes to bed at 10:30?   (**D**) What time does he go to bed?

II   *Write sentences. Use the words below.*

1. John / late / always / is / . ___John is always late.___

2. at 9:00 / never / arrives / He / . _____

3. arrives / at 9:15 / usually / He / . _____

4. eat / do / Where / you / usually / ? _____

5. have / you / always / at noon / Do / lunch / ? _____

III   *Complete this paragraph. Use the correct form of* **have** *or* **be**.

Dana ___is___ an artist. She _____ 25 years old. She _____ from Ohio, but she
　　　　　1.　　　　　　　　　　　**2.**　　　　　　　　　　　　**3.**

lives in Florida now. She lives with four other artists. They _____ a big house. It
　　　　　　　　　　　　　　　　　　　　　　　　　　　　　　　　　4.

_____ a garden in the front. They also _____ a turtle and a parrot. The parrot's name
5.　　　　　　　　　　　　　　　　　**6.**

_____ Sammy. The bird _____ loud and funny. It sits outside and says, "Please don't
7.　　　　　　　　　　　**8.**

eat the flowers."

IV   *Complete these conversations. Use the words in parentheses.*

A. AMANDA: (What / she / do) ___What does she do___ ?
　　　　　　　　　　　　　　　　　　　　　　　1.

　　KATHY: She's a manager.

　　AMANDA: (Where / she / work) _____ ?
　　　　　　　　　　　　　　　　　　　　　　　2.

　　KATHY: At a bank.

　　AMANDA: (What time / she / start) _____ ?
　　　　　　　　　　　　　　　　　　　　　　　3.

　　KATHY: She starts at nine.

　　AMANDA: (How long / she / stay) _____ ?
　　　　　　　　　　　　　　　　　　　　　　　4.

　　KATHY: She stays until six.

　　AMANDA: That sounds like a good job.

(continued)

B. **MATT:** (Who / live / in that house) _____ ?
1.

PETER: Tim and Jessica Olson.

MATT: (What / they / do) _____ ?
2.

PETER: He's a graphic artist, and she's a TV news reporter.

MATT: (they / have / children) _____ ?
3.

PETER: Yes, they do. They have two sons and a daughter.

MATT: (the boy on the bike / their son) _____ ?
4.

PETER: Yes, that's Ben. He's a nice kid.

▶ *To check your answers, go to the Answer Key on page RT-1.*

The Present Progressive: Statements

Ron isn't studying. He's working.

Grammar in Context

🎧 *Read this conversation.*

JEREMY: Hello.

DANNY: Hey, Jeremy? This is Danny.

JEREMY: Hi, Danny. Where are you? What's going on?
Are you with Hiro and Ron?

DANNY: No. Hiro**'s studying**.

JEREMY: Don't tell me Ron**'s studying** too.

DANNY: No. Ron **isn't studying**. He**'s working**. I'm
with Matt. We're at the video store on Jackson
Avenue. We**'re looking** at the new games. Why
don't you come over?

JEREMY: I can't. I**'m watching** my sister and brother.

DANNY: Bring them along.

JEREMY: Impossible. They**'re watching** videos and
waiting for my Uncle Steve. Today's Ben's
birthday, and Uncle Steve has some computer
games for him.

DANNY: Cool. Maybe Ben wants some help.

JEREMY: Sure. Come on over. My grandma **is making**
vegetable soup and lasagna. My grandpa **is
baking** a cake. Stay for dinner.

DANNY: Thanks. We can play games all night.

JEREMY: Great. See you soon.

Words

🎧 *Do you know these words? Read the words. Write new words in your notebook.*

look at

wait for

lasagna   vegetable soup

Expressions

🎧 *Do you know these expressions? Read the conversations. Write new expressions in your notebook.*

1. **A:** *What's going on?*
   B: Hiro's studying.

2. **A:** *Come on over.*
   B: Thanks. *See you soon.*

Working Together

A *Practice the conversation in the opening reading with a partner.*

B *Practice the conversation that follows with a partner. Use the words in the box.*

department store / suits	electronics store / TVs	hardware store / tools
shoe store / running shoes	sports store / basketballs	

A: Hello.

B: Hi, Joe. This is Bill.

A: Are you calling from home?

B: No. I'm calling from the _____ store. They're having a sale on _____.

Grammar Presentation

THE PRESENT PROGRESSIVE: STATEMENTS

Affirmative Statements		
am	*is*	*are*
I **am listening**.	He **is talking**. She **is talking**. It **is raining**.	We **are listening**. You **are talking**. They **are talking**.
I**'m** listening.	He**'s** talking. She**'s** talking. It**'s** raining.	We**'re** listening. You**'re** talking. They**'re** talking.

Negative Statements		
am not	*is not*	*are not*
I **am not talking**.	He **is not listening**. She **is not reading**. It **is not snowing**.	We **are not working**. You **are not listening**. They **are not working**.
I**'m not** talking.	He**'s not** listening. Jeremy **isn't** listening. She**'s not** talking. Annie **isn't** talking. It**'s not** snowing.	We**'re not** talking. Tim and I **aren't** talking. You**'re not** talking. You and Annie **aren't** talking. They**'re not** talking. Tim and Jeremy **aren't** talking.

GRAMMAR NOTES

EXAMPLES

1. Use the **present progressive** to talk about an action that is **happening now**.

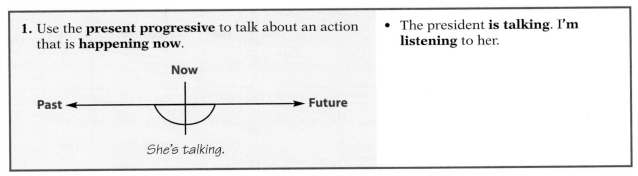

- The president **is talking**. I**'m listening** to her.

2. Use a form of *be* + the **verb** + *-ing* to form the present progressive.

- I **am listening**. (listen)
- She **is talking**. (talk)
- He is wri**ting**. (write)

NOTE: If the **base verb ends in** *-e*, drop the *-e* and add *-ing*.

If the **base verb is one syllable** and it ends in consonant + vowel + consonant, **double the last consonant**. Then add *-ing*.

- She is run**ning**. (run)
- They're sit**ting**. (sit)
- We're shop**ping** (shop)

EXCEPTION: **Do not double** the last consonant if it is *w*, *x*, or *y*.

- We're gro**wing** tomatoes.
- He's fi**xing** his computer.
- She's pla**ying** ball.

---

3. We often use **contractions** in speaking and informal writing.

- He**'s** playing ball.
- I**'m** reading.
- They**'re** smiling.

---

4. Use a form of *be* + *not* + the **verb** + *-ing* for **negative statements**.

- I**'m not wearing** a hat.

There are **two contractions** for *is not* and *are not*.

- Jeremy **isn't talking**. OR He**'s not talking**.
- Annie and Ben **aren't reading**. OR They**'re not reading**.

---

5. *Be*, *have*, *like*, *need*, and *want* are **non-action (stative) verbs**. We usually use these verbs in the **simple present**, not the present progressive.

- Kathy **is** a lawyer.
- Mary **likes** spaghetti.
- Bob **doesn't have** a car.
- I **need** water now.
- I **don't want** coffee.

NOTE: Look at Units 10 and 11 for more practice with these verbs.

---

6. When you want to connect **one subject** with **two verbs, do not repeat** a form of *be*.

- **He's eating** and **watching** TV.

  NOT: He's eating and ~~is~~ watching TV.

Focused Practice

1 | DISCOVER THE GRAMMAR

Read this conversation. Underline the statements in the present progressive.

DANNY: That's a funny picture. Who's that?

JEREMY: It's me. In middle school. At a school picnic.

DANNY: <u>You're kidding.</u>

JEREMY: No. Really! I'm wearing baggy jeans and a funny hat. The sun was really strong.

DANNY: Oh. Well, what are you doing?

JEREMY: I'm playing ball with Joe.

DANNY: That's Joe? He looks very unhappy.

JEREMY: He is. He's not enjoying that picnic. He has allergies.

2 | WHAT'S GOING ON?   *Grammar Notes 1–4*

Complete these sentences. Use the present progressive.

1. I _____'m waiting OR am waiting_____ for the number 4 bus. It's late.
      (wait)

2. Ben _____ TV. He _____ homework.
            (watch)   (not, do)

3. They _____. They _____ games.
            (work)   (not, play)

4. We _____ chicken. We _____ lasagna.
            (make)   (not, make)

5. I _____ from school. I _____ from home.
            (call)   (not, call)

6. She _____. She _____ the bus.
            (drive)   (not, take)

7. It _____. It _____.
            (rain)   (not, snow)

3 | THE OLSON FAMILY

Look at the picture. Write about the people and the cat. Use the present progressive. Choose from the verbs in the box.

do	eat	play	sit	wear
drink	~~make~~	read	sleep	write

1. Jessica _____ *is making* _____ chicken. She _____ *'s not making* _____ lasagna.
           (not)

2. Tim _____ at his desk and _____ a letter.

3. Jeremy _____ pasta. He _____ soda.

4. Ben and Annie _____ cards. They _____
                                                   (not)
   homework.

5. The cat _____ a hat and _____ a book.

6. No one _____. They're all awake.

4 | CLOTHES FOR WORK

Seven years ago

Today

A Tim Olson works for Arthur Andrews Company. Read this article from his company newsletter.

Arthur Andrews Company
EMPLOYEE NEWS & VIEWS

Good-bye Suits, Hello Sweaters

Look at us seven years ago. Now take a look at us today. What's the difference? That's right. We're not wearing suits. We're all wearing casual clothes. It's Casual Friday. Some men are wearing turtleneck sweaters. Some are wearing shirts. Some women are wearing pants with sweaters. Others are wearing skirts.

Tim Olson says, "Casual Friday is a great idea. I'm saving money. And I'm much more comfortable." Pam Cooper says, "I love the new look."

But not everyone likes the change. Todd Stuart says, "I'm not happy. I like wearing a suit to work."

Are Casual Fridays here to stay? At this time, we just don't know.

B True or False? Write **T** or **F** on the line.

_F_ **1.** Seven years ago: No one at Arthur Andrews Company is wearing a suit.

____ **2.** Today: The men at Arthur Andrews Company are wearing suits, but the women aren't.

____ **3.** Tim Olson is happy. He's saving money.

____ **4.** Everyone is happy with the new policy.

5 | TICKETS TO A CONCERT

Grammar Notes 1–4

🎧 *Listen to this conversation. Then listen again and complete the sentences.*

JEREMY: Hi, guys. How's it going?

ANNIE: OK.

BEN: Fine.

JEREMY: Busy?

ANNIE: Well, _____*I'm writing a story*_____.
1.

BEN: And _____ TV.
2.

JEREMY: Too bad. I have tickets to a rap concert.

ANNIE: Tickets to a rap concert? _____
3.

anymore.

BEN: And _____.
4.

JEREMY: Well, come on. Let's go. The concert is in 20 minutes. Just one thing . . .

ANNIE: What?

JEREMY: Don't tell Mom and Dad about our school reports. Wait a week.

BEN AND ANNIE: _____.
5.

6 | EDITING

Correct these sentences. There are 10 mistakes. The first mistake is already corrected. Use contractions with pronoun subjects.

1. She wearing a new T-shirt today.

2. We no are eating pasta now.

3. They're make chicken right now.

4. He reading the newspaper now.

5. It no is raining today.

6. I no drinking water. I drinking soda.

7. She isn't talk. She's listen.

8. You not listening to me.

Communication Practice

7 | **WHERE ARE THEY? WHAT ARE THEY DOING?**

🎧 *Listen to this conversation. Then listen again and complete the chart.*

	Where are they?	**What are they doing?**
Dad		
Mom		
Grandma		
Grandpa		

8 | **PERSONAL RESPONSES**

Check (✓) the true statements. Then read your statements aloud. Compare them with a partner's.

☐ I'm waiting for a letter.   ☐ I'm not waiting for a letter.

☐ Our teacher is wearing a suit.   ☐ Our teacher isn't wearing a suit.

☐ The sun is shining today.   ☐ The sun isn't shining today.

☐ It's raining today.   ☐ It's not raining today.

9 | WHAT ARE THEY WEARING?

A *Work with a partner. Look at the second picture in Exercise 4 on page 111. Label the following clothes items:*

| a blouse | pants | a shirt | a skirt | a sweater | a turtleneck | a vest |

B *Describe one of the people in the picture. Your partner points to the person.*

Example: This person is wearing a turtleneck sweater.

10 | WHAT'S DIFFERENT?

Picture A

Picture B

A *Study the two pictures. Find five differences.*

Example: In Picture A the man is cooking hot dogs. He's not cooking hot dogs in Picture B. He's cooking chicken.

B *Take photos of your class on different days. Compare the photos.*

The Present Progressive: *Yes / No* Questions

Is Annie studying?

Grammar in Context

🎧 *Read these conversations.*

TIM: Hi, hon. Happy anniversary!

JESSICA: Thanks. You too.

TIM: Everyone OK? **Is Jeremy watching** Ben and Annie?

JESSICA: No. Jeremy's at a ball game with Steve.

TIM: Oh. **Is Mrs. Brody babysitting?**

JESSICA: No. Kelly Brown is. You know her.

[Later—Jessica calls Kelly.]

KELLY: Hello?

JESSICA: Hi, Kelly. This is Mrs. Olson. How's everything? **Are the children listening** to you?

KELLY: Sure. Everything's great.

JESSICA: So **are you helping** Ben with his math?

KELLY: No, not now. He's baking cookies. He's a really sweet kid.

JESSICA: Thanks. **Is Annie studying** for her science test?

KELLY: I think so. Her friend Gail is here. They're in Annie's room. It's quiet. They're probably studying.

JESSICA: Hmm. Well, I'm sure they are. Can you check?

KELLY: OK, Mrs. Olson. Look. Don't worry. Everything's cool. Enjoy your anniversary.

JESSICA: Thanks, Kelly. We'll be back around 11:00.

KELLY: Bye.

115

Words

🎧 *Do you know these words? Read the words. Write new words in your notebook.*

meals

an anniversary

breakfast

lunch

dinner

get a haircut

Expressions

🎧 *Do you know these expressions? Read the conversations. Write new expressions in your notebook.*

1. A: Is everything OK?
B: Sure. Don't worry. **Everything's cool.**

2. A: Are the children quiet?
B: Yes, but I'll **check on** them.

3. A: We'll **be back around 11:00**.
B: OK.

Working Together

A *Practice the conversations in the opening reading with a partner.*

B *Look at the Dennis the Menace cartoon. Match the questions and answers.*

_____ **1.** Are the parents leaving?

_____ **2.** Is the babysitter eating?

_____ **3.** Are the parents walking in the door?

_____ **4.** Is the little boy eating a sandwich?

a. Yes, he is.

b. No, she's not.

c. No, they're not.

d. Yes, they are.

DENNIS THE MENACE

"The sitter is sleeping. Now you need to pay me. Right?"

Grammar Presentation

THE PRESENT PROGRESSIVE: *YES / NO* QUESTIONS

Yes / No Questions	Short Answers			
Am I **working**?	Yes, you **are**.	No, you**'re not**.	OR	No, you **aren't**.
Is he **sleeping**?	Yes, he **is**.	No, he**'s not**.	OR	No, he **isn't**.
Are they **playing**?	Yes, they **are**.	No, they**'re not**.	OR	No, they **aren't**.

GRAMMAR NOTES

EXAMPLES

1. In a *yes / no* question, put *am*, *is*, or *are* before the subject.	subject • Statement: You **are** working. subject • Question: **Are** you working?
2. We often use **short answers** in speaking and informal writing.	**A:** Are you doing your homework? **B: Yes, I am.** OR **Yes.** **C: No, I'm not.** OR **No.**
3. Don't use contractions in affirmative short answers.	**A:** Is he reading? **B:** Yes, **he is**. NOT: Yes, ~~he's~~.

Focused Practice

1 | DISCOVER THE GRAMMAR

Check (✓) the yes / no *questions in the present progressive.*

_____ **1.** Are you sure?

__✓__ **2.** Are they sleeping?

_____ **3.** Is it snowing?

_____ **4.** Do they have homework?

_____ **5.** Are they doing their homework?

_____ **6.** Does Kelly usually babysit?

_____ **7.** Is she babysitting today?

2 | QUESTIONS AND ANSWERS
Grammar Notes 1–3

Match these questions and answers.

___c___ **1.** Is it raining?

_____ **2.** Are you still reading?

_____ **3.** Is he doing his homework?

_____ **4.** Are they wearing suits?

_____ **5.** Am I doing the right exercise?

_____ **6.** Is she smiling?

a. No, he's not. He's playing.

b. No, they're wearing jeans.

c. No, but it's cloudy.

d. Yes, I am. It's a long book.

e. No, she's crying.

f. Yes, you are.

3 | A PHONE CALL FOR KELLY
Grammar Notes 1–3

A *Write statements and* yes / no *questions in the present progressive. Use the words in parentheses.*

KELLY: Hello.

SUSAN: Kelly? It's me, Susan. So, tell me. Is Jeremy there?

KELLY: Uh . . . sure. Right here with me.

SUSAN: Oh, you're so lucky. __Are you watching TV together_____?
    1. (you / watch TV together)

KELLY: Yeah. _____.
    2. (we / watch / a video)

SUSAN: _____?
    3. (you / watch a romance)

KELLY: Uh-huh. _____ *Sleepless in*
    4. (We / watch)

Seattle.

SUSAN: Awesome. _____?
    5. (Jeremy / wear / his cool basketball jacket)

KELLY: Sure. And he wants to take me to a concert.

SUSAN: Wow!

KELLY: Hey, Susan. _____. _____ here with me.
    6. (I / kid)   **7. (Jeremy / not / sit)**

_____ together. He isn't even
    8. (We / not / watch a video)

here. _____ a silly basketball
    9. (Jeremy and his uncle / watch)

game. And—Jeremy doesn't even know I exist.

🎧 **B** *Listen and check your work.*

4 | **QUESTIONS AND ANSWERS**   *Grammar Note 1*

Complete the questions and answers using the present progressive. Use the words in parentheses. Use contractions when possible.

1. A: _____*Is Ben doing homework*_____?
            (Ben / do homework)

    B: No, he _____. _____.
                                          (He / watch a movie)

2. A: _____?
            (you / wear / a new hat)

    B: No, _____. That's my new haircut.

3. A: _____?
                  (it / rain)

    B: _____. Take an umbrella.

4. A: _____?
                (the baby / sleep)

    B: _____. He was, but he isn't anymore.

5. A: _____?
          (they / celebrate their anniversary)

    B: _____. They're having a big party.

5 | **EDITING**

Correct these conversations. There are 13 mistakes. The first mistake is already corrected.

1. A: ~~He~~ *He's* playing cards.

    B: No, he not. He's playing chess.

2. A: Are you wear my T-shirt?

    B: Yes, I am. Is that OK?

3. A: Is raining?

    B: Yes, it's.

4. A: Are they read in the living room?

    B: No. They read in the bedroom.

5. A: Steve working hard?

    B: Yes, is he.

6. A: Am sitting in the right seat?

    B: Yes, you are. You're in 7B.

7. A: Is she do her homework?

    B: I don't know.

8. A: Are they eat breakfast?

    B: I think so.

9. A: He getting a haircut?

    B: I'm not sure.

Communication Practice

6 | A TELEPHONE CONVERSATION

🎧 *Listen to the telephone conversation between Steve and his sister, Jessica. Then listen again and check (✓)* **Yes**, **No**, *or* **No Information**.

	Yes	No	No Information
1. Is Steve working hard?	☐	☐	☐
2. Is Tim listening to the conversation?	☐	☐	☐
3. Is Steve writing for a newspaper and teaching?	☐	☐	☐
4. Are Jessica and Steve talking about their parents?	☐	☐	☐

7 | HOW'S YOUR MEMORY?

A *Look at the Dennis the Menace cartoon. Label these items in the picture.*

| a coat |
| a glass of milk |
| glasses |
| a sandwich |
| shoes |
| a sofa |

DENNIS THE MENACE

"The sitter is sleeping. Now you need to pay me. Right?"

B *Write five* yes / no *questions about the cartoon. Use the present progressive.*

1. _____

2. _____

3. _____

4. _____

5. _____

C *Ask classmates your questions. Answer their questions.*

8 | GAME: CHARADES

A *Write a sentence in the present progressive. Use one of these verbs.*

bake	daydream	eat	play	sleep	write
cook	drink	listen to	read	watch	

B *Give your sentence to a classmate. That classmate acts out your sentence.*

C *The class asks* yes / no *questions to guess the action.*

Example: **Class:** Are you watching a scary movie?
            You: Yes, I am.
                     OR
                     No, I'm not.

16 The Present Progressive: *Wh-*Questions

What are you making?

Grammar in Context

🎧 *Read these conversations.*

ANNIE: Hey, Mom. Dad's driving down the street. **Where's he going?**

JESSICA: To the store.

ANNIE: **Why is he going** to the store now?

JESSICA: We're out of milk.

ANNIE: Oh. What's for dinner?

JESSICA: Your favorite!

ANNIE: My favorite? Really? What?

JESSICA: Fish stew.

ANNIE: Mom! Come on! Are you kidding?

JESSICA: Yes, I'm kidding.

[Later]

JEREMY: Hi, Mom. **Who are you talking to?**

JESSICA: Dad. He's at the supermarket.

JEREMY: Oh. **What are you making?**

JESSICA: Tacos and beans.

JEREMY: Mmm. Super. I'm starved. Mom, this is my friend Yoshio.

JESSICA: It's nice to meet you, Yoshio. Can you stay for dinner?

YOSHIO: It's nice to meet you too. Yes, I would love to stay for dinner. Thank you.

JESSICA: Wonderful. Now, Jeremy, why don't you go and help Ben?

JEREMY: Again? **What's he doing?**

JESSICA: He's writing a report for school. He needs help on the computer.

JEREMY: Oh, all right. These kids!

Words

🎧 *Do you know these words? Read the words. Write new words and expressions in your notebook.*

| pizza | tacos and beans | stew | chicken and rice | spaghetti and meatballs |

Expressions

🎧 *Do you know these expressions? Read the conversations. Write new expressions in your notebook.*

1. **A:** Why is Dad going to the store?
   B: We're ***out of*** milk.

2. **A:** ***What's for*** dinner?
   B: Tacos and beans.
   A: ***Super.*** I'm ***starved***.

3. **A:** ***Come on***! Are you kidding?
   B: Yes, I'm kidding.

4. **A:** ***Why don't you*** go and help Ben?
   B: All right.

Working Together

A *Work in small groups. Practice the conversations in the opening reading.*

B *Look at the pictures. Ask and answer questions. Say what the people are eating.*

Example: **A:** What's he eating?
B: He's eating spaghetti and meatballs. What's she eating?

Grammar Presentation

THE PRESENT PROGRESSIVE: *WH-* QUESTIONS

Wh- Questions about the Object	Short Answers
What are you **making**?	Spaghetti.
Where are you **going**?	To the store.
Why is Dad **going** to the store now?	We're out of milk.
Who are you **talking** to?	Dad.
How are you **doing**?	Fine.

Wh- Questions about the Subject	Short Answers
Who is singing?	Dad. OR Dad is.

GRAMMAR NOTES

EXAMPLES

1. Begin *wh-* **questions** in the present progressive with a question word like *what*, *where*, *why*, *who*, or *how*. Use *am*, *is*, or *are* + the *-ing* form of the verb.	*Wh-* word + *be* + subject + *-ing* form • **What** are you making? • **Where** is he going?
2. Use *who* to ask about a **person**.	A: **Who** is singing in the shower? B: Mom (is). A: **Who** are you talking to? B: Dad. He's at the supermarket.
3. Use *why* to ask for **reasons**.	A: **Why** is Dad going to the store now? B: We're out of milk.
4. In informal conversation, **answers** are often **short**.	A: Who's singing? B: **Dad (is).** A: Where's Dad going? B: **To the store.**

🎧 Pronunciation Note

In *yes / no* **questions**, your voice goes up at the end of the question:

Are you watching TV now?

In *wh-* **questions**, your voice goes up in the middle of the question and down at the end:

What are you watching?

Focused Practice

1 | DISCOVER THE GRAMMAR

Circle the wh- *question word. Then match the* wh- *questions and the short answers.*

__e__ **1.** (What) are you making?   **a.** Mom is working late.

_____ **2.** Who's playing the guitar?   **b.** Jeremy is. He's practicing for his concert.

_____ **3.** How's it going?   **c.** To work. It's 8:30.

_____ **4.** Where's Jessica going?   **d.** Great. How are things with you?

_____ **5.** Why is Dad making dinner?   **e.** Pizza. Your favorite.

2 | CONVERSATIONS   *Grammar Notes 1–4*

Put the words in the right order. Then match the questions and short answers.

Questions   **Answers**

1. wearing / you / black / are / Why / ?

  Why are you wearing black?
_____   _____ **a.** My favorite meal—
                                                              tacos and beans.

2. shower / a / Who / taking / is / ?

_____   __1__ **b.** It's my favorite color.

3. feeling / morning / this / you / are / How / ?

_____   _____ **c.** Pretty sick.

4. is / What / making / Grandma / ?

_____   _____ **d.** Jeremy is. He has a
                                                              date.

3 | WRITE QUESTIONS   *Grammar Notes 1–4*

Write questions in the present progressive for the following answers. Use the words in parentheses and **Where, How, What, Why,** *or* **Who.**

1. A: ___*Why is Dad making*___ dinner?   **B:** Mom's still at work.
          (Dad / make)

2. A: _____?   **B:** To their favorite restaurant for dinner.
          (Grandma and Grandpa / go)

3. A: _____ you?   **B:** My cousin. He's from Hawaii.
          (visit)

4. A: _____?   **B:** Spaghetti. Your favorite.
          (you / make)

5. A: _____ in school?   **B:** Great. She loves it.
          (your daughter / do)

4 | EDITING

Correct these conversations. There are eight mistakes. The first mistake is already corrected.

1. **A:** Why ~~Uncle Steve is~~ sleeping? *is Uncle Steve*

   B: He not feeling well.

2. **A:** Who singing in the shower?

   B: Jeremy's.

3. **A:** Why you are studying, Jeremy?

   B: I have a biology test tomorrow.

4. **A:** Why you wearing a suit today?

   B: My other clothes are dirty.

5. **A:** Who you talking to?

   B: Dad. He's at the supermarket.

6. **A:** What she wearing?

   B: A blue suit.

Communication Practice

5 | INTONATION

🎧 **A** *Listen to these questions. Write an up arrow (↑) if the voice goes up at the end. Write a down arrow (↓) if the voice goes down at the end.*

Examples: What are you doing? ↓

Is it broken? ↑

1. Is Jeremy taking a shower?

2. Why is Jeremy taking a shower?

3. Is Mom making dinner?

4. What's she making?

5. Are Grandpa and Grandma coming?

6. What's Uncle Steve doing?

7. Why is he sleeping now?

8. Is he sleeping in the living room?

🎧 **B** *Listen again and repeat. Then read the questions to a partner. Take turns.*

6 | AGAIN?

🎧 *Listen to this conversation. Then listen again and answer the questions. Use long answers.*

1. Who is Annie talking to? _____

2. What is Jeremy doing? _____

3. Why? _____

4. What is Mom doing? _____

5. What is Uncle Steve doing? _____

6. Why? _____

7. How is Uncle Steve feeling? _____

7 | INFORMATION GAP: FAMOUS PLACES

Work with a partner.

Student B, turn to the Information Gap on page IG-3 and follow the instructions there.

Student A, read the sentences below to Student B. Student B names the places.

1. People are speaking Arabic. I'm visiting Egypt. I'm riding a camel. *(The Great Pyramid, Giza)*

2. I'm speaking English. I'm visiting Canada. I'm looking at a waterfall. *(Niagara Falls)*

3. People are speaking Portuguese. I'm visiting Brazil. I'm riding a cable car up a mountain. *(Sugar Loaf Mountain, Rio de Janeiro)*

Now listen to Student B. Look at the pictures and name the places.

The Empire State Building, New York City

Kilimanjaro

Acapulco Beach, Acapulco

V Review Test

I *Complete these conversations. Circle the correct letter.*

1. MAIKO: Hi, Jeremy. This is Maiko. What are you doing?

JEREMY: I'm _____ the radio.

(**A**) listening to   (**C**) listening

(**B**) listen   (**D**) listen to

2. ANNIE: _____ Grandma and Grandpa going?

BEN: To the store. We need ice cream.

(**A**) What are   (**C**) Why are

(**B**) Where are   (**D**) How are

3. JEREMY: Who's taking a shower?

BEN: _____

(**A**) Is Dad.   (**C**) It Dad.

(**B**) Dad's.   (**D**) Dad is.

4. PEDRO: Why _____ laughing?

MARIA: Because that joke is funny.

(**A**) you   (**C**) you are

(**B**) are you   (**D**) you're

5. STEVE: Is it raining there?

TIM: _____

(**A**) No, it's raining.   (**C**) Yes, it is.

(**B**) No, it's.   (**D**) Yes, it's.

II   *Look at the picture of the Johnson family. Complete the sentences. Use the present progressive forms of the verbs in the box. Use contractions with subject pronouns.*

| make | play | read | sing | sit | sleep | ~~visit~~ | watch |

Judy Johnson _____*is visiting*_____ her parents in Michigan this week. It's a typical
1.

evening. Mr. Johnson _____ dinner. Mrs. Johnson and Judy _____
2.   3.

folk songs, and Mrs. Johnson _____ the piano. Ken and his grandmother
4.

_____ on the sofa; he _____ the newspaper, and she
5.   6.

_____ television. Prince and Princess, the cats, _____ on different
7.   8.

chairs.

III   *Put the words in the correct order. Make conversations.*

1. A: doing / Annie / What's   *What's Annie doing* _____?

   B: game / She's / a / playing   _____.

2. A: playing / Ben / Is / too   _____?

   B: playing / with / cat / the / he's / No,   _____.

3. A: laughing / you / Why / are   _____?

   B: The / is / cat / wearing / a / hat   _____.

4. A: Jessica / going / is / Where   _____?

   B: supermarket / the / going / to / She's   _____.

IV *Aunt Hattie is asking Steve about his birthday party. Write questions with **what**, **who**, or **why** in the present progressive. Use the words in parentheses.*

STEVE: Hello?

AUNT HATTIE: Hi, Steve. This is Aunt Hattie. Happy birthday!

STEVE: Hi, Aunt Hattie! Thanks a lot. We're having a great time.

AUNT HATTIE: That's great. _____ *What's everybody doing?* _____?

1. (everybody / do)

STEVE: Well, let's see. Annie and Ben are playing a game.

AUNT HATTIE: _____?

2. (they / play)

STEVE: Cards. And Dad is making dinner.

AUNT HATTIE: _____?

3. (he / make dinner)

STEVE: Well, he's a great cook. Don't you remember?

AUNT HATTIE: Oh, yes. That's right. _____?

4. (he / make)

STEVE: Pizza. And it looks delicious.

AUNT HATTIE: Good. You know, I hear music. _____?

5. (sing)

STEVE: Mom and Jessica. They sound good, right?

AUNT HATTIE: They sure do. And _____?

6. (play the guitar)

STEVE: Jeremy is. He's really a good guitarist.

AUNT HATTIE: Yes, I'm sure he is. Well, may I speak with your mother?

STEVE: Sure, Aunt Hattie. Just a minute.

▶ *To check your answers, go to the Answer Key on page RT-2.*

UNIT

17

Possessive Nouns; *This / That / These / Those*

I like those shoes.

Grammar in Context

🎧 *Read this conversation.*

MARK: Judy, do I look OK?

JUDY: Yeah. You look really sharp. What's the occasion?

MARK: I'm having dinner with Kathy and her parents. It's her **parents'** anniversary. They're taking us to The Water Grill.

JUDY: **That's** terrific. Is **that** a new jacket?

MARK: It's my **brother's** jacket.

JUDY: It's nice.

MARK: Are **these** suspenders OK?

JUDY: Sure. They go well with **that** tie and **those** shoes.

MARK: Thanks. Actually they aren't mine. They're my **roommate's**.

JUDY: Oh yeah? Is *anything* yours?

MARK: Uh-huh. **This** new goatee. It's all mine.

JUDY: Oh. I see. You know, **that** goatee makes you look like a doctor.

MARK: A doctor? No kidding. I guess **that's** good. Now I need to remember—**Kathy's** mom is Bea Harlow, and her dad is Lee White.

JUDY: Relax, Mark. They're going to love you!

Words

🎧 *Do you know these words? Read the words. Write new words in your notebook.*

a tie

a sports jacket

slacks

shoes

Expressions

🎧 *Do you know these expressions? Read the conversations. Write new expressions in your notebook.*

1. A: You **look sharp**.
   B: Thanks.

2. A: **You know**, you look like a professor.
   B: **I guess** that's good.

3. A: A doctor?
   B: **No kidding.**

Working Together

A *Practice the conversation in the opening reading with a partner.*

B *Work in small groups. Compliment your classmates.*

Example: **PAT:** Maria, that hat is beautiful!
         MARIA: Thanks. It was a present from my
                grandmother. That's a very nice sweater,
                Pat. Is it new?
         PAT: Thank you. Yes, it is.

Grammar Presentation

POSSESSIVE NOUNS; *THIS / THAT / THESE / THOSE; THAT'S*

Possessive Nouns	
Singular	**Plural**
My **sister's** car is red. The **actress's** name is Rosa.	My **parents'** car is blue. Her **daughters'** names are Tina and Marie.

This / That / These / Those	
Pronouns	**Adjectives**
This is my cell phone. **That** is your jacket. **These** are my keys. **Those** are your keys.	**This** cell phone is great. **That** tie is Steve's. **These** keys don't work. **Those** keys are Steve's.

That's
A: It's their 30th anniversary. **B: That's** great.
A: He's in the hospital. **B: That's** too bad.
A: I'm studying tonight. **That's** why I can't come to the party.

GRAMMAR NOTES

EXAMPLES

1. Possessive nouns show **belonging**.	• I'm wearing my **roommate's** shoes. *(The shoes belong to my roommate.)* • She's wearing **Joe's** hat. *(The hat belongs to Joe.)*
2. To show belonging, add an **apostrophe (')** + *-s* to a singular noun or an irregular plural noun. Add only an **apostrophe (')** to a plural noun ending in *-s*.	• That's my **father's** jacket. • Where's the **women's** restroom? • It's her **parents'** anniversary. • It's the **Becks'** house.

3. *This*, *that*, *these*, and *those* can be **pronouns** or **adjectives**.

REMEMBER: *This* and *that* are **singular**; *these* and *those* are **plural**.

Use *this* and *these* for things that are **near**. Use *that* and *those* for things that are **away** from you.

- **This** is my cell phone. *(pronoun)*
- **This cell phone** is new. *(adjective)*
- **These** are my sunglasses. *(pronoun)*
- **Those sunglasses** on **that table** over there are Robert's. *(adjectives)*

4. *That's* is often used in speaking and informal writing. It refers to the idea that was just stated.

A: I really like her parents.
B: **That's** great.

A: I really don't like her brother.
B: **That's** too bad.

A: He's in Boston. **That's** why he's not here.

🎧 Pronunciation Note

The *'s* in a possessive noun sounds like /s/, /z/, or /ɪz/:

/s/: *This is my aunt's telephone number.*
/z/: *When's your uncle's birthday?*
/ɪz/: *Those are Ross's glasses.* (Note that /ɪz/ makes an extra syllable.)

Reference Note
For more practice with *this*, *that*, *these*, **and** *those* as pronouns, see Units 2 and 4.

Focused Practice

1 | DISCOVER THE GRAMMAR

Read these sentences. Underline **this, that, these,** *and* **those.** *Circle the possessive nouns.*
Then match the sentences.

__c__ **1.** Let's visit (Kathy's) grandmother.

_____ **2.** Are those your father's glasses?

_____ **3.** This is my sister's friend Melanie.

_____ **4.** Mark's car is in the auto repair shop.

_____ **5.** She has a broken leg.

a. Nice to meet you. I'm Kathy's friend Mark.

b. What's the problem? I hope it's not the brakes again.

c. That's a good idea. She loves visitors.

d. That's too bad.

e. No, they're not. They're my mother's.

2 | AT THE RESTAURANT

A *Complete these conversations.* Use **this**, **that**, **these**, *or* **those**.

1. **KATHY:** Mom, Dad, ____*this*____ is

Mark. Mark, _____ are

my parents.

MARK: Nice to meet you.

BEA HARLOW: Good to meet you.

2. LEE WHITE: Bea, is _____ your phone?

BEA: No, Lee. I think it's Kathy's.

KATHY: It is, Dad.

3. MARK: _____'s an unusual ring. It's very

interesting.

BEA: Thanks. _____ ring is about 100 years old. It was my

great-grandmother's ring.

4. **BEA:** How do you like the food?

MARK: _____ steak is delicious!

KATHY: And _____ vegetables melt in your mouth. How's the chicken, Mom?

BEA: Excellent, as always.

5. LEE: Bea, do you see _____ men over there? I think the tall man is Adam Katz.

BEA: You're right. What a small world! Let's go say hello.

B *Complete these conversations.* Write the possessive form of the nouns in parentheses.

1. **KATHY:** Excuse me. Where's the _____ restroom?
(women)

WAITER: It's over there, next to the telephones.

2. **LEE:** Mark, is your _____ home nearby?
(parents)

MARK: Yes. They live in Redmond. It's just a few miles away.

3. BEA: Lee, are these your car keys?

LEE: No, they're _____.
(Kathy)

3 | WHAT'S IN A WOMAN'S NAME?

Grammar Note 2

Complete this reading. Use the words in parentheses in the possessive.

Women in the United States are free to choose their family name when they marry.

Many women change their name to their _____*husband's family name*_____. For example,
1. (husband / family name)

before _____ married Bill Beck, she was Mary Meyers. After her
2. (Steve Beck / mother)

marriage, she became Mary Beck.

But some women don't change their name. _____, Bea
3. (Kathy White / mother)

Harlow, married Lee White. She is still Bea Harlow after 30 years of marriage. Today some

women are keeping their name and adding their _____. For
4. (husband / name)

example, _____, Jill, is married to Joe Smith. Her married name
5. (Kathy / sister)

is Jill White-Smith. So a woman's last name doesn't always match her husband's.

4 | THAT'S GREAT

Grammar Note 4

Complete these conversations. Use the expressions in the box.

| That's a good idea. | ~~That's great.~~ | That's right. | That's too bad. |

1. A: Her parents really like me.

B: *That's great.*

2. A: My boss is impossible.

B: _____

3. A: The Water Grill is on Third Street, isn't it?

B: _____

4. A: Let's rent that video.

B: _____

5 | PRONUNCIATION

🎧 *Listen to the sentences. Write the possessive noun. Then listen again and check (✓) the last sound of the possessive noun.*

Possessive Noun	/s/	/z/	/ɪz/
1. *mother's*		✓	
2.			
3.			
4.			
5.			
6.			

6 | EDITING

Correct this reading. There are six mistakes. The first mistake is already corrected.

My family loves to eat out. On my ~~parents~~ *parents'* anniversary we go to a Chinese restaurant. That's because my parent's love Chinese food. On my brother birthday we go to an Italian restaurant. My brother loves Italian food. On my sister birthday we go to a Mexican restaurant. That because her favorite food comes from Mexico. And on my birthday we go to a different restaurant every year because *I* like to try different places. These year I want to try a Brazilian restaurant.

Communication Practice

7 | HOW DID DINNER GO?

🎧 *Listen to the conversation. Then listen again and circle the correct letter.*

1. _____ have boats.
   a. Mark's dad and Kathy's dad
   b. Mark's friend's dad and Kathy's dad
   c. Mark's friend and Kathy's friend's dad

2. _____ is in the hospital.
   a. Kathy's mom's friend
   b. Kathy's mom
   c. Kathy's aunt

3. _____ is worried.
   a. Kathy's mom
   b. Mark's friend
   c. Kathy's friend

4. _____ doesn't like Mark's goatee.
   a. Kathy's mom
   b. Kathy's dad
   c. Kathy

5. _____ likes Mark's tie and suspenders.
   a. Kathy
   b. Mark's roommate
   c. Mark's friend

8 | WHAT'S DIFFERENT?

Picture A   Picture B

A *Look at the pictures. What's different in Picture B?*

Example: In Picture B, Renee is wearing Amy's hat. Juan is wearing . . .

B *One student leaves the room. The other students exchange glasses, backpacks, watches, shoes, and so on. The student returns and talks about the changes.*

9 | THAT'S GREAT / THAT'S TOO BAD

Work with a partner. Complete these conversations. Then read them to the class.

Example: **A:** I have free tickets for the ball game.
B: That's great.
A: I don't have time to finish my homework.
B: That's too bad.

A: I have _____.

B: That's great.

A: I don't have _____.

B: That's too bad.

B: I'm _____.

A: That's great.

B: I'm not _____.

A: That's too bad.

Count and Non-count Nouns; *Some* and *Any*

I usually have a bagel and coffee.

Grammar in Context

🎧 *Read these news interviews.*

JESSICA: Hello, everyone. This morning we're interviewing people about their eating habits . . . Excuse me, sir, do you eat breakfast?

MAN: Yes, I do.

JESSICA: What do you have?

MAN: I usually have **a bagel** and **a cup of coffee**.

JESSICA: That's all? Do you have **any juice** or anything else to drink?

MAN: Nope. That's all—just **a bagel** and **coffee**. I'm always in a hurry. Bye.

JESSICA: OK. Thanks. Bye.

JESSICA: Now, here's our next person. Ma'am, what do you have for breakfast?

WOMAN 1: I never eat breakfast.

JESSICA: Nothing at all?

WOMAN 1: No. I'm on **a diet**. I'm *always* on **a diet**.

JESSICA: OK. Thank you . . .

JESSICA: And what about you, ma'am? What do you have for breakfast?

WOMAN 2: Oh, I usually have **a bowl of cereal** and **some yogurt** with **fruit—a banana**, **a peach** or **an orange**, or **some strawberries**. And I have **a glass of juice**.

JESSICA: Hmm. That sounds healthy.

WOMAN 2: Yes, I always eat **a good breakfast**.

JESSICA: All right, thanks. Let's see what our next person says . . .

Words

🎧 *Do you know these words? Read the words. Write new words in your notebook.*

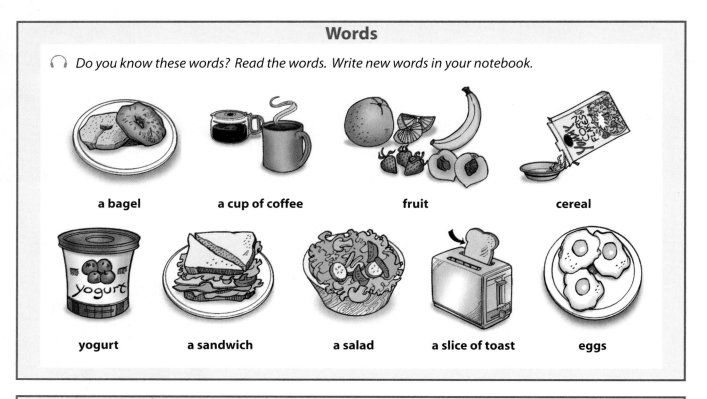

a bagel	a cup of coffee	fruit	cereal
yogurt	a sandwich	a salad	a slice of toast	eggs

Expressions

🎧 *Do you know these expressions? Read the conversations. Write new expressions in your notebook.*

1. A: I never eat breakfast.
   B: *Nothing at all?*
   A: No. I'm *on a diet*.

2. A: *What about you,* ma'am?
       What do you have?
   B: I usually have cereal and eggs.

Working Together

A *Practice the conversations in the opening reading with three partners.*

B *Tell your partners what you usually have for breakfast.*

   Example: I usually have toast and eggs and coffee for breakfast. I also have some yogurt.

C *Read Annie's composition with a partner and answer the question. Then check your answer on page P-2.*

My Favorite

   I love vegetables. This is about my favorite vegetable dish. It has lettuce, tomatoes, and carrots. Sometimes it has cauliflower and broccoli. I always eat it with dressing. It's usually in a bowl, but it can also be on a plate. Can you guess what it is?

Grammar Presentation

COUNT AND NON-COUNT NOUNS; *SOME* AND *ANY*

Count Nouns		Non-count Nouns
Article + Singular Noun	Plural Noun	
an orange **a** sandwich	orange**s** sandwich**es**	yogurt water

Quantifiers: *Some* and *Any*	
Count Nouns	**Non-count Nouns**
A: Do you have **any** oranges? **B:** Yes, I have **some**. OR No, I don't have **any**.	**A:** Do you have **any** bread? **B:** Yes, I have **some**. OR No, I don't have **any**.

GRAMMAR NOTES

EXAMPLES

1. Count nouns refer to separate things. It is **easy to count** them. To form the plural of most count nouns, add **-s** or **-es**.

- **one** orange, **two** eggs, **three** bagels

- orange   orange**s**
- sandwich   sandwich**es**

2. Non-count nouns refer to things that are **difficult to count**.

We use **quantifiers** to help us count non-count nouns. Some quantifiers are: *a bowl of, a slice of, a bottle of, a glass of,* and *a cup of.*

- I love **coffee**.
- Bring me **a cup of coffee**.
- Ben likes **bread**.
- Please bring him **a slice of bread**.
- I want **cereal**.
- Please bring me **a bowl of cereal**.

a cup of (coffee)

a slice of (bread)

a bowl of (cereal)

a bottle of
(mineral water)

a glass of (water)

Some and *any* are also quantifiers.

- I want **some cereal**. I don't want **any bread**.

3. Use **singular verbs** with **non-count nouns**.	• Rice **is** good for you. NOT: Rice ~~are~~ good for you.

4. Use *a* or *an* before **singular count nouns**. Use *a* before words that start with consonant sounds. Use *an* before words that start with vowel sounds. Use *some* (or no word) with **plural count nouns** and **non-count nouns**.	• Steve wants **a banana**. *(starts with a consonant sound)* • I want **an orange**. *(starts with a vowel sound)* plural count noun • We have **(some) oranges** in the refrigerator. non-count noun • I drink **(some) juice** every morning.

5. Use *some* in **affirmative statements**. Use *any* in **negative statements** and in **questions**. NOTE: You can use *some* in a **question**, especially when you are offering something.	• I have **some** fruit. • I don't have **any** fruit. • Do you have **any** fruit? • Do you want **some** fruit? *(offer)*

6. Use **plural count nouns** or **non-count nouns** to talk about things you **like** or **dislike** in general. (Don't use *a* or *an*.)	• I like **oranges**. I don't like **yogurt**. NOT: I like ~~an orange~~. I don't like ~~some~~ yogurt.

Reference Notes
For more information about **plural nouns**, see Appendix 6 on page A-6.
For a list of **non-count nouns and quantifiers**, see Appendix 8 on page A-8.

Focused Practice

1 | DISCOVER THE GRAMMAR

*Read this paragraph. Find the foods. Write them in the correct column. Write the word
that goes with it:* **a**, **an**, **some**, *or another quantifier.*

My favorite meal is lunch—my big meal of the day. I start with a bowl of soup. I usually

have some crackers with it. Next, I have some meat: maybe a piece of chicken or a slice of roast

beef. I also have some vegetables: maybe some carrots, some peas, or some beans. I almost

always have a salad. For dessert, I sometimes have a piece of pie, and I usually have some

fruit—an orange, or an apple, or a banana. Occasionally, I have a bowl of ice cream. I usually

drink a cup of coffee. Once in a while I have a cup of tea. I'm never hungry after lunch.

Count Nouns

some crackers

_____

_____

_____

_____

_____

_____

_____

Non-count Nouns

a bowl of soup

_____

_____

_____

_____

_____

_____

_____

2 | AT THE RESTAURANT

Grammar Notes 2, 4, 6

Complete this conversation. Choose the correct word in parentheses.

WAITER: All right, folks. What would you like?

MARY: I'd like _____*some*_____ spaghetti and
     1. (a bag of / some)

_____ coffee.
     2. (a bag of / some)

WAITER: Of course. And for you, young man?

BEN: I want _____ peanut butter
     3. (a / some)

sandwich. Is that OK, Grandma?

(continued)

MARY: Yes, that's fine. But how about _____ salad to go with it?
   4. (a slice of / a)

BEN: I don't like _____ salad, Grandma.
   5. (a / Ø*)

MARY: All right. But you need something green. Or maybe _____ fruit.
   6. (a / some)

   Maybe _____ banana?
   7. (a / some)

BEN: OK, Grandma. I like _____ bananas.
   8. (Ø / some)

WAITER: All right. For you, young lady?

ANNIE: I'd like _____ pizza. And _____ orange.
   9. (a slice of / a bowl of)   10. (a / an)

WAITER: Of course. And to drink?

MARY: Can you bring them each _____ milk?
   11. (a / a glass of)

WAITER: Certainly. Be right back with your drinks.

3 | A PARTY

Grammar Note 5

*Complete this conversation. Use **some** or **any** and the nouns in parentheses.*

AMANDA: Josh, we need ___*some things*___ for the party tonight. Can you go to the store
   1. (things)

   now?

JOSH: Sure. I know we don't have _____. And we don't have
   2. (soda)

   _____. What else?
   3. (chips)

AMANDA: We need _____. And we need _____. But let me
   4. (fruit)   5. (olives)

   check . . . Oh, yes! Get _____. Don't get _____.
   6. (black olives)   7. (green olives)

JOSH: OK. Anything else? Do you want _____?
   8. (ice cream)

AMANDA: Good idea. Get _____.
   9. (chocolate ice cream)

* Ø = no article or quantifier

4 | EDITING

Correct these conversations. There are six mistakes. The first mistake is already corrected.

1. **A:** Do you like a ~~bagel~~? *bagels*

   B: No, I don't. But I like a sandwich.

2. **A:** Can I bring you some coffee?

   B: No, thanks. I don't drink a coffee.

3. **A:** Are we having egg for lunch?

   B: Yes, we are. We're also having a yogurt.

4. **A:** Does the plant need water?

   B: No, it doesn't need some water.

Communication Practice

5 | I CAN'T BELIEVE THIS PLACE!

🎧 *Listen to Mark and Judy talk with a waiter. Read the statements. Then listen again and check* **T (true)**, **F (false)**, *or* **NI (no information)**. *Correct the false statements.*

	T	F	NI	
1. The restaurant is serving lunch now.	☐	☐	☐	_____
2. Judy wants chips and salsa.	☐	☐	☐	_____
3. The restaurant has iced tea.	☐	☐	☐	_____
4. Mark likes tea.	☐	☐	☐	_____
5. The restaurant is out of salsa.	☐	☐	☐	_____
6. The restaurant has mineral water.	☐	☐	☐	_____
7. The soda is expensive.	☐	☐	☐	_____
8. Mark and Judy like the restaurant.	☐	☐	☐	_____

6 | WHAT DO YOU LIKE TO EAT?

Write about the food you like and don't like. Compare your likes and dislikes with a partner's. Which things are the same? Which are different? Tell the class.

Example: **A:** I like chips and salsa. I don't like peas. I hate green olives!

B: I don't like chips and salsa. But I hate green olives too! I like to eat pizza and chocolate ice cream.

A: *[to class]* I like chips and salsa, but she doesn't. We both hate green olives. She likes pizza and chocolate ice cream.

Grammar in Context

🎧 *Read this conversation.*

CLERK: May I help you?

KEN: Yes, I'm looking for **a** new sports jacket. I have **an** interview tomorrow.

CLERK: Oh, you're in luck! We're having **a** sale on sports jackets.

KEN: You are? Great!

CLERK: What size?

KEN: Forty-two.

CLERK: OK. Be right back.

CLERK: All right. Do you like any of these?

KEN: Yes! I really like **the** blue **one**.

CLERK: Do you want to try it on?

KEN: Sure.

CLERK: How does it feel?

KEN: Really comfortable. How does it look, Laura?

LAURA: Well, it's pretty bright. And it's casual. How about that black **one**? It's more formal.

KEN: All **the** black **ones** are dull—really boring.

LAURA: OK. It's up to you.

Words

🎧 *Do you know these words? Read the words. Write new ones in your notebook.*

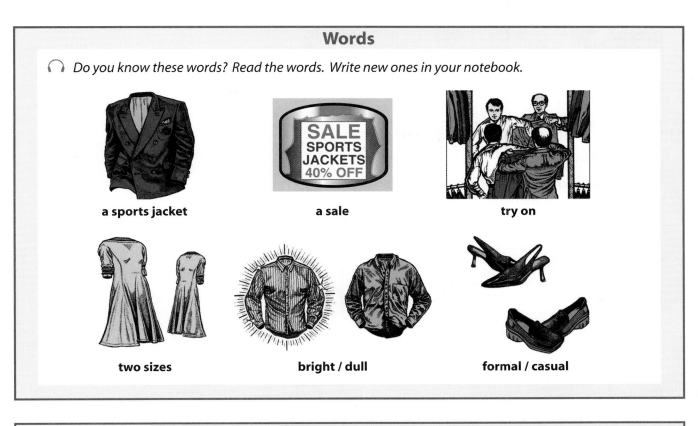

a sports jacket   **a sale**   **try on**

two sizes   **bright / dull**   **formal / casual**

Expressions

🎧 *Do you know these expressions? Read the conversations. Write new expressions in your notebook.*

1. **A:** You're *in luck*.
   B: Great!

2. **A:** Can I *try it on*?
   B: Sure. *Be right back.*

3. **A:** I want to get it.
   B: OK. It's *up to you*.

Working Together

A *Practice the conversation in the opening reading with two partners.*

B *Work with a partner. Look at the pictures. Which objects do you like? Tell your partner.*
Use **one** *or* **ones**.

Example: I like the expensive suit. I don't like the cheap one.

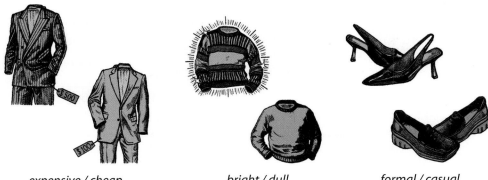

expensive / cheap   *bright / dull*   *formal / casual*

Grammar Presentation

A / An and The; One / Ones

Indefinite Articles (A / An)	
Singular Nouns	**Plural Nouns**
I'm looking for **a suit**. I have **an interview** tomorrow.	**Suits** are expensive. I don't like **interviews**.

The Definite Article (The)	
Singular Nouns	**Plural Nouns**
I like **the** blue **suit**.	I don't like **the** black **suits**.

One and Ones	
Singular Pronouns	**Plural Pronouns**
I like **the** blue **one**.	I don't like **the** black **ones**.

GRAMMAR NOTES

EXAMPLES

1. Use **a** or **an** (**indefinite articles**) before a **singular count noun**. Use **a** before a **consonant** sound. Use **an** before a **vowel** sound.

- I'm looking for **a jacket**.
- I have **an interview** tomorrow.

▶ **BE CAREFUL!** Don't put **a** or **an** before a non-count noun or a plural noun.

- **Meat** is expensive. (*indefinite—in general*)
- I usually wear **jackets**.
  NOT: I like a̶ meat.
  NOT: I have a̶ jackets.

2. Use **the** (the **definite article**) for specific things that the speaker and listener know about.

You can use **the** before singular count nouns, plural count nouns, and non-count nouns.

SALESPERSON: Do you like **the** black suit?
CUSTOMER: No, but I like **the** blue suit.

- **The shirt** is too small.
- **The apples** are green.
- **The coffee** is delicious.

3. Use **the** when there is only one of something.

- I really like **the** gray **suit**.
  (There is only one gray suit in the store.)
- **The sun** is bright today.
  (There is only one sun.)

4. Use *the* when you talk about something for the second time.

- Jessica made pasta and meatballs. **The pasta** was delicious. **The meatballs** were spicy.

5. Use *one* to replace a **singular noun**. Use *ones* to replace a **plural noun**.

- They have three **suits** on sale. I like the blue **one**. I don't like the black **ones**.

Focused Practice

1 | DISCOVER THE GRAMMAR

Read these conversations and look at the underlined words and expressions. Circle the correct explanation.

1. A: <u>The sun</u> is bright today!   (one / more than one) sun

   B: Yes. You need <u>a hat</u>.   (a hat in general / a specific hat)

2. A: Where's <u>the cat</u>?   (one / more than one) cat

   B: She's sleeping on <u>the sofa</u>.   (one / more than one) sofa

3. A: Do you have <u>a car</u>?   (a car in general / a specific car)

   B: No, I don't. <u>Cars</u> are expensive.   (cars in general / specific cars)

4. A: Do you like <u>the jackets</u>?   (all of the jackets / some of the jackets)

   B: I only like <u>the red one</u>.   (one red jacket / more than one red jacket)

2 | PRONUNCIATION

🎧 *Listen to these conversations. Write **a** or **an** in each blank.*

1. A: What do you want for your birthday, Mary?

   B: I want ___*a*___ good novel. And I want _____ umbrella— _____ red one.
                   1.   **2.**   **3.**

2. A: Annie, is someone at the door?

   B: Yes, there's _____ man outside. He's _____ old man.
                       4.   **5.**

3. A: Grandma, I have _____ interview tomorrow.
                          6.

   B: Oh, good, Ken. I hope it's _____ good interview.
                              7.

3 | KEN AND LAURA

Complete the next part of Ken and Laura's conversation. Choose from the words in parentheses. If no article or quantifier is needed, write Ø.

CLERK: Do you need anything else?

KEN: Yes, I need _____Ø_____ dress shoes.
          1. (a / the / Ø)

CLERK: OK. _____ dress shoes are over here . . .
          2. (A / The)

What size?

KEN: Ten medium.

LAURA: I like _____ black ones. What do you
          3. (a / the / Ø)

think?

KEN: No. They're dark and formal. And I don't like

_____ style.
4. (a / the / Ø)

CLERK: What about these?

KEN: Cool! I like them.

CLERK: Do you want to try them on?

KEN: Yes, please.

CLERK: How do they feel?

KEN: Perfect. Laura, what do you think?

LAURA: Well, _____ shoes look nice. But they're casual. This is for _____ interview.
          5. (a / the / Ø)   6. (a / an / Ø)

KEN: Don't worry. They're fine.

4 | EDITING

Correct this letter. There are 10 mistakes. The first mistake is already corrected.

> Dear Kathy,
>
>   Josh and I have ~~an~~ *a* great house! House is very big, but it's also a old one. It needs work. It has the nice living room, but the colors are terrible. Each wall is the different color. There's a orange wall, an yellow wall, a blue wall, and the red wall. We need to repaint.
>
>   We want you to see a house. Give me the call.
>
> Love,
>
>   Amanda

Communication Practice

5 | LET'S GO OUT TONIGHT

🎧 *Listen to this conversation. Then listen again and circle the correct answers.*

1. There is (one / more than one) concert.

2. Josh and Amanda have (one / more than one) dog.

3. They have (one / more than one) photograph.

4. They have (one / more than one) house.

5. They have (one / more than one) umbrella.

6. They have (one / more than one) car.

6 | STYLES

*Work with a partner. Look at the pictures. Tell your partner about the clothes you like and don't like, and why. Use **the** and **one / ones** in your statements.*

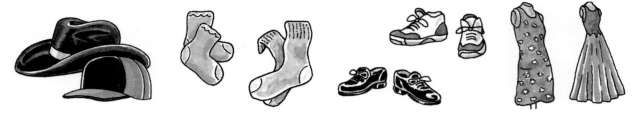

Example: **A:** I like the first hat. I like the color.
B: I like the second one.
OR I like the first one too.

7 | WHAT'S WRONG WITH THIS PICTURE?

*Work in small groups. Talk about what you see. Use **a**, **an**, or **the**. Then tell the class.*

Example: I see a car in the store. . . .

Can / Can't

I can't understand her message.

Grammar in Context

🎧 *Read this conversation.*

MARK: Judy, Steve, thanks for coming.

JUDY: Hi, Mark. What's the problem?

MARK: I have a message from Kathy on my answering machine. She leaves a phone number, but I **can't get** all the numbers. Listen.

[Phone message with lots of noise in the background]

> Hi, Mark. It's Kathy. I can't meet you today. Please call me at 796-774 —.
> It's important. Call right away, please.

STEVE: **Can** you **hear** the last number?

JUDY: No, I **can't**. Kathy sounds a little upset. Do you think she's in trouble? **Where can** she **be**?

MARK: I don't know. She left her cell phone here.
Look. I need to take this package to *The Daily Times*. **Can** you **do** me a favor? Wait here in case Kathy calls again?

STEVE: Of course. Go! And don't worry. Judy and I **can get** her phone number.

MARK: You **can**?

STEVE: Sure. Now take it easy. I'm sure Kathy's fine.

MARK: Thanks. I'll be back soon.

Words

🎧 *Do you know these words? Read the words. Write new words in your notebook.*

a cell phone

a phone number

Hi Mark. This is Judy. I can't meet you. I…

a phone message

Expressions

🎧 *Do you know these expressions? Read the conversations. Write new expressions in your notebook.*

1. A: *Thanks for coming.*
   B: No problem.

2. A: Can you *do me a favor*? Wait here in case Kathy calls?
   B: *Of course.*

3. A: I think Kathy's *in trouble*.
   B: *Take it easy.* I'm sure she's OK.

Working Together

A *Practice the conversation in the opening reading with three partners.*

B *Discuss the following with a partner.*

Steve says, "Judy and I can get her phone number." How can they do that?

Grammar Presentation

CAN / CAN'T

Affirmative and Negative Statements

Subject	Can / Can't	Base Form of Verb
I You He / She / It We You They	**can** **can't**	**help**.

Yes / No Questions

Can you **do** me a favor?
Can he **understand** French?

Short Answers

Yes, I **can**.
No, he **can't**.

Wh- Questions

Where can she **be**?
What can I **do**?
Who can help?

GRAMMAR NOTES

EXAMPLES

1. *Can* is a **modal**. A modal changes the meaning of the verb that follows. *Can* has different meanings, including **ability**, **possibility**, and **request**.

- I **can understand** German. *(ability)*
- I **can meet** you at four. *(possibility)*
- **Can** you **do** me a favor? *(request)*

2. Use the **base form** of the verb **after** *can*.

▶ **BE CAREFUL!** Do not use *to* after *can*. Do not add *-s* to verbs that follow *can*.

- I **can speak** Spanish.
- You **can get** there by bus or by train.
  NOT: He can ~~to speak~~ English.
  NOT: He can ~~speaks~~ English.

3. *Cannot* is the negative form. *Can't* is the contraction. We usually use *can't* in speaking and informal writing.

- I **cannot help** you.
- I **can't help** you.

4. For **questions** (*yes / no* questions or *wh-* questions), put *can* before the subject (unless the subject is *who* or *what*).

- **Can** she **speak** English?
- How **can** we **help**?
- Who **can help**?
- What **can happen** next?

🎧 Pronunciation Note

When *can* is followed by a base form verb, we usually pronounce it /kən/ or /kn/ and stress the base form verb: *I can SPEAK Spanish*.

In sentences with *can't* followed by a base form verb, we stress both *can't* and the base form verb: *I CAN'T SPEAK French*.

Focused Practice

1 | DISCOVER THE GRAMMAR

A *Read this conversation. Underline sentences with **can** and **can't**. Circle the sentence in which **can** is a request.*

B *Now write the sentence in which* can *is a request.*

_____

JUDY: OK. Can you really get the phone number?

STEVE: I think so.

JUDY: How can you do it?

STEVE: Well, we know the first six numbers—796-774. Right?

JUDY: Uh-huh.

STEVE: There are only 10 possibilities for the seventh. We can try all of them.

JUDY: Good idea. Let's try them.

STEVE: 796-7740 . . . an answering machine.

796-7741 Hello? Is Kathy White there? . . . Sorry, wrong number.

796-7742 Hello? Is Kathy White there? . . . Yes. The police station?

Can I speak with Ms. White?

[To Judy]

She's at the police station.

Hello, Kathy. . . . Are you OK? . . . Uh-huh. Oh. Uh-huh. OK.

JUDY: Well?

STEVE: She's fine, but she wants Mark to meet her there.

2 | AT THE POLICE STATION

Grammar Notes 1–3

A *Complete this conversation. Use the phrases in the box.*

> Can she remember her grandma's number
> Can you help her
> Can you two wait for her grandmother
> ~~She can't speak~~
> you can speak a little Chinese

KATHY: Mark, this is Mei Liang. She was lost in the park.

She was very, very upset. _____*She can't speak*_____ a word of English.
                                                   1.

MARK: Oh? Poor kid!

KATHY: Mark, _____. _____?
                              2.   3.

MARK: Well, let me see. I hope she can understand Mandarin.

[Mark speaks with Mei Liang.] . . .

[To Kathy] Uh . . . She lives with her grandmother.

KATHY: That's good to know. _____?
                                              4.

MARK: *[Speaks with Mei Liang]* She can't remember the number, but her grandmother's

name is Li Li Wang and they live in Kent.

OFFICER: I'm looking it up in the phone book. . . . We've got her number. Thank you.

_____?
       5.

MARK: Sure.

OFFICER: *[Calls Li Li Wang]* Her grandmother is on the way. She's really upset.

🎧 **B** *Now listen to the conversation and check your work.*

3 | EDITING

Correct these sentences. There are six mistakes. The first mistake is already corrected. Add
can *in one more place.*

1. Li Li Wang ᵃ understand English, but she can't speak it well.
            can

2. Mei Liang Wang can't speaks English. She can to speak Mandarin Chinese.

3. Mei Liang is a good ice skater. She can skates very well.

4. Mei Liang sing well, but she can't not dance.

Communication Practice

4 | CAN OR CAN'T?

A *Listen to these sentences. Then listen again and check the word you hear.*

1. can ☐ can't ☐   **3.** can ☐ can't ☐   **5.** can ☐ can't ☐

2. can ☐ can't ☐   **4.** can ☐ can't ☐   **6.** can ☐ can't ☐

B *Complete these conversations. Use* **can** *or* **can't**.

1. A: We _____ hear you.
   B: Sorry. Is that better?

2. A: We _____ hear you.
   B: That's good.

3. A: I _____ believe it.
   B: It's true.

4. A: I _____ believe it.
   B: Well, I can't.

5. A: I _____ see the board.
   B: Then change your seat.

6. A: I _____ see the board.
   B: Good. Please read the sentence on the board.

C *Now choose a conversation. Read* **A**. *Your partner reads* **B**.

5 | DRAMA

Complete these conversations with a partner. Read them to the class.

1. A: Can I please speak to_____?

   B: I'm sorry. _____.

   A: Please tell _____ I called.

2. A: Can you do me a favor? Can you_____?

   B: I'm sorry, I can't. I just can't do it. Please understand.

   A: _____?

   B: _____.

6 | THINK OF THE POSSIBILITIES

Work in groups. You have five minutes. Make a list of all the things you can do in a car. The group with the longest list wins.

   Example: 1. We can drive.
                  2. We can listen to the radio.

7 | TIC TAC TOE

Walk around the class. Find someone who can do each thing. Write the name of the student below the picture. When you have three names in any direction, you win.

Example: **MARIA:** Can you water ski?
   KEIKO: Yes, I can. *(Maria writes Keiko's name in the box with "water ski.")*

water ski

speak Mandarin

change a tire

play the guitar

understand Italian

play tennis

play golf

dance well

play chess

I *Complete these conversations. Circle the correct letter.*

1. JESSICA: Do we have any fruit?

  TIM: _____

  (**A**) Yes, I have.

  (**B**) No, we have some.

  (**C**) No, we don't have any.

  (**D**) Yes, they don't have any.

2. KATHY: _____

  JOSH: Sure. Hold on.

  (**A**) Can you please speak with Amanda?

  (**B**) Do you know Amanda?

  (**C**) Is Amanda your sister?

  (**D**) Can I speak with Amanda?

3. CLERK: Do you like the dark blue jacket?

  KEN: _____

  (**A**) No, but I like the brown one.

  (**B**) Yes, I like the red one.

  (**C**) No, I don't like tan jackets.

  (**D**) Yes, I need a jacket.

4. CLERK: _____

  KEN: Very comfortable.

  (**A**) How does it look?

  (**B**) How much does it cost?

  (**C**) How does it feel?

  (**D**) How can I help you?

5. CLERK: Do you like John's tie?

  KEN: _____

  (**A**) Yes, I like the ties.

  (**B**) No, I'm not.

  (**C**) Yes, but I don't like it.

  (**D**) No, I don't like it.

II *Complete these conversations. Use the words in parentheses.*

1. **ANNIE:** What can I have for breakfast?

   JESSICA: _____ *How about a slice of toast* _____?
   (toast / How / of / about / a / slice)

2. **KATHY:** _____?
   (look / it / does / How)

   AMANDA: Really great. It's your color.

3. **CLERK:** _____?
   (shoes / the / like / Do / black / you)

   KEN: No, but I really like the brown ones.

4. **JESSICA:** Is there a message from Ben?

   TIM: _____.
   (I / Yes, / his / can't / but / message / understand)

5. **KELLY:** _____?
   (guitar / Jeremy / the / Can / play)

   JESSICA: Yes, he plays very well.

III *Annie and Ben are making breakfast for their parents. Look at the picture. Write sentences about what they have and don't have. Use **some** and **any**.*

1. (eggs) *They have some eggs.*
2. (coffee) _____
3. (juice) _____
4. (fruit) _____
5. (bagels) _____
6. (milk) _____

IV *Complete these paragraphs with **a**, **an**, **the**, **one**, and **ones**.*

Josh and Amanda are talking with ___*a*___ car salesman. They need _____ new car.
1. 2.

They see a lot of cars, expensive _____ and cheap _____. Josh wants to buy
3. 4.

_____ expensive car. Amanda wants to buy _____ cheap _____.
5. 6. 7.

Right now _____ salesman is showing them two cars, _____ old red car and
8. 9.

_____ new blue car. Josh wants _____ blue _____. Amanda wants _____ red
10. 11. 12. 13.

_____.
14.

V | *Write sentences with the words in parentheses. Use **It's** and a possessive noun with **-'s** or **-'**.*

1. (Jeremy / guitar) *It's Jeremy's guitar.* _____

2. (Annie / cat) _____

3. (the / men / department) _____

4. (the / women / department) _____

5. (Jessica / parents / house) _____

▶ *To check your answers, go to the Answer Key on page RT-2.*

UNIT

The Simple Past: Regular Verbs (Statements) **21**

The party was fun, but we missed you.

Grammar in Context

🎧 *Read these e-mail messages.*

Kathy,

Thanks for the chocolates. Everyone **enjoyed** them. The party was a blast, but we all **missed** you, especially Mark. He **looked** like a lost dog. :>(

How's Boston? How's the convention?

Judy

Judy,

Once again, happy birthday!

Boston is terrific :)! The convention was another story.

I **arrived** here late Monday night. Tuesday I **worked** from 7:00 in the morning until 10:00 at night. Wednesday I **started** at 7:00 and **didn't finish** until 9:00 at night. Thank goodness, the convention **ended** last night.

This morning I **checked out** of my hotel and I'm staying with my cousin Ted for a couple of days. He's a really nice guy. I'd like you to meet him.

Again, I'm so sorry I **missed** your party.

Kathy

Hi Kathy,

Who's this secret cousin? I'd love to meet him.

Judy

Words

🎧 *Do you know these words? Read the words. Write new ones in your notebook.*

a hotel

a convention

a presentation

Expressions

🎧 *Do you know these expressions? Read the conversations. Write new expressions in your notebook.*

1. A: The party was *a blast*.
   B: Sorry I missed it.

2. A: The movie was great, but the restaurant was *another story*.
   B: Too bad.

3. A: Is the convention over?
   B: Yes, *thank goodness*.

4. A: I want you to meet my cousin.
   B: *I'd love to.*

Working Together

A *Read the e-mail messages in the opening reading with a partner.*

B *Look at the pictures in **Words**. Tell a story. Use the words in the box.*

| ~~attended~~ | Grand | listened | stayed | convention | presentation |

A man _____*attended*_____ a travel agents' _____ in Seoul, Korea. He
_____ at the _____ Hotel. He _____ to a
_____ about travel in Asia.

Grammar Presentation

THE SIMPLE PAST: REGULAR VERBS (STATEMENTS)

Affirmative		
Subject	Past Form Verb	
I You He She It We You They	**arrived**	at 2:00 P.M.

Negative			
Subject	*Did not*	Base Form of Verb	
I You He She It We You They	**did not (didn't)**	**arrive**	at 3:00 P.M.

PAST TIME EXPRESSIONS

Past Time Expressions		
Yesterday	*Ago*	*Last*
yesterday morning **yesterday** evening	two days **ago** a month **ago**	**last** night **last** week

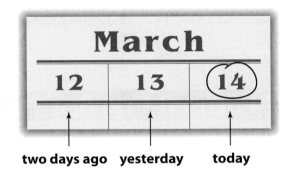

two days ago   yesterday   today

GRAMMAR NOTES

EXAMPLES

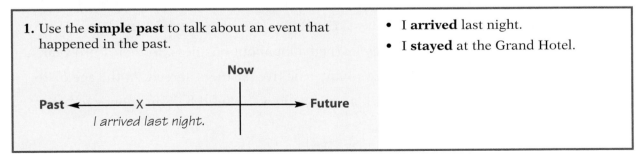

1. Use the **simple past** to talk about an event that happened in the past.

- • I **arrived** last night.
- • I **stayed** at the Grand Hotel.

Past ◄——X—— Now ——► Future
I arrived last night.

2. **Regular verbs** in the simple past **end in -*ed***. If the base form ends in -*e*, add only -*d*. If the base form ends in -*y* after a consonant, change the *y* to *i* and add -*ed*.

- • I stay**ed** at a hotel.   base form (stay)
- • I arriv**ed** yesterday.   (arri**ve**)
- • I stud**ied** all night.   (stu**dy**)

3. Use ***did not*** + the **base form** of the verb for a **negative statement** in the simple past.	• She **did not stay** at the hotel.
We usually use ***didn't*** for speaking and informal writing.	• She **didn't stay** at the hotel.

4. Time expressions come at the **beginning** or the **end** of a sentence.	• **Last night** I arrived in Boston.
	• I arrived in Boston **last night**.

🎧 Pronunciation Note

The regular simple past verb ending has three sounds: **/t/**, **/d/**, and **/ɪd/**. The sound of the past ending depends on the last sound of the base form of the verb.

> *I missed you.* **/t/**
> *She arrived at 7:00 P.M.* **/d/**
> *He insisted.* **/ɪd/** (= extra syllable)

Reference Notes
For the **past of *be***, see Unit 7.
For **irregular past verbs**, see Unit 22.
For more about the **spelling and pronunciation of the simple past of regular verbs**, see Appendix 14 on page A-16.

Focused Practice

1 | DISCOVER THE GRAMMAR

A *Read about Kathy's cousin. Underline the 10 simple past verbs. The first one is already underlined for you.*

Ten years ago Ted Geller <u>graduated</u> from college. A year after graduation, Ted and four friends started an online business. For three years they worked very hard. They hired and fired a lot of people. They learned a lot about business. In their third year, a big company offered to buy their company. The five partners agreed. At the age of 26, Ted ended up without a job but with a lot of money. He used half his money to help poor children. Ted's an unusual man.

B *Write the base form of the underlined words.*

graduate	_____	_____	_____
_____	_____	_____	_____
_____	_____		

2 | A FLOWER SHOP
Grammar Notes 1–2

Complete the sentences with the past form of the verbs in the box. Use each verb once.

graduate	~~help~~	learn	open	stay	work

Jane loves flowers. As a child she always _____*helped*_____ her mother in their garden.
1.

Six years ago she _____ from art school. She _____ in a flower
2.   3.

shop after graduation. She _____ at the flower shop for three years. She
4.

_____ a lot about flowers and about the flower business. Three years ago she
5.

_____ her own flower shop. Today her flower shop is doing very well.
6.

3 | LAST WEEKEND
Grammar Notes 1–3

*Look at the pictures. Complete the sentences. Use the affirmative or negative of the verbs
in the box.*

Saturday

Sunday

clean	play	rain	stay	watch

Saturday it _____*rained*_____ all day long. Judy _____ home. She
1.   2.

_____ her apartment. Then she _____ TV. She _____
3.   4.   5.

tennis.

Sunday it _____. It was a beautiful day. Judy _____ home. She
6.   7.

_____ her apartment. She _____ tennis in the park.
8.   9.

4 | EDITING

Correct the mistakes in the messages. There are five mistakes. The first mistake is already corrected.

1. I'm sorry I ~~did miss~~ *missed* your call. Please leave your name and a short message.

2. Hi, Ted. This is Al. I am arrived this morning. My phone number is 345-9090.

3. Hello, Ted. This is Melissa. I yesterday talked to Ellen. She loved your speech.

4. Hi, Ted. This is Judy. Sorry I was missed your call. Call me. I have some exciting news.

5. Hi, Uncle Ted. This is Mickey. I received this morning your gift. It's awesome. Thank you so much. I love the game.

Communication Practice

5 | THANKS FOR THE FLOWERS

🎧 *Listen to these three phone messages. Then listen again and complete the sentences.*

Message from	
1. _____	Thanks for the _____. They arrived _____.
2. _____	He's still _____. Let's meet at _____, not _____.
3. _____	She _____ a really good _____ a couple of _____ _____. It's on tonight at _____ o'clock on Channel _____.

6 | PRONUNCIATION

A *Complete the sentences with **last**, **ago**, or **yesterday**. Then read the sentences. Underline the past verb forms. Write the base form of the verb.*

Sentence	Base Verb	/t/	/d/	/ɪd/
1. He graduated from college _____ year.				
2. They started a business 10 years _____.				

Sentence	Base Verb	/t/	/d/	/ɪd/
3. They worked for 10 hours _____.				
4. They hired many people _____ month.				
5. They learned a lot _____ year.				
6. A company wanted to buy their business three years _____.				
7. They agreed to the sale _____ afternoon.				

🎧 **B** *Now listen and check (✓) the sound of the **-ed**.*

7 | TRUE OR FALSE

Work in small groups. Write four true sentences and one false sentence about yourself in the past. Read your sentences to your group. Your group guesses the false sentence. Use the ideas in the box or your own ideas.

like a food	play a sport	watch _____ on TV _____
listen to a kind of music	travel to a place	

Example: **A:** I played soccer in high school.
I didn't like candy as a child.
I listened to classical music in high school.
I traveled to Kenya five years ago.
I watched *Star Trek* on TV last night.
B: You didn't really travel to Kenya five years ago.
C: You didn't really listen to a lot of classical music in high school.
D: You liked candy as a child.
A: I really traveled to Kenya five years ago. I listened to a lot of classical music in high school. D's right. I liked candy as a child.

8 | A GOOD FRIEND

Work in pairs. Tell about a friend. Use the following verbs in the past.

live	study	visit	work

Example: My friend Kel lived in Turkey for 10 months. He studied Turkish there. He worked hard in school. In his free time he visited different cities in Turkey.

Grammar in Context

🎧 *Read this conversation.*

KATHY: Hi, Amanda. Say, where **were** you and Josh on the weekend? I **called** and **left** a message.

AMANDA: Well, we **had** an adventure.

KATHY: You **did**?

AMANDA: Yes. We **went** out of town on Saturday. We **left** at 3:00. About 4:00 it **started** to snow. In half an hour the snow **was** really deep.

KATHY: Oh no! **Did** you **stop**?

AMANDA: Yeah. We **had** to. I **tried** to call for help, but my cell phone **was** dead. Then it **got** dark. We **put on** all our warm clothes, so we **were** OK.

KATHY: **Did** you **have** anything to eat?

AMANDA: **Yes, we did**, actually. We **had** some cookies and chocolate bars. We **ate** those right away. And we **had** some water. We **drank** it during the night.

KATHY: **Was** it cold?

AMANDA: Freezing! Fortunately, we **had** our sleeping bags. But we **didn't sleep** much.

KATHY: Then what **happened**?

AMANDA: In the morning a snowplow **came** along and **cleared** the road.

KATHY: Wow! That's scary. I'm glad you're OK.

AMANDA: Thanks. Me too.

Words

🎧 *Do you know these words? Read the words. Write new ones in your notebook.*

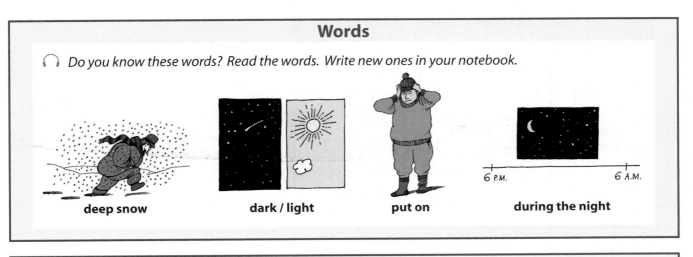

deep snow   **dark / light**   **put on**   **during the night**

Expressions

🎧 *Do you know these expressions? Read the conversations. Write new expressions in your notebook.*

1. A: Where were you on the weekend?
   B: We went **out of town**.

2. A: Did you call for help?
   B: I tried to, but **my cell phone was dead**.

Working Together

A *Practice the conversation in the opening reading with a partner.*

B *Last month Tim, Jessica, Jeremy, Annie, and Ben Olson went camping. Look at the picture. Each partner asks four past questions. Use the words in the box.*

Examples: **A:** Did it snow?   **B:** Did they sleep in tents?
              B: No, it didn't.   **A:** Yes, they did.

enjoy their breakfast

rain

sleep in beds

sleep in sleeping bags

sleep in tents

snow

stay in a motel

take their dog with them

Grammar Presentation

THE SIMPLE PAST: IRREGULAR VERBS (STATEMENTS)

Statements	
Affirmative	**Negative**
I **ate** the cookies.	I **did not eat** the chocolate.
You **had** the chocolate.	You **didn't have** the cookies.
She **drank** soda.	She **didn't drink** water.
We **went** camping in September.	We **didn't go** in August.

THE SIMPLE PAST: REGULAR AND IRREGULAR VERBS (*YES / NO* QUESTIONS)

Did	Subject	Base Form	
	I	**wake**	you up?
	you	**sleep**	late?
	he	**stay**	home?
Did	it	**snow**?	
	we	**eat**	all the cookies?
	they	**take**	warm clothes?

Short Answers	
Affirmative	**Negative**
Yes, you **did**.	No, you **didn't**.
Yes, we **did**.	No, we **didn't**.
Yes, he **did**.	No, he **didn't**.
Yes, it **did**.	No, it **didn't**.
Yes, you **did**.	No, you **didn't**.
Yes, they **did**.	No, they **didn't**.

GRAMMAR NOTES

EXAMPLES

1. Remember that **regular verbs** end in **-ed** in the simple past.

- It **started** to snow.   **start**

Irregular verbs have **different forms** in the simple past. (*See the verbs in Note 5.*)

- I **ate** my sandwich.   **eat**
- We **went** out of town.   **go**

2. For a **negative sentence** in the simple past, use **did not** + the **base form** of the verb. Use the contraction **didn't** + the **base form** in conversation and informal writing.

- He **did not sleep** much.
- He **didn't sleep** much.

▶ BE CAREFUL! Don't use *did* or *didn't* with the past tense form of the verb.

NOT: He ~~didn't slept~~ much.

---

3. To make a *yes / no question* in the simple past, use *did* + the **subject** + the **base form** of the verb.

- **Did** you **stop**?
- **Did** he **eat** anything?

---

4. You can use *did* or *didn't* in the **short answer** in the simple past.

A: Did it snow?
B: Yes, it **did**. OR Yes.
   No, it **didn't**. OR No.

---

5. Here are some common **irregular verbs** and their simple past forms.

Base Form	Simple Past	Base Form	Simple Past	Base Form	Simple Past
buy	**bought**	get	**got**	put	**put**
come	**came**	go	**went**	see	**saw**
do	**did**	have	**had**	sleep	**slept**
eat	**ate**	leave	**left**		

Reference Note
For more about **irregular verbs and their simple past forms**, see Appendix 11 on page A-14.

Focused Practice

1 | DISCOVER THE GRAMMAR

Read this conversation. Underline the three yes / no questions in the simple past. Then circle the irregular verbs in the simple past.

YOSHIO: Wow! I'm starved. Let's go have lunch.

JEREMY: Why are you so hungry? <u>Did you eat breakfast?</u>

YOSHIO: Not really. I got up at 8:15. I just drank a glass of orange juice. That's all I had time for. Did you eat anything this morning?

JEREMY: Sure. I always do. I had my usual big breakfast.

YOSHIO: What did you have?

JEREMY: Scrambled eggs, toast, cereal, juice, and milk. Why did you get up late? Did you stay up late last night?

YOSHIO: Yes. I went to a movie and got home about 11:00. Then I studied for a couple of hours.

2 | ONE OF THOSE DAYS

Grammar Notes 1–2, 5

Complete these sentences about Jason Mendoza's day. Use the simple past of the verbs in parentheses.

Yesterday Jason _____*had*_____ one of those days. He _____ at 8:00. He
                    1. (have)   2. (get up)

_____ in a hurry, so he _____ a shower. He _____ a
      3. (be)   4. (not, take)   5. (eat)

piece of toast and _____ a cup of black coffee for breakfast. Jason
                        6. (drink)

_____ the house at 8:20, but his car was in the shop, so he _____
      7. (leave)   8. (take)

the bus. He _____ at the office at 10:00 A.M. His boss _____ him
                 9. (arrive)   10. (see)

come in and _____ happy. At lunchtime, Jason _____ to a
                 11. (not, be)   12. (go)

restaurant, but he _____ enough money to pay. He _____ the
                        13. (not, have)   14. (not, leave)

office until 7:30 P.M. He _____ home at 9:00 P.M. It was just one of those days.
                              15. (get)

3 | QUESTIONS

Grammar Note 3

Complete the conversations. Write yes / no *questions with the words in the box.*

Verbs	call	get up	go	~~have~~	leave	rain
Subjects	I	it	Jeremy	~~you~~	you and Amanda	your parents

1. A: _____*Did you have*_____ breakfast this morning, Ken?

　　B: Yes. I had cereal, eggs, toast, and tea.

2. A: Josh, _____ early this morning?

　　B: No, we didn't. We slept until 10:00 A.M. It's Saturday, remember?

3. A: Mary, _____ in Seattle yesterday?

　　B: Yes, it did. It rained all day.

4. A: _____ to the movie with you?

　　B: Yes, he did. Ben went too. We all really enjoyed it.

5. A: I'm sorry, Mark. _____ too late?

　　B: No. It's only 9:45. What's up?

6. A: _____ on vacation, Jessica?

　　B: Yes, they did. They left at 6:30 this morning for Jamaica.

4 | EDITING

Correct the mistakes in the postcard. There are eight mistakes. The first mistake is already corrected.

Dear Rose,

Greetings from beautiful Jamaica! Thanks for taking us to

the airport. Our flight ~~not leave~~ *didn't leave* until 1 P.M., so the plane didn't

arrived until 10:30. We was really tired when we get to the hotel.

But that is two days ago. Now the sun is shining and it's warm.

Yesterday we go swimming at the beach. I buy some great

gifts for people. Today we sleeped until 9:30!

Hope everything is OK in Seattle. Is it cold?

Love,

Mary

TO:
Rose Corgatelli
3677 49th Ave. SW
Seattle, WA 98116
USA

Communication Practice

5 | AN INTERVIEW WITH YOSHIO

🎧 *Listen to the school interview with Yoshio. Then listen again. Check (✓)* **Yes**, **No**, *or* **No Information**.

	Yes	No	No Information
1. Yoshio came to the United States four months ago.	☐	☐	☐
2. Yoshio was born in Hamamatsu.	☐	☐	☐
3. Yoshio has two sisters and one brother.	☐	☐	☐
4. Yoshio played soccer in high school.	☐	☐	☐
5. Yoshio has a black belt in karate.	☐	☐	☐
6. Yoshio climbed Mount Everest when he was 14.	☐	☐	☐
7. Yoshio's family took a trip to the United States when he was a teenager.	☐	☐	☐
8. They went to Seattle on that trip.	☐	☐	☐
9. Yoshio likes the Seattle area.	☐	☐	☐

6 | ASK OTHER PEOPLE

You have five minutes to ask your classmates seven yes / no *questions. Use the question phrases in the box and a past time expression. Report interesting answers.*

Question phrases		
drink tea for breakfast	go out of town	see a movie
eat at a fast-food restaurant	go to bed after midnight	sleep in a tent
get up after 10:00 A.M.		

Past time expressions		
last month	last weekend	this morning
last night	on Monday	yesterday
last summer		

> **Example:** **A:** Did you go to bed after midnight last night?
> **B:** Yes, I did. I studied until 3:00 A.M.

7 | A DAY TO REMEMBER

Work in small groups. Look at the pictures. Write a story about what happened to Andy and Doris. Use simple past verbs. Write one false sentence in your story. One person in your group reads your story to the class. The class says "That's not true" when you read your false statement.

> **Example:** Andy and Doris left their house at 9:00 A.M. The weather . . .

The Simple Past: *Wh-* Questions

Why did you do it?

Grammar in Context

🎧 *Read this conversation between Josh and Amanda and Amanda's part of a telephone conversation with her brother Rob.*

JOSH: Amanda. It's for you. It's your brother. He says it's important.

AMANDA: Thanks, Josh . . . Hi, Rob. What's up? . . . Oh no! Are you OK? . . . **When did it happen?** . . . **Where did it happen?** . . . Are you there now? . . . **Why did you *drive* there? Why did you go *there*?** . . . Does Dad know? . . . Sorry. I think Dad needs to know.

[Amanda hangs up.]

JOSH: **What happened?**

AMANDA: Rob had a car accident this morning.

JOSH: How is he?

AMANDA: He's fine, but the car isn't. He wanted to get some videos, and he didn't want to walk to the store. He took Dad's car. Anyway, he saw a parking spot in front of the video store. He tried to park there and accidentally hit a sign. He broke the headlights and dented the bumper.

JOSH: That's too bad.

AMANDA: What's worse, he drove Dad's car without Dad's OK.

JOSH: Uh-oh.

AMANDA: He didn't want to go to Dad's auto repair shop. He's at a new body shop. This body shop wants $600 to fix the car today.

JOSH: Poor Dad.

AMANDA: What do you mean "poor Dad"? Poor Rob.

Words

🎧 *Do you know these words? Read the words. Write new ones in your notebook.*

an accident

headlights

a bumper

an auto repair shop

Expressions

🎧 *Do you know these expressions? Read the conversations. Write new expressions in your notebook.*

1. A: *It's for you.* It's your brother.
   B: Thanks.

2. A: *What's worse*, he drove without Dad's OK.
   B: *Uh-oh.*

3. A: Poor Dad.
   B: *What do you mean* "poor Dad"?

Working Together

A *Practice the conversation in the opening reading with a partner.*

B *Look at the opening conversation. Work with a partner. Answer these questions.*

1. What happened to Rob?

2. Where did it happen?

3. When did it happen?

4. Why did Rob go to a new auto repair shop?

Grammar Presentation

THE SIMPLE PAST: *WH-* QUESTIONS

Questions				
Wh- Question Word	**Did**	**Subject**	**Base Form of Verb**	
Where		it	**happen**?	
When	**did**	the accident	**occur**?	
Why		he	**go**	there?
Who		he	**drive**	with?

Answers
In front of the video store.
In the morning.
He wanted to get a video.
He drove alone.

Questions about the Subject
Who drove?
What happened?

Answers
Rob (did).
He had a car accident.

More Irregular Verbs	
Base Form	**Simple Past**
break	**broke**
drive	**drove**
do	**did**
find	**found**
hit	**hit**
say	**said**
teach	**taught**
wear	**wore**
win	**won**
write	**wrote**

GRAMMAR NOTES

EXAMPLES

1. Most *wh-* questions **in the simple past** use a ***wh-*** **word** + ***did*** + the **subject** + the **base form** of the verb.	**A: When did** he **call**? **B:** At 11:00 in the morning.

2. *Wh-* questions **about the subject** use a ***wh-*** **word** + the **simple past form** of the verb. ▶ **Be careful!** Do not use *did* with questions about the subject.	**A: Who called?** **B:** My brother called. Not: Who ~~did~~ call?

🎧 Pronunciation Note

Wh- questions usually have rising-falling intonation: **A:** What did he **eat**?
 B: Pasta.

To show surprise, stress the question word and use rising intonation: **A:** He ate a snake.

B: *What* did he eat?

Reference Note
For a list of **common irregular past forms**, see Appendix 11 on page A-14.

Focused Practice

1 | DISCOVER THE GRAMMAR

Read this conversation. Underline the wh- *questions.*

A: Guess what? I saw Tom Cruise.

B: Really? <u>Where did you see him?</u>

A: On Oak Street.

B: What time did you see him?

A: It was about 3:00 in the afternoon.

B: What did he look like?

A: Like Tom Cruise, of course.

B: Did you ask for his autograph?

A: Yes, I did.

B: What did he say?

A: He said, "Here you go," and signed his name.

Tom Cruise

2 | AN EMERGENCY

Grammar Notes 1–2

Complete the conversation. Use the words in parentheses.

JOSH: You know, I once drove without a license.

AMANDA: _____ *When did you do that* _____?
   1. (you / When / do / did / that)

JOSH: Oh, about 10 years ago. I was 15, and I went to my grandmother's house.

AMANDA: _____?
   2. (you / Why / there / did / drive)

JOSH: It was impossible to get to her home by bus. She called and said she was sick.

   My parents were away for the day.

AMANDA: So _____?
   3. (happened / what)

JOSH: Well, I drove to her house. She was really sick. I took her to the hospital.

AMANDA: _____?
   4. (How long / the drive / did / take)

JOSH: About 30 minutes.

AMANDA: _____?
   5. (your / parents / What / say / did)

JOSH: They said I did the right thing. I got my license the next month.

3 | WHO DID THESE THINGS?

Grammar Note 2

Write questions in the simple past. Begin with **Who**. *Use the words in parentheses.*

1. (go to the post office last week) _____ *Who went to the post office last week* _____?

2. (eat sushi last night) _____?

3. (teach you to ride a bicycle) _____?

4. (come late today) _____?

5. (visit you last weekend) _____?

6. (give you a special gift last year) _____?

4 | INTONATION—INFORMATION AND SURPRISE

Grammar Notes 1–2

⌒ **A** *Listen to these two conversations.*

1. A: I'm buying a newspaper.

 B: What did you say? *(B didn't hear A. B is asking for information.)*

2. A: I'm getting married this afternoon.

 B: *What* did you say? *(B is surprised.)*

⌒ **B** *Listen to these questions. Check (✓)* **Information** *or* **Surprise**.

	Information	Surprise
1. When did they arrive?	✓	☐
2. When did they arrive?	☐	☐
3. How did she get there?	☐	☐
4. How did she get there?	☐	☐
5. What did you say?	☐	☐
6. What did you say?	☐	☐
7. Who came to your house?	☐	☐
8. Who came to your house?	☐	☐

C *Work with a partner. Read one of the questions in Part B. Your partner gives the number of the question you read.*

5 | EDITING

Correct the conversations. There are four mistakes. The first mistake is already corrected.

A: Hello. This is Rob Peck. I'd like to report an accident.

B: Thank you, Mr. Peck. What time ^did^ the accident occur?

A: At 9:30 this morning.

B: Where did it happened?

A: It happened on Oak Street between First and Second Avenues.

B: How it did happen?

A: A cat ran into the street. The car ahead of me stopped suddenly, and I hit it.

B: Thank you for reporting the accident.

*   *   *

C: What the insurance company say?

A: Nothing. Just "Thank you for reporting the accident."

Communication Practice

6 | WHAT DID DAD SAY?

🎧 *Listen to this telephone conversation between Amanda and Rob. Listen again and answer the questions.*

1. What did Rob promise to pay for? _____

2. When did he start work? _____

3. How many hours did he work yesterday? _____

4. How many hours did he work the day before? _____

7 | SAME AND DIFFERENT

Work with a partner. Interview your partner about his or her past. Student A, write five things that were the same for both of you. Student B, write five things that were different.

Examples: **1. A:** What sports did you play in high school?
B: I played soccer.
A: I played soccer too.

We both played soccer in high school.

2. B: Where did you go on your last vacation?
A: I went to the beach.
B: I went to the mountains.

On my last vacation, I went to the beach. Juan went to the mountains.

8 | THINGS I DID

Work with a partner. Complete these sentences. Then your partner asks you wh- *questions about the information. Answer your partner's questions.*

I saw _____.

I went to _____.

I found _____.

Example: **A:** I saw a beautiful bird.
B: Where did you see it?
A: I saw it in East Park.
B: When did you see it?
A: Last weekend.
B: What did it look like?
A: It had beautiful red feathers.

9 | SURVEY

Ask three classmates three questions about their childhood. Use the suggestions in the box or your own ideas.

give you nice gifts	read stories to you	teach you to ride a bike
help you with homework	teach you to drive	

Example: **A:** Who taught you to ride a bike?
B: Nobody did. I can't ride a bike.
C: My father.
D: My friend did.

I *Complete these conversations. Circle the correct letter.*

1. STEVE: Sorry I'm late. _____

    TIM: That's OK.

(**A**) I miss the train.   (**C**) I missed the train.

(**B**) Do I miss the train?   (**D**) I do miss the train.

2.   **ROB:** What happened?

  AMANDA: _____

(**A**) Dad got a traffic ticket.   (**C**) Did it happen to you?

(**B**) It happened last night.   (**D**) It happened during the night.

3.   **TIM:** How was the movie?

  STEVE: It was a blast. _____

(**A**) Everyone really enjoyed it.   (**C**) Everyone really is enjoying it.

(**B**) Everyone really enjoys it.   (**D**) What was the movie about?

4.   **TIM:** _____

  STEVE: At my house.

(**A**) Why did your friends stay there?   (**C**) Where did your friends stay?

(**B**) Did your friends stay at your house? (**D**) Did your friends stay at a hotel?

5.   **TIM:** _____

  STEVE: Last night about 9:00.

(**A**) Why did they leave?   (**C**) When do they leave?

(**B**) Who left last night?   (**D**) When did they leave?

II *Complete the paragraph. Use the simple past and the verbs in parentheses.*

Steven Spielberg is a popular movie director all over the world. He always

_____ *liked* _____ movies. His father was an engineer, but Spielberg _____
  1. (like)   **2. (not, like)**

engineering. At 12, he _____ his first film. At 13, he _____ a prize
                          3. (complete)   **4. (receive)**

for a 40-minute movie. He _____ to study film at the University of Southern
                            5. (want)

California, but he _____ into the film program there. That famous film school
                      6. (not, get)

_____ a big mistake. He _____ to California State University in
  7. (make)   **8. (go)**

Long Beach instead. At 20, he _____ a job with Universal Pictures. Spielberg
                                 9. (get)

was the director of many popular movies, such as *Jaws*, *E.T.*, *Raiders of the Lost Ark*,

Schindler's List, and *War of the Worlds*. In the future he will probably direct many more.

III *Complete this conversation. Use the simple past and the verbs in parentheses.*

KATHY: _____ *Did* _____ you _____ *go* _____ to Judy's party?
                                                       1. (go)

MARK: Yes, I _____. It _____ fun, but I _____ you.
                  2. (do)   **3. (be)**   **4. (miss)**

KATHY: _____ you really _____ me?
                                              5. (miss)

MARK: I certainly _____.
                         6. (do)

KATHY: Well, I missed you too. So tell me, what _____ they _____?
                                                                                  7. (serve)

MARK: Thai food—that's Judy's favorite.

KATHY: _____ she _____ nice gifts?
                                     8. (get)

MARK: I don't know. She _____ them.
                              9. (not, open)

KATHY: What _____ you _____ her?
                                          10. (give)

MARK: I _____ her a gift card to an art store.
             11. (give)

KATHY: That _____ a good idea.
                   12. (be)

MARK: _____ you _____ her anything in Boston?
                                    13. (get)

KATHY: Yes, I _____ her a sweatshirt.
                    14. (buy)

MARK: Cool.

IV *Write the question about the underlined words.*

1. **MARY:** *Where did you go?*

   JESSICA: We went <u>to the country</u>.

2. **MARY:** _____

   JESSICA: We left <u>at 10:00 in the morning</u>. The drive took five hours.

3. **MARY:** _____

   JESSICA: It took five hours <u>because we had a flat tire on the way</u>.

4. **MARY:** _____

   JESSICA: <u>Jeremy</u> changed the tire.

5. **MARY:** _____

   JESSICA: We got home <u>at midnight</u>.

▶ *To check your answers, go to the Answer Key on page RT-2.*

UNIT

Subject and Object Pronouns

24

Why don't you give them some chocolates?

Grammar in Context

🎧 *Read this conversation.*

CARLOS: Kathy, **you**'re an American. What's a good gift?

KATHY: For what?

CARLOS: For the party at Bill's house on Saturday. I want to get **him** a gift.

KATHY: Right. Let **me** think.

CARLOS: How about flowers?

KATHY: Well, **I** suppose so. But **you** don't usually give flowers to a man.

CARLOS: **He** has a wife. Can **I** give **them** to **her**?

KATHY: Hmm. **I**'m not sure.

CARLOS: What about a CD of some cool Latin music? **I** know **he** likes music.

KATHY: No. Not appropriate. **You** don't give your boss a CD.

CARLOS: Well, what do **you** suggest?

KATHY: Why don't **you** give **them** some chocolates? **He**'s always eating **them** at his desk.

CARLOS: OK, good idea. A box of chocolates. Now, another question.

KATHY: What?

CARLOS: Tomiko and **I** need a ride to the party. Can you take **us**?

KATHY: For a price.

CARLOS: For a price? What do **you** mean?

KATHY: Get **me** a box of chocolates too.

CARLOS: **I** don't believe **you**. **You**'re not serious, are **you**?

KATHY: No, just kidding! **I**'ll pick **you** up at 6:30 on Saturday.

Words

🎧 *Do you know these words? Read the words. Write new ones in your notebook.*

flowers

chocolates

a ride

Expressions

🎧 *Do you know these expressions? Read the conversations. Write new expressions in your notebook.*

1. A: Does he like flowers?
  B: Well, *I suppose so*.

2. A: How about some flowers?
  B: *I don't think so.*

3. A: What about a CD?
  B: No. *Not appropriate.*

4. A: Why don't you give them some chocolates?
  B: *Good idea.*

Working Together

A *Practice the conversation in the opening reading with a partner.*

B *Take turns. Ask your partner about the following gifts for Carlos's boss.*

a CD	a DVD	fruit	nuts
chocolates	flowers	money	a watch

Example: A: What about flowers?
     B: I think it's OK to give them to him. OR I don't think they're a good gift.

Grammar Presentation

SUBJECT AND OBJECT PRONOUNS

Subject Pronouns			
Subject	Verb	Object Pronoun	Object Noun
I You He She We You They	gave	them	chocolates.

Object Pronouns			
Subject	Verb	Object Pronoun	Object Noun
They	gave	me you him her us you them	a CD.

GRAMMAR NOTES

EXAMPLES

1. *I*, *you*, *he*, *she*, *it*, *we*, and *they* are **subject pronouns**. They replace a subject noun.

- **The boys** need a ride to the party. **They** don't have a car.

2. *Me*, *you*, *him*, *her*, *it*, *us*, and *them* are **object pronouns**. They replace an object noun.

subject   object
noun   noun
- **Bill** loves **chocolates**.

subject   object
pronoun   pronoun
- **He** loves **them**.

Object pronouns often come **after prepositions** like *to* or *for*.

- Give **them to him**.
- The chocolates are **for him**.

3. NOTE: *You* and *it* are both subject and object pronouns.

subject   object
- **You**'re kidding. I don't believe **you**.

subject   object
- **It**'s Latin music. He likes **it**.

4. The pronoun *you* is the same for singular and plural.

- I don't believe **you**. (*you* = Kathy)
- See **you** at 6:30. (*you* = you and Tom)

When *you* is **plural**, we sometimes add the word *both* to make the sentence clearer.

- See **you both** at 6:30.

Focused Practice

1 | DISCOVER THE GRAMMAR

Read this conversation. Underline the subject pronouns. Circle the object pronouns.

STEVE: <u>You</u> like parties. Right?

AMANDA: I love (them.) Why?

STEVE: Well, we're having a party on Sunday at my apartment. You and Josh are both invited. Are you free at three o'clock?

AMANDA: I think so. What's the occasion?

STEVE: It's Jessica's birthday, but I don't know what to get. What's a good gift? Any ideas?

AMANDA: How about some CDs? Does she like music?

STEVE: Yes. She listens to it all the time.

AMANDA: Good. Get her some CDs. Now, tell me again. What's your new address?

STEVE: 14 Vine Street, Apartment 202.

AMANDA: OK. See you then.

2 | HOW ABOUT A BOOK?   *Grammar Notes 1–2*

Complete these conversations with subject and object pronouns.

  1. A: It's Jessica's birthday on Sunday. What's a good gift for ___*her*___?

  B: How about a book? _____ loves to read.

  2. A: It's Mark's birthday next week. What's a good present?

  B: Well, _____ likes CDs. Get _____ a CD.

  3. A: Our car is in the shop. Can _____ give _____ a ride to the party?

  B: Sure. I'll pick _____ up at 5:00.

  4. A: The Johnsons are having a party on Saturday. What's a good gift for _____?

  B: _____ love flowers.

  5. A: Hello? Steve? Is _____ raining there? Do I need my umbrella?

  B: Yes, bring _____. It's raining hard.

  6. A: My friends are visiting from Portland. _____'re a lot of fun.

  B: Well, bring _____ on Saturday. We have plenty of food.

3 | WHY DON'T YOU GET THEM SOME FLOWERS?

Grammar Note 2

1. a travel book

2. a tennis racquet

3. a vest

4. a DVD

*Write a suggestion for each picture. Use **Why don't you get** + object pronoun + object noun.*

1. _____

2. _____

3. _____

4. _____

4 | EDITING

Correct this invitation. There are six mistakes. The first mistake is already corrected.

Dear Sarah,

Jim and ~~me~~ are having a party on Saturday, June 10, at 3:00. Is for our son, Bob, and our daughter, Sally. They birthdays are both in June. You and Stan are invited. Please don't bring they any presents. Are just having a band and lots of food, but no gifts. Please come! Give John and I a call if you can come.

See you soon,

Doris

Communication Practice

5 | WHO ARE THEY FOR?

🎧 *Listen to Tim and Jessica's conversation. Then listen again and complete the chart. Use the words in the box.*

Colors				
blue	green	orange	red	white
Gifts				
a CD	a DVD	a game	something special	a tennis racquet

Color of Box	Who is it for?	Gift
	Cousin Martha	
	Mom and Dad	
	Jeremy	
	Ben and Annie	
	Jessica	

6 | WHAT'S A GOOD GIFT?

Write down the names of five people. Work with a partner. Talk about a good gift for each person. Then tell the class.

Example: A: It's my brother's birthday tomorrow. What's a good gift for him?
B: Hmm. How old is he?
A: Ten.
B: Maybe a DVD?
A: I don't think so.
B: OK, then why don't you get him a soccer ball?
A: Good idea.
OR
A: It's my brother's birthday tomorrow. What's a good gift for him?
B: What does he like?
A: He loves sports.
B: How about a tennis racquet?
A: I don't think so.
B: OK, then how about a soccer ball?
A: Good idea.

How much / How many; Quantity Expressions

How many days were you away?

Grammar in Context

🎧 *Read this conversation.*

STEVE: Welcome back.

JESSICA: Thanks.

STEVE: How was Ecuador?

JESSICA: Great.

STEVE: **How many days** were you away?

JESSICA: Ten. We were in the capital, Quito, and on the Galápagos Islands.

MARK: The Galápagos Islands? That sounds exciting. **How much time** did you spend there?

TIM: Not much. Only four days. But it was fantastic. We took about a hundred photos. And we ate and slept on a boat.

MARK: Really? **How many people** were on the boat?

JESSICA: Twelve including us. All very interesting people.

STEVE: I'll bet. **How much** did the trip cost?

JESSICA: Don't ask.

MARK: Well, nothing beats travel.

TIM: You said it.

Galápagos Islands

Quito

193

Words

🎧 *Do you know these words? Read the words. Write new ones in your notebook.*

an island

the capital

Expressions

🎧 *Do you know these expressions? Read the conversations. Write new expressions in your notebook.*

1. A: How many days were you *away*?
   B: Five days.

2. A: It was fun.
   B: *I'll bet.*

3. A: How much did it cost?
   B: *Don't ask.*

4. A: Nothing beats travel.
   B: *You said it.*

Working Together

A *Practice the conversation in the opening reading with three partners.*

B *Tell your partner about an interesting place you visited.*

How much time did you spend there?

How many people did you go with?

How many photos did you take?

How much did it cost to go there?

Grammar Presentation

HOW MUCH / HOW MANY

Count Nouns	Non-count Nouns
A: How many photos did you take? **B: A lot.** (I took a lot of photos.) **Not many.** (I didn't take many photos.) **A few.** (I took a few photos.) **Sixty.** (I took 60 photos.)	**A: How much time** did you spend there? **B: A lot.** (We spent a lot of time there.) **Not much.** (We didn't spend much time there.) **A little.** (We spent a little time there.) **Six days.** (We spent six days there.)

GRAMMAR NOTES

EXAMPLES

1. Use *how many* + a **plural count noun** to ask about a quantity of something. Use *how much* + a **non-count noun** to ask about an amount.	plural count noun **A: How many days** were you there? **B:** Fifteen. non-count noun **A: How much time** did you spend there? **B:** A lot.

2. *A lot*, *a few*, *a little*, *not many*, and *not much* are **general** expressions. *A lot* tells that an amount is large. *A few*, *a little*, *not many*, and *not much* tell that amounts are small.	**A:** How many people were on the boat? **B: Not many.** (a small quantity) **A:** How much time did you spend in Quito? **B: Not much.** (a small amount)

3. Numbers also answer questions with *how many*. Numbers give an **exact** amount.	**A:** How many days were you there? **B: Ten days.**

4. Use *how much* to ask about the **cost** of something. We often use *how much* **without a noun**.	• **How much** was the trip? • **How much** did the trip cost? • **How much (money)** did it cost?

Reference Note
For more about **count and non-count nouns**, see Unit 18.

Focused Practice

1 | DISCOVER THE GRAMMAR

Reread the opening conversation. Answer the questions. Choose from the words in the box.

A lot	A lot—almost 100	Two—Quito and the Galápagos Islands
10 days	12 people	

1. How many photos did they take? _A lot—almost 100_____.

2. How much time did they spend in Ecuador? _____.

3. How much money did they spend? _____.

4. How many people were on the boat to the Galápagos Islands? _____.

5. How many places did they visit? _____.

2 | A STUDENT TRIP

Grammar Notes 1, 3–4

Read about this trip to Washington, D.C. Match the questions and answers below.

Come to Washington, D.C.!
See the beautiful cherry blossoms.
Visit the White House. See the Capitol.
INCLUDES:
• round-trip airfare from Seattle
• 2 nights, 3 days at the Best Eastern
• double rooms
• lunch and dinner for 3 days
• sightseeing tour of Washington, D.C.
• free bus from airport to hotel
All this for only $650!

1. How many days is the trip? __b__   **a.** Two.

2. How many meals does the trip include? _____   **b.** Three.

3. How much does the trip cost? _____   **c.** Six.

4. How many people share a room? _____   **d.** Nothing.

5. How much is the bus ride from the airport? _____   **e.** $650 from Seattle.

3 | A SHORT VACATION

*Read this ad for a trip to Boston. Then write questions with **how much** or **how many** to complete the conversation below.*

VISIT BOSTON!

Includes:
- **Round-trip airfare from Seattle**
- **5 days and 4 nights at Motel 9**
- **4 to a room**
- **Delicious breakfast every day**
- **3-hour sightseeing tour of Boston**

ONLY $800!

Visit the Freedom Trail, Faneuil Hall, Quincy Market, and Old North Church

JUDY: I'm thinking of visiting New York or Boston.

MARK: Well, here's an ad for a trip to Boston.

JUDY: *How much does the trip cost* OR *How much does it cost* _____?
                                                 1.

MARK: $800.

JUDY: _____?
                                                 2.

MARK: Five days.

JUDY: Do they provide meals?

MARK: Some.

JUDY: _____?
                                                 3.

MARK: Five breakfasts.

JUDY: Do you have your own room?

MARK: Uh, no.

JUDY: _____?
                                                 4.

MARK: Four people to a room.

JUDY: That's not for me.

MARK: Oh, well. It's a good price.

4 | EDITING

Correct the mistakes in this questionnaire. There are five mistakes. The first mistake is already corrected.

1. **A:** How ~~much~~ *many* people are there in your family?

   B: Five.

2. **A:** How many book do you read in a month?

   B: Not much.

3. **A:** How much time do you spend online?

   B: Not many time.

4. **A:** How much trips do you take in a year?

   B: Two or three.

Communication Practice

5 | A RADIO BROADCAST

A *Complete these questions. Use* **how much** *or* **how many**.

1. _____ travel books did John Phillips write? _____

2. _____ children did he have? _____

3. _____ grandchildren did he have? _____

4. _____ money did John Phillips have? _____

5. _____ people did he leave his money to? _____

6. _____ time did his children spend with him? _____

B *Now listen to the radio broadcast and answer the questions in Part A.*

6 | I ATE A LOT OF ICE CREAM LAST NIGHT

*Write four sentences with **a lot of**. Use the verbs in the box. Your partner asks for an exact amount.*

buy	drink	eat	find	see	spend	visit	write

Example: **A:** I drank a lot of coffee yesterday.
B: How much did you drink?
A: Eight cups.

7 | HABITS

A *Work in small groups. Take turns. Ask questions with **how much** and **how many**. Your classmates answer with **a lot**, **a little**, **a few**, **not much**, **not many**, **some**, or **none**, or give an exact amount. Use the ideas in Exercise 4, the ones in the box, or your own ideas.*

clothes / buy in a month

e-mail messages / get in a week

money / give to charity in a year

movies / watch in a month

people / help in a week

time / spend on the telephone in a day

Example: **A:** How much time do you spend online?
B: Not much. About 10 minutes a day.

B *Write four of your questions and your classmates' answers. Report the results.*

Question	Student 1	Student 2	Student 3	Student 4
1.				
2.				
3.				
4.				

Example: Juan doesn't spend much time online: about 10 minutes a day.

Grammar in Context

🎧 *Read this conversation.*

AMANDA: Well, Josh, here we are. Now what?

JOSH: We need to find a place to stay . . . **There's** an information booth over there. Let's go ask.

AMANDA: OK, hon. Lead the way.

ATTENDANT: May I help you?

JOSH: Yes, thanks. We're looking for a place to stay. **Are there** any youth hostels around here?

ATTENDANT: Well, **there's** one near here, but it's kind of late. They're probably full by now. What about a bed-and-breakfast?

JOSH: Aren't bed-and-breakfasts pretty expensive?

ATTENDANT: Not always. **There are** a few inexpensive ones. Would you like me to check?

AMANDA: Please do. *[A few moments later . . .]*

ATTENDANT: Good news. **There's** a nice bed-and-breakfast about half a kilometer from here, and they have a room. It's very reasonable. They can hold it for an hour.

JOSH: That's great! Can you tell us how to get there?

ATTENDANT: **There's** an Underground station just outside. Take the Circle Line west three stops. Here's an Underground map.

AMANDA: We're starved. **Are there** any good fast-food restaurants around here?

ATTENDANT: **There's** a nice snack bar right there. **Is there** anything else I can help you with?

AMANDA: No, but thank you very much.

ATTENDANT: My pleasure. Enjoy your stay in London.

Words

🎧 *Do you know these words? Read the words. Write new ones in your notebook.*

a youth hostel

a bed-and-breakfast

an Underground station (a subway station)

a snack bar

Expressions

🎧 *Do you know these expressions? Read the conversations. Write new expressions in your notebook.*

1. A: Let's go ask.
   B: OK. *Lead the way.*

2. A: *Would you like me to* check?
   B: *Please do.*

3. A: They can *hold* the room for an hour.
   B: That's great. Can you tell us how to get there?

4. A: Thank you very much.
   B: *My pleasure. Enjoy your stay.*

Working Together

A *Practice the conversation in the opening reading with two partners.*

B *Work in small groups. Use the words or phrases in the box to ask about your city, town, or neighborhood.*

amusement parks	a bank	a metro (a subway)	parks
art museums	a mall	movie theaters	a stadium

Example: **A:** Is there a metro (a subway) in your city?
B: No, there isn't.
OR
Yes, there is.
Are there any movie theaters in your neighborhood?
C: Yes, there are. There are two.

Grammar Presentation

THERE IS / THERE ARE

Statements	
Singular	**Plural**
There is a bank on this block.	**There are** three **banks** on this block.
There isn't a bank near here.	**There aren't** any **banks** around here.

Questions and Answers	
Singular	**Plural**
A: **Is there sugar** in the coffee?	A: **Are there** any **museums** in the town?
B: Yes, **there is.** OR No, **there isn't.**	B: Yes, **there are.** OR No, **there aren't.**

GRAMMAR NOTES

EXAMPLES

GRAMMAR NOTES	EXAMPLES
1. Use *there is* or *there's* to state facts about a person or thing.	• **There is a message** for you. OR • **There's a message** for you.
Use *there are* if the noun is plural.	• **There are** two **postcards** from Rome.
We often use *there is* or *there are* to tell the location of people or things.	• **There is a snack bar** over there. • **There are** two **snack bars** over there.
2. To state a **negative fact**, you can use *there isn't a / an* or *there aren't any*.	• **There isn't a** subway in this city. • **There aren't any** theaters near here.
3. To make a **question**, put *is* or *are* before *there*.	• **Is there** a bank near here? • **Are there** any stores in this area?

| 4. Use *there* both in **questions** and in **short answers**. | **A:** **Is there** a pool in our hotel?
B: Yes, **there is.** OR No, **there isn't.** OR No, **there's not.**

A: How many rooms **are there** on this floor?
B: **There are** eight. |

| 5. Use *there's* in speaking and informal writing. (*There's = There is*)

▶ **BE CAREFUL!** Don't use a plural noun after *there's*. | • **There's** a mall two kilometers from here.

• **There are** some beautiful paintings in this house.

NOT: ~~There's~~ some beautiful paintings in this museum. |

| 6. Use *there* the **first time** you talk about something. Use *it* or *they* after that. | **A:** Is there a bank around here?
B: Yes, **there** is. **It**'s on the corner of First Avenue and Barton Street.

A: Are **there** any theaters near here?
B: Yes, **there** are several. **They**'re in the mall. |

Focused Practice

1 | DISCOVER THE GRAMMAR

Read Amanda and Josh's conversation at their bed-and-breakfast. Underline all the uses of **there is** *and* **there are**. *Draw an arrow between* **there** *and the noun it refers to.*

MRS. BRADY: Good evening. You must be Josh and Amanda Wang. Welcome. Can you please sign the guest book? 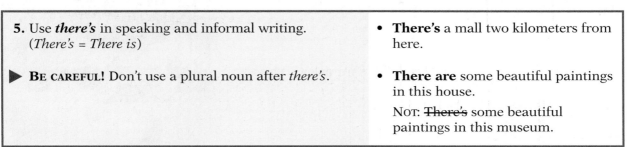There's a pen right over there.

JOSH: Thank you. We're glad there's a room for us.

MRS. BRADY: Actually, there are two rooms to choose from, one on the second floor and one on the third. The one on the third floor has a nice view, but there isn't an elevator, unfortunately.

AMANDA: Oh, that's fine. We'd like the one with the nice view. Is there a bath in the room?

MRS. BRADY: No, there isn't. Sorry about that. There's just one bathroom per floor. But we don't have many guests. So, let's see . . . breakfast goes from 7:00 until 9:00. There's tea in your room, and there are also some nice biscuits. Your room is up that stairway over there. We'll see you in the morning.

JOSH: Thanks a lot. See you then.

2 | OUT AND ABOUT IN LONDON
Grammar Notes 1, 3–6

Complete Josh and Amanda's breakfast conversation. Choose from the items in parentheses.

HANS: What are your plans for today?

AMANDA: We're going to the Tower of London.

_____Is there_____ a bus we can take?
1. **(Is there / There's)**

HANS: Yes, _____. The number 78 bus
2. **(there is / it is)**

will get you there. And _____ a
3. **(there's / there are)**

bus stop down the block.

JOSH: Great . . . Hmm. What about lunch?

_____ any good places to eat near the Tower?
4. **(Is there / Are there)**

HANS: Yes, _____ a great Indian restaurant near the Tower, and
5. **(there's / it's)**

_____ some other restaurants close by. _____ all pretty
6. **(they're / there are)**   7. **(They're / There are)**

cheap. So have a great day. See you this evening.

3 | MEANWHILE, BACK IN SEATTLE
Grammar Notes 3–4

Annie Olson is writing a report about London. She is calling the Public Library Quick Information line. Write her questions. Use **how many** + *noun* + **are there** *and* **how much** + *noun* + **is there**.

LIBRARIAN: Quick Information. May I help you?

ANNIE: Yes. I'm writing a report about Britain, and I need some information.

LIBRARIAN: All right. What do you need to know?

ANNIE: First, about London: _____How many people are there_____ in London today?
1. **(people)**

LIBRARIAN: Let's see . . . There are about 7,619,000 people in London.

ANNIE: OK. _____ in London?
2. **(rain)**

LIBRARIAN: Let's see . . . about 29.7 inches a year.

ANNIE: OK, thanks. And _____?
3. **(snow)**

LIBRARIAN: In the city the snowfall is rarely more than 1 inch per year.

ANNIE: And _____?
4. **(theaters)**

LIBRARIAN: There are over a hundred theaters in the city.

ANNIE: Thanks very much. I really appreciate it.

LIBRARIAN: My pleasure. Glad to help.

4 | AN ACCIDENT REPORT

Grammar Note 6

Josh and Amanda are driving in London. Complete this radio accident report. Use **there**, **it**, *or* **they**.

Good afternoon. This is Pamela Robinson reporting.

_____*There*_____ is a major traffic jam on the M-3.
1.

About an hour ago, a truck carrying oranges hit a milk

truck. Fortunately, no one was hurt. But right now

_____ 's milk all over the highway.
2.

_____ is causing traffic problems.
3.

_____ are also oranges everywhere.
4.

_____ are about 10 police officers at the
5.

scene. _____ are directing traffic. Stay tuned for more information.
6.

5 | EDITING

Correct Amanda's letter to Kathy. There are six mistakes. The first mistake is already corrected.

⊰ Brady's Victoria Bed-and-Breakfast ⊱

Dear Kathy,

                                        There are

    Greetings from London! We're having a wonderful time. ~~It's~~ so many interesting things to

see and do here! They are interesting little shops on every street, and there's lots of fun

things to buy. I hope my suitcase is big enough. They are also a lot of great museums; we went

to the Tower of London yesterday, and we're going to the British Museum today. We're staying

at a really nice bed-and-breakfast. There's a nice, comfortable place, and they are lots of

interesting people from different countries staying here.

    I have to sign off now; we're ready to go to the museum. Say hi to Mark and everyone else.

Love,

Amanda

Communication Practice

6 | ON THE TRAIN

🎧 *Listen to Josh and Amanda's conversation on the train to Manchester. Listen again and answer each question in a complete sentence.*

1. How many other people are there in Josh and Amanda's compartment?

_____

2. According to Josh, are there a lot of or a few differences between British and American English?

_____

3. What is the American word for *biscuits*?

_____

4. What is the American word for *Underground*?

_____

5. Is there an Underground in Seattle?

_____

6. Is there a monorail in Seattle?

_____

7. According to Helen, how many nice bed-and-breakfasts are there near the train station in Manchester?

_____

7 | A MEMORY GAME

Form two teams. Everyone is going on a trip. Everyone has a suitcase with something special in it. Each person describes his or her special item:

I have a _____ _____.

*The other team must repeat all the items in sentences with **there**, **it**, and **they**. The team that remembers the most items wins.*

> **Example:** **TEAM A:** I have a cheap DVD player in my suitcase.
> **TEAM B:** There's a DVD player in Alicia's suitcase. It's cheap.
> **TEAM A:** I have two blue soccer balls in my suitcase.
> **TEAM B:** There's a DVD player in Alicia's suitcase. It's cheap. There are two soccer balls in Yoshi's suitcase. They're blue . . .

Review Test VIII

| Complete these conversations. Circle the correct letter.

1. ANDREA: _____

    JUDY: There are a lot of people—about 20.

(**A**) How many people are there in your class?

(**B**) How much space is there in your class?

(**C**) Do you have many classes?

(**D**) How many people is there in your class?

2. BEN: Dad, are there computers at your office?

    TIM: _____

(**A**) Of course there is.

(**B**) Of course they are.

(**C**) Of course there are.

(**D**) Of course it is.

3. JUDY: _____

    MARK: Sorry. My car's in the shop.

(**A**) Can you give me a ride to the party?

(**B**) Are you going to the party?

(**C**) What time does the party start?

(**D**) Can I go to the party?

4. JEREMY: Dad, I don't know what to get you and Mom for your anniversary.

    TIM: _____

(**A**) Why don't you get her some flowers?

(**B**) Why don't you get us some flowers?

(**C**) Why don't you get me some flowers?

(**D**) Why don't you get them some flowers?

II *Write questions about the underlined expressions. Use* **how much** *or* **how many**.

1. A: _How many days were you away?_____

B: We were away <u>10 days</u>.

2. A: _____

B: We drove <u>about a thousand miles</u>.

3. A: _____

B: <u>Four people</u> went on the trip.

4. A: _____

B: The trip cost <u>about a thousand dollars</u>.

III *Look at the picture. Complete the paragraph with the correct choices.*

It's Jeremy's eighteenth birthday party. There are _____*a lot*_____ of Jeremy's friends

1. (a lot / not many)

at the party, and everyone is having a good time. _____ of the kids are singing

2. (A few / Much)

songs. _____ of them are dancing. There's a DVD playing on TV, but not

3. (Some / A little)

_____ of the kids are watching it. There's not _____ pizza left, but

4. (many / much)   **5. (many / much)**

there is _____ cake.

6. (some / a few)

IV *Complete the paragraphs with* **there is, there are, it is, it has,** *or* **they are.** *Capitalize where necessary.*

In downtown Madison today, _____*there are*_____ a lot of stores. _____

1.   2.

large and modern. _____ a movie complex. _____ 12 theaters in

3.   4.

it. _____ no big companies in Madison, but _____ a lot of smaller

5.   6.

businesses. _____ a beautiful concert hall near downtown Madison.

7.

_____ very new—only two years old.

8.

Today _____ two high schools in Madison. _____ both very

9.   10.

modern. _____ about a thousand students in each high school.

11.

_____ computers in every classroom in these high schools. _____

12.   13.

a large sports stadium in Madison. Both schools use it.

▶ *To check your answers, go to the Answer Key on page RT-3.*

UNIT

27 Noun and Adjective Modifiers

I'm a young chemistry teacher.

Grammar in Context

🎧 *Read these personal ads from* The Seattle Daily.

The Seattle Daily

❤ ❤ ❤ ❤ *Love Lines* ❤ ❤ ❤ ❤

MEN	WOMEN
A. Am I for you? Are you interested in a **35-year-old**, **fun-loving** man? I'm **easygoing**. I enjoy **jazz** bands and **sandy** beaches. I'm looking for a **kind**, **sensitive** woman.	**A.** Let's get together. **Artistic 20-year-old** woman looking for an **artistic** man.
B. Rich **80-year-old**, **active**, **healthy**, **young-at-heart** man. Wants to enjoy life with a **lively middle-aged** woman.	**B. 19-year-old computer science** major. Enjoys tennis, mysteries, and **fast** cars. Looking for a **smart** guy with **similar** interests.
C. Tall, slim, **25-year-old chemistry** teacher. Enjoys **bird**-watching and **nature** walks. Looking for a woman with **similar** interests.	**C. 75-year-old** woman. **Rich**, **funny**, **warm**, and **honest**. Enjoys **spy** films and **abstract** art. Looking for a **younger** man with **similar** interests.

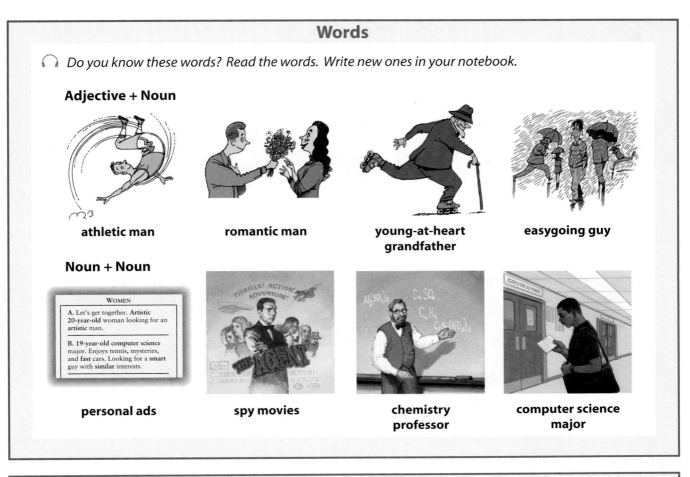

Words

🎧 *Do you know these words? Read the words. Write new ones in your notebook.*

Adjective + Noun

athletic man **romantic man** **young-at-heart grandfather** **easygoing guy**

Noun + Noun

WOMEN

A. Let's get together. **Artistic** **20-year-old** woman looking for an **artistic man.**

B. **19-year-old computer science** major. Enjoys tennis, mysteries, and **fast cars.** Looking for a **smart guy** with **similar** interests.

personal ads **spy movies** **chemistry professor** **computer science major**

Expressions

🎧 *Do you know these expressions? Read the conversations. Write new expressions in your notebook.*

1. A: Are you ***interested*** in computer science?
   B: Yes, I like it a lot.

2. A: Let's ***get together***.
   B: OK. When?

Working Together

A *Read the personal ads on page 210 with a partner.*

B *Are there any possible matches? Why or why not?*

Example: A: I think man C and woman B are a match. They're in similar fields.
   B: I don't think so. Computer science and chemistry are very different. And he likes nature walks. She likes fast cars. I don't think they're a match.

Grammar Presentation

DESCRIPTIVE ADJECTIVES

Subject	*Be*	Adjective
This woman	is	**artistic**.
These women	are	

Subject	*Be*		Adjective	Noun
She	is	an	**artistic**	woman.
They	are			women.

NOUN MODIFIERS

		Noun	Noun
We saw	a	**spy**	film.
	two		films.

DESCRIPTIVE ADJECTIVE + NOUN MODIFIER

		Adjective	Noun	Noun
He's	a	**young**	**computer**	scientist.
She's	an	**excellent**	**tennis**	player.

GRAMMAR NOTES

EXAMPLES

1. Adjectives and nouns can **describe (modify) nouns**. They give more information about the main noun.

- I like **romantic** music.
  (adjective · noun)
- He's a **tennis** player.
  (noun · noun)

2. Adjectives can come **after the verb** *be* or **before a noun**.

- She is **artistic**.
- She's an **artistic** woman.

3. BE CAREFUL! Adjectives can end in *-ing*, *-ly*, and *-ed*.

- She's an **interesting** woman.
- She's **lively** and **friendly**.
- She's never **bored**.

4. Some adjectives contain **two or more words**.

- She's **fun-loving** and **young-at-heart**.

5. **Do not add -s** to an adjective or a noun modifier.

- He's looking for a **fast** car.
- He likes **fast** cars.
- He wants a **leather** jacket.
- He likes **leather** jackets.
  Not: He likes ~~fasts~~ cars.
  He likes ~~leathers~~ jackets.

6. Before a singular count noun:
Use *a* before a modifier that begins with a **consonant sound**. Use *an* before a modifier that begins with a **vowel sound**.

- She's **a young** woman.
- It's **a travel** magazine.
- She's **an artistic** woman.
- It's **an art** school.

7. When both an **adjective** + a **noun modify a noun**, the **adjective** comes **first**.

- I have a **new leather** jacket.
- He's a **good tennis** player.

Focused Practice

1 | DISCOVER THE GRAMMAR

Complete these sentences. Underline the adjective modifiers. Circle the noun modifiers.
Use each item once.

__c__ **1.** He's a (biology)   **a.** walks.

_____ **2.** He likes to take long   **b.** interests.

_____ **3.** We are listening to a jazz   **c.** major.

_____ **4.** They have similar   **d.** books.

_____ **5.** He likes to read grammar   **e.** shop.

_____ **6.** Let's meet in front of the gift   **f.** band.

_____ **7.** She's a famous movie   **g.** stew.

_____ **8.** My favorite dish is chicken   **h.** shirts.

_____ **9.** They both like modern   **i.** actor.

_____ **10.** He always wears cotton   **j.** art.

2 | MAN C

Grammar Notes 1–6

Complete these conversations. Use the words in parentheses in the correct word order.

A: How does he dress?

B: He usually wears ___*an old leather jacket*___,
  1. (old / an / jacket / leather)

_____, and _____.
  2. (cotton / black / T-shirts)   3. (jeans / baggy)

A: What does he drive?

B: He drives _____
  4. (sports / black / car / a)

A: Where does he live?

B: He lives in a _____
  5. (house / brick / small)

  with a _____
  6. (garden / beautiful / rock)

  in front.

3 | JILL'S DATE

Grammar Notes 1–6

A *Complete the sentences. Use the words in the box.*

blue	~~coffee~~	hungry	major	nice	pancakes	~~shop~~
blueberry	delicious	juice	math	orange	polite	

CLARA: So, Jill. How was your date?

JILL: OK. We met at 11:00 in front of the ___*coffee*___ ___*shop*___. I had
                                              1.   2.

_____ _____. They were _____. He just drank
       3.   4.   5.

a glass of _____ _____. I guess he wasn't
                6.   7.

_____.
       8.

CLARA: What did you talk about?

JILL: School mostly. He's a _____ _____. He plans to teach.
                                      9.   10.

CLARA: What did he wear?

JILL: He wore a light _____ shirt and jeans.
                              11.

CLARA: Are you going to go out again?

JILL: I don't know. He was _____ and _____.
                                    12.   13.

B *Listen and check your work.*

4 | EDITING

Correct this letter to advice columnist Dahlia. There are seven mistakes. The first mistake is already corrected.

Dear Dahlia,

My boyfriend, Joe, is wonderful. He's ~~a~~ kind, honest, and intelligent. He has an job good and a heart kind. There's only one problem. He doesn't like to spend money. We always watch TV at his house, and he doesn't even have TV cable. Sometimes we go to frees concerts and picnics. I have fun with Joe, but I want to do differents things. Do you have any suggestions?

Sincerely,

Rosa

Communication Practice

5 | A DESCRIPTION OF MIA

Listen to the conversation between Ken and his friend Brian. Listen again and find Brian's friend Mia. Put a circle around Mia.

6 | QUALITIES OF PEOPLE I KNOW

Work in small groups.

A *Match the words and their opposites.*

_____	**1.** friendly	**a.**	stingy
_____	**2.** kind	**b.**	unfriendly
_____	**3.** generous	**c.**	serious
_____	**4.** honest	**d.**	dishonest
_____	**5.** funny	**e.**	cold
_____	**6.** warm	**f.**	mean

B *Use adjectives to describe your neighbor, sister or brother, cousin, aunt or uncle, a friend, boss, or doctor. Write six sentences and read them to your group. Begin three sentences with* **I have a / an** _____. *Begin three sentences with* **My** _____ **is** _____.

Examples: I have a generous uncle.
My doctor is serious and kind.

7 | MATERIALS AND FABRICS IN OUR CLASS

A *Do you know these words? If not, look them up in your dictionary.*

brick	cotton	denim	glass	leather	nylon	paper	wool

B *Work with a partner. Look around your classroom. Describe 10 things by their material or fabric.*

Examples: a leather belt, a nylon jacket

C *Add an adjective to each item in Part B.*

Examples: an interesting leather belt, a colorful nylon jacket

D *Write five sentences with the items in Part B.*

Example: Won Il is wearing an interesting leather belt.

8 | PERSONAL ADS

Answer one of the personal ads on page 210. Post your answer on the wall. Read your classmates' answers.

Example:

Dear Am I for You,

    I think you are for me. I'm easygoing, and I love jazz bands and walks on the beach.

    I'm an artist. I love to read and write and talk. I'm 26 years old. There's one other thing. I love cats. I have six cats. Is that OK? Please e-mail me at catlovers@qol.com.

    Sincerely,

    You're for Me

Grammar in Context

🎧 *Read this conversation.*

KEN: So when's the party?

LAURA: Saturday night at about eight.

MARTY: How many people are coming?

LAURA: I've got 15 on the list.

MARTY: What about music? I can bring my rap and metal CDs.

KEN: Get real! We want to dance, right? Rap is bad for dancing, and metal is **worse**.

MI YOUNG: Let's have rock. It's a lot **better** for dancing.

LAURA: OK. My **older** brother has a lot of rock CDs. Now, what about food?

KEN: How about steak? We can barbecue some steak.

MI YOUNG: Let's get pizza. It's **easier** and **quicker than** steak. And it's **cheaper**.

KEN: OK, sounds good. And what about entertainment? Besides dancing, I mean.

MARTY: How about watching some videos?

LAURA: Well . . . I'm tired of them. Games are **more interesting than** videos.

KEN: Hey, I know a really funny new game. It's called, "Who's **faster**? Who's **smarter**? Who's **funnier**?" We can play that.

MI YOUNG: Sounds good.

The party

Words

🎧 *Do you know these words? Read the words. Write new ones in your notebook.*

| a list | entertainment | a game |

Expressions

🎧 *Do you know these expressions? Read the conversations. Write new expressions in your notebook.*

1. A: How about pizza?
B: OK. ***Sounds good.***

2. A: ***What about*** dinner?
B: Let's have fish.

3. A: ***How about*** watch***ing*** videos?
B: I'm ***tired of*** them. Games are more interesting.

Working Together

A *Practice the conversation in the opening reading with three partners.*

B *Write the names of two movies. Which is better? Which is more interesting? Tell your partners your opinion.*

> **Example:** In my opinion, *Million Dollar Baby* is better than *War of the Worlds*. It's a lot more interesting.

Grammar Presentation

COMPARATIVE ADJECTIVES

Comparative Adjectives with *-er*				
		Comparative Adjective	*than*	
The train	is	**quicker**	**than**	the bus.
The bus	is	**cheaper**.		

Comparative Adjectives with *more*				
		Comparative Adjective	*than*	
Movies	are	**more interesting**	**than**	television.
They	're	**more expensive**		too.

GRAMMAR NOTES

EXAMPLES

1. Use the comparative form of an adjective + *than* to compare **two** people, places, or things.

We **can omit** *than* when the context is clear.

- Ken is **taller than** Laura.
- Pizza is **quicker than** steak.
- It's **cheaper**. (cheaper than steak)

2. To form the comparative of **short (one-syllable)** adjectives, **add -er** to the adjective. If the adjective **ends in -e**, just add **-r**.

young → young**er**
- Laura is **younger than** Ken.
larg**e** → larg**er**
- New York is **larger than** Chicago.

3. To form the comparative of **two-syllable** adjectives that **end in -y**, change the **y** to **i** and add **-er**.

eas**y** → eas**ier**
- Pizza is **easier than** steak.

4. To form the comparative of most adjectives of **two or more syllables**, use *more* before the adjective.

crowded → **more** crowded
- New York is **more crowded than** Chicago.
interesting → **more** interesting
- This book is **more interesting than** that one.

5. The adjectives *good* and *bad* have **irregular** comparative forms.

good → **better**
- Rock is **better than** metal for dancing.

bad → **worse**
- Rap is **worse than** metal for dancing.

6. Use *which* to ask about a comparison of things or places.

Use *who* to ask about people.

A: Which is **better**, rock or rap?
B: I think rock is **better** (**than** rap).

A: Who's older, you or your cousin?
B: I am. I'm 25 and he's 23.

Focused Practice

1 | DISCOVER THE GRAMMAR

A *Look at the opening reading.* Place the adjectives in bold in the proper category.

Short Adjectives	Adjectives That End in *-y*	Long Adjectives	Irregular Adjective Forms
			worse

B *Complete these sentences with the best endings on the right.*

1. Level 1 is easier __*e*__

2. The bus is cheaper _____

3. The book was more interesting _____

4. A taxi is quicker _____

5. The original movie was better _____

6. The weather on Friday was worse _____

a. than the movie.

b. than the remake.

c. than the train.

d. than the weather on Thursday.

e. than level 2.

f. than a bus.

2 | COMPARE THE PEOPLE

Grammar Notes 2–4, 6

Look at this picture. Compare the people. Use the words in parentheses.

1. (Marty / Ken / tall) _Ken is taller than Marty._____.

2. (Marty / Ken / old) _____.

3. (Marty's clothes / Ken's clothes / colorful) _____.

4. (Mi Young / Laura / short) _____.

5. (Mi Young's hair / Laura's hair / dark) _____.

6. (Lisa / David / good) _____ at dancing.

7. (Jason / Maia / bad) _____ at singing.

3 | MAKE CONVERSATIONS

Grammar Notes 1–6

Complete these conversations. Put the words in the right order.

1. A: worse, / cafeteria food / is / Which / restaurant food / or

  _Which is worse, cafeteria food or restaurant food_____?

  B: is / worse / cafeteria food / think / I

  _____.

2. A: father / you / taller / Are / your / than

  _____?

  B: heavier / he's / but / Yes,

  _____.

3. A: Paris / than / Is / interesting / more / Marseilles

_____?

B: expensive / Yes, / more / but / it's

_____.

4. A: *War of the Worlds* / better, / *Cinderella Man* / is / or / Which

_____?

B: think / *War of the Worlds* / better / I / is

_____.

4 | EDITING

Ben wrote a composition comparing dogs and cats. Correct his composition. There are seven mistakes. The first mistake is already corrected.

Ben Olson

Dogs Rule

                                       better
In my opinion, a dog is a ~~gooder~~ pet than a cat. I know because

we have a dog and a cat at home. Here are my reasons. First, a dog is

friendly than a cat. My dog is more happy to see me when I come home.

My cat just doesn't care. Second, a dog is activer. I always take my

dog for a walk. I can't do that with my cat. She only wants to sleep.

Third, a dog is more interesting than a cat. My dog is a lot more

playful that my cat. He knows a lot of tricks. My cat doesn't know any

tricks at all. She's a lot boring. Last, a dog is more protectiver than a

cat. My dog barks if anyone comes to the house. The cat just runs and

hides. I think dogs rule.

Communication Practice

5 | KEN'S CLASSES

🎧 *Listen to Ken's conversation with his grandmother. Read the statements. Then listen again. Check (✓)* **True**, **False**, *or* **No Information**.

	True	False	No Information
1. Ken's classes are easier than they were last semester.	☐	☐	☐
2. Ken is taking a Spanish class this semester.	☐	☐	☐
3. Ken is better at music than he is at art.	☐	☐	☐
4. The art teacher's tests are easier than the music teacher's tests.	☐	☐	☐

6 | COMPARING GAMES

Work in groups. Compare two games. One person asks questions with **which**. *The others answer. Use the adjectives in the box. Report to the class.*

difficult	easy	exciting	interesting	popular

Example: **A:** Which is more interesting, chess or checkers?
B: I think chess is more interesting than checkers.

We compared chess and checkers. Chess is more difficult than checkers. It is also a more interesting game. In our country, chess is more popular than checkers.

7 | A CLASS SURVEY

Work in teams of four. On the chart, write down two items for each topic. Each team member gives his or her opinion on the topic, and then asks the other team members for their opinions on the same topic. Use the comparative adjective. Use **which** *for the things and* **who** *for the people. Write the number of group members with the same opinion. Discuss with the class.*

Example: Which is harder—algebra or psychology?

Topic / Adjective	Item 1	Number	Item 2	Number
School subject / hard	*algebra*	*3*	*psychology*	*1*
Actor / funny				
Music / good for dancing				
Activities / interesting				

Superlative Adjectives

What was the best thing about your trip?

Grammar in Context

🎧 *Read this conversation.*

MARK: Welcome back, world travelers!

AMANDA: Thanks. We *feel* like world travelers.

KATHY: So come on—tell us all about it. What was **the best** thing about your trip?

AMANDA: Well, for me it was just being in London. That was **the most exciting** place.

JOSH: Yeah, London was great. But Stonehenge was **the most interesting** place we saw.

AMANDA: Yes, but it was also **the worst** part of the trip. We camped out near Stonehenge. Did you know this is **the hottest** summer in Europe in 10 years? There was no rain for weeks—until the night we camped out. It rained hard, and we got really wet. It was **the most terrible** night I can remember.

MARK: You guys are always having adventures. Did anything unusual happen on your trip?

AMANDA: **The** two **scariest** things happened when we were driving. Tell them, Josh.

JOSH: Well, we had a flat tire at night. But **the most dangerous** thing happened when I made a turn on one of those traffic circles and ended up going in the wrong direction. You know they drive on the left there? Suddenly there were cars everywhere—honking their horns. I pulled off to the side of the road, and it turned out OK.

MARK: Tell you what: If we ever take a trip together, let me drive, all right?

Words

🎧 *Do you know these words? Read the words. Write new ones in your notebook.*

It's pouring rain.

She's getting soaked.

a flat tire

honking your horn

Expressions

🎧 *Do you know these expressions? Read the conversations. Write new expressions in your notebook.*

1. **A:** London was the most exciting place.
   B: *I agree.*

2. **A:** What did you do?
   B: I pulled off the road. It *turned out OK*.

3. **A:** *Tell you what*: If we take a trip together, let me drive.
   B: OK.

Working Together

A *Practice the conversation in the opening reading with three partners.*

B *Tell a partner about your best or most interesting trip.*

Example: **A:** My best trip was my trip to China.
 B: Why?
 A: Well, we saw the Great Wall. It was beautiful and impressive. And we met a lot of nice people.
 B: My most interesting trip was . . .

Grammar Presentation

SUPERLATIVE ADJECTIVES

Superlative Adjectives with *-est*			
		Superlative Adjective	
It	was	**the warmest**	night of all.

Superlative Adjectives with *the most*			
		Superlative Adjective	
Stonehenge	was	**the most interesting**	place we saw.

GRAMMAR NOTES

EXAMPLES

1. Use the **superlative form** of an adjective to **compare three or more** people, places, or things.	• It was **the coldest** day of the year.
2. To form the superlative of **short (one-syllable)** adjectives, use *the* before the adjective and **add -est** to the adjective. If the adjective **ends in e**, add *-st*. If a one-syllable adjective ends in a consonant, a vowel, and a consonant, double the final consonant (except *w*, *x*, or *y*).	strange → **the** strange**st** • I had **the strangest** dream. hot → **the** hot**test** • It's **the hottest** summer in 10 years.
3. To form the superlative of **two-syllable** adjectives that **end in -y**, use *the* before the adjective, change the *y* to *i*, and add *-est*.	scary → **the** scar**iest** • **The scariest** thing happened when we were driving.
4. To form the superlative of **longer** adjectives, use *the most* before the adjective.	fantastic → **the most** fantastic • London is **the most fantastic** place.
5. The adjectives *good* and *bad* have **irregular** superlative forms.	good → **the best** • That was **the best** part of our trip. bad → **the worst** • That was **the worst** part.

6. We sometimes use a **possessive** adjective (*my*, *his*, *her*, *your*, *our*, *their*) in place of *the*.

- It was **my scariest** experience.

Reference Note
For the **comparative form of adjectives**, see Unit 28.

Focused Practice

1 | DISCOVER THE GRAMMAR

A *Read Amanda and Kathy's conversation about the trip to Britain. Underline the four uses of superlative adjectives.*

KATHY: Did you guys buy anything nice on the trip?

AMANDA: Well, Josh bought a new stamp for his collection. And I found these three blouses in an open-air market. This pink one was <u>the cheapest</u> one I saw, and it was also the prettiest.

KATHY: Yeah, it is pretty. Actually, I think that red one is the most beautiful.

AMANDA: Really? It was also the most expensive one.

B *Complete this chart.*

Adjective	Comparative Adjective	Superlative Adjective
scary	*scarier*	the scariest
cold		
	quicker	
		the most wonderful
		the most amazing
	better	
bad		

2 | THE NICEST PEOPLE

Read more about Josh and Amanda's trip to Britain. Complete this conversation. Use the superlative form of the words in parentheses.

MARK: Did you meet any interesting people on your

trip?

JOSH: We sure did—a lot. But

_____the nicest ones_____ were some
1. (the / nice / ones)

people we met on a country road in Scotland.

KATHY: Really? What happened?

AMANDA: Well, it was _____ of
2. (the / long / day)

the year—June 21st. And it was also

_____. We were driving late, and it was almost dark. Then
3. (the / hot / day)

we had a flat tire.

MARK: Did you fix it?

JOSH: No. We had a rental car, and it was _____. Too cheap, I
4. (the / cheap / model)

guess. There was no spare tire. We didn't know what to do. But then these

Scottish people came along and stopped. Their names were Ben and Jean

Alexander.

AMANDA: Yes. They were _____. They drove us to
5. (the / sweet / people)

_____ and took us to a car shop. Then they drove us to a
6. (the / near / town)

hotel. The next day they took us to a restaurant, and we had

_____ ever. We hope we can see them again sometime.
7. (the / delicious / lunch)

3 | EDITING

Correct the thank-you note. There are six mistakes. The first mistake is already corrected.

Dear Ben and Jean,

> We're back from our trip to Britain now. It was our ~~wonderfulest~~ *most wonderful* trip ever, and Scotland was the most prettiest part of the trip. Thanks so much for all your help. We're so happy you came along when you did. The next time we take a vacation we won't rent the most cheap model, and we won't rent from that company again. It's the worse rental company we know of. No spare tire—how ridiculous! Actually, it was the ridiculous thing that happened on the trip.
>
> Thanks also for that wonderful lunch. It was the most good meal we had on the whole trip. We hope to take you to a nice restaurant in Seattle sometime. Do you have any plans to come to this part of the world?
>
> Best,
>
> Amanda and Josh Wang

Communication Practice

4 | JOSH'S STAMP COLLECTION

🎧 *Listen to Josh tell Mark and Kathy about his stamps. Then listen again and complete his description of each stamp. Use the adjectives in the box.*

the biggest	the most colorful	the newest
the most artistic	the most valuable	the oldest

1. The Egyptian stamp is _____

2. The Italian stamp is _____

3. The Brazilian stamp is_____

4. The Austrian stamp is _____

5. The Korean stamp is_____

6. The Swiss stamp is _____

5 | SPORTS

Work with a partner. Look at the box. Circle three sports. Then compare them. Use the superlative form of the adjectives.

Sports						
baseball	basketball	football	skiing	soccer	swimming	tennis
Adjectives						
boring	dangerous	difficult	easy	exciting	interesting	popular

Example: **A:** Which sport do you think is the most boring?

B: I think swimming is the most boring. What do you think?

6 | DISCUSSION

A *Work in small groups. List five cities, five holidays, and five actors.*

Cities	Holidays	Actors

B *Compare the cities, the holidays, and the actors. Use superlatives. For example, discuss the following:*

1. Which city is the most beautiful? The oldest? The most international? The most crowded?

2. Which holiday is the most important? The longest? The shortest? The most exciting?

3. Who's the best male actor? The best female actor? The most popular? The oldest? The youngest? The funniest?

Example: **A:** I think Rio de Janeiro is the most beautiful city of all.

B: Really? I don't agree. I think . . .

C *Tell the class about your discussion.*

30 Prepositions of Time: *In, On, At*
See you on Saturday at 2:30.

Grammar in Context

Read these conversations.

TIM: Tim Olson.

FELIX: Hello, Tim! This is Felix Maxa. Do you remember me? We met **in August** on the train to Seattle.

TIM: Felix! Of course! It's great to hear from you. How are you doing?

FELIX: Wonderful. Say, I called to invite you and your wife to our house for a barbecue.

TIM: That sounds like fun. We'd really like that. When is it?

FELIX: **On Saturday**, the 20th, **in the afternoon**.

TIM: I think we're free. But I need to check with Jessica. Can I call you back?

FELIX: Sure.

[Later—phone rings]

FELIX: Hello?

TIM: Hi, Felix. This is Tim. I e-mailed Jessica, and she e-mailed back. We're free **on the 20th**. We can come to the barbecue.

FELIX: Great!

TIM: What's the address?

FELIX: We're at 819 40th Avenue. From 45th, turn left on Stone Way and then right on 40th. It's the third house on the right, a light blue two-story.

TIM: OK. What time?

FELIX: Come **at about 2:30**.

TIM: Great. Can we bring anything?

FELIX: Just yourselves.

TIM: OK. Thanks a lot. I'm looking forward to it. See you **on Saturday at 2:30**. Bye.

FELIX: Good-bye.

Words

🎧 *Do you know these words? Read the words. Write new ones in your notebook.*

a barbecue

a two-story house

Expressions

🎧 *Do you know these expressions? Read the conversations. Write new expressions in your notebook.*

1. A: Can I **call you back**?
   B: Sure.

2. A: **We're free** on the 20th.
   B: Great!

3. A: Can we bring anything?
   B: **Just yourselves.**

4. A: See you at the barbecue on Saturday.
   B: I'm **looking forward to** it.

Working Together

A *Practice the conversation in the opening reading with a partner.*

B *Look at the pictures. Say when each event is.*

Example: The Chess Club barbecue is on Saturday, the 20th of May, at 2:30 P.M.

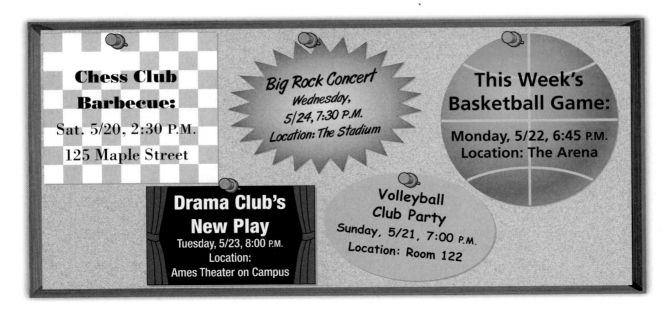

Chess Club Barbecue:
Sat. 5/20, 2:30 P.M.
125 Maple Street

Big Rock Concert
Wednesday,
5/24, 7:30 P.M.
Location: The Stadium

This Week's Basketball Game:
Monday, 5/22, 6:45 P.M.
Location: The Arena

Drama Club's New Play
Tuesday, 5/23, 8:00 P.M.
Location:
Ames Theater on Campus

Volleyball Club Party
Sunday, 5/21, 7:00 P.M.
Location: Room 122

Grammar Presentation

PREPOSITIONS OF TIME: *IN, ON, AT*

In		On		At
in 2007 **in** January **in** the morning	**in** the afternoon **in** the evening	**on** Saturday **on** January 20 **on** weekends	**on** holidays **on** weekdays **on** the 10th	**at** 2:30 P.M. **at** dinnertime **at** night

GRAMMAR NOTES

EXAMPLES

1. Use *in* with **years**, **months**, and **parts of the day**, and in expressions like *in a few minutes*. ▶ **BE CAREFUL!** Don't use *in the* with **night**. Use *at*.	• I was born **in 1988**. • We were in Japan **in August**. • The barbecue is **in the afternoon**. • Can I call you back **in a few minutes**? • The game is **at night**. NOT: The game is ~~in the~~ night.
2. Use *on* with **days of the week** and **dates**, and in expressions like *on weekdays*, *on weekends*, and *on weeknights*.	• The barbecue is **on Saturday**. • It's **on January 21**. • I often go to the movies **on weekends**.
3. Use *at* with **times** and in expressions like *at night* and *at dinnertime*.	• The party starts **at 7:00 at night**. • We always have good conversations **at dinnertime**.

Focused Practice

1 | DISCOVER THE GRAMMAR

*Read Tim's e-mail to Jessica. Find and underline all time expressions with **in, on,** and **at.***

Hi Honey, I couldn't reach you on the phone. Do you remember Felix Maxa? He's the man from Romania; I met him on the train <u>in August</u>. Felix called and invited us to a barbecue at their house. Their house is near the university. The barbecue is on the 20th, at 2:30. I know we have something planned on Sunday afternoon, but I don't think we have anything on Saturday. Are we free? Please get back to me right away. Love, Tim

2 | AT THE BARBECUE

Grammar Notes 1–3

*Complete this conversation. Use **in, on,** or **at.***

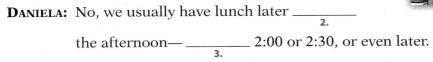

TIM: This is a nice big meal. Is lunch the biggest

meal in Romania?

FELIX: Yes, it is, actually. We don't eat very much for

dinner.

JESSICA: Are mealtimes the same as here? I mean, for

example, do you eat lunch __*at*__ noon
          1.

like we do?

DANIELA: No, we usually have lunch later _____

          2.

the afternoon— _____ 2:00 or 2:30, or even later.
          3.

TIM: What about breakfast? I usually have breakfast _____ 6:45 or 7:00. Is it
          4.

similar in Romania?

FELIX: Well, we usually have breakfast a bit later—_____ 7:30 or so.
          5.

JESSICA: So it's a long time between breakfast and lunch. You must get hungry.

DANIELA: Well, people usually have a snack, like a sandwich, _____ the late morning—
          6.

_____ 11:30 or so.
          7.

FELIX: It's different _____ weekends, of course. We get up later.
          8.

TIM: I'd like to visit Romania sometime.

DANIELA: Well, Felix and I are going back to Romania _____ a few days—on separate
          9.

flights, unfortunately. But we'll send you a postcard.

JESSICA: Great.

3 | MORE QUESTIONS FOR FELIX AND DANIELA

Grammar Notes 1–3

Complete these questions and answers. Add necessary words.

1. A: What time / be / dinner

What time is dinner _____?

   B: Dinner / be / usually / 7:00 or 7:30

_____.

2. A: What time / people / start work / morning

_____?

   B: People / usually / start work / 8:00

_____.

3. A: What / people / do / evenings

_____?

   B: They / often / watch TV / evenings

_____.

4. A: What / people / do / weekends

_____?

   B: They / often / visit friends / weekends

_____.

4 | EDITING

Correct the statements below. There are 10 mistakes. The first mistake is already corrected.

1. Daniela is leaving Seattle ~~in~~ *on* Monday, January 25, on 12:00 noon.

2. Her flight arrives in Chicago in 6:00 at the evening.

3. Her flight to London leaves at 7:30 in the night.

4. Flight 774 arrives in London in 11:30 on the morning.

5. Her flight to Bucharest leaves in 2:00 P.M. in January 26.

6. It arrives in Bucharest at 6:05 at evening.

Communication Practice

5 | FELIX'S FLIGHT

🎧 *Listen to the telephone conversation. Then listen again and complete the chart. Use* **in**, **on**, *or* **at**.

Day, month, and date Felix leaves Seattle	Time first flight leaves Seattle	Time second flight leaves Seattle	Day, month, and date Felix returns to Seattle

6 | FIND OUT

Work with three partners. Ask questions. Complete the chart. Tell the other groups one thing you learned.

Example: **A:** What do you never do on Sundays?
B: I never study on Sundays.

	You	Student 1 _____	Student 2 _____	Student 3 _____
never / on Sundays				
rarely / in July				
usually / on weekdays				
almost never / in the evening				
almost always / at night				

7 | INFORMATION GAP: WHEN IN THE WORLD?

Work in pairs.

Student B, look at the Information Gap on page IG-4. Follow the instructions there.

*Student A, get information from Student B. Ask questions with **when** or **what time**. Then answer Student B's questions. Use the phrases in the box. Use **in, on,** or **at** in each answer.*

Example: **A:** When do Americans vote?
            B: Americans usually vote on a Tuesday.
                 When do the French vote?
            A: The French usually vote on a Sunday.

Student A's questions

1. Americans / vote / ?

2. summer normally begin / in the Southern Hemisphere / ?

3. afternoon / begin / ?

4. Brazilians / celebrate / Carnaval / ?

5. fall normally begin / in the Southern Hemisphere / ?

Carnaval in Brazil

Student A's answers

12:00 midnight	July 1	December 21	September	a Sunday

▶ *To check your answers, go to the Answer Key on page P-2.*

8 | GAME: *IN, ON, AT*

Write down the date and time of a big event in your life.

Examples: My sister got married on June 3, 2003, in the evening.
                I graduated from college on May 15, 2000, in the afternoon.

Then tell the class about the event. Do not tell them the date or time. Your classmates ask a maximum of 10 yes / no questions to guess the date and the time of the event.

Example: **A:** I got married.
            B: Did you get married in July?
            A: No, I didn't.
            C: Did you get married in June?
            A: Yes, I did.

Review Test

I *Complete these conversations. Circle the correct letter.*

1. **JUDY:** Is the meeting in the morning?

    MARK: _____

    (**A**) Yes. It's in the afternoon.   (**C**) No. It's at night.

    (**B**) When?   (**D**) It wasn't in the morning.

2. **TIM:** When are you free?

    ALLEN: _____

    (**A**) On the 10th at 2:00 P.M.   (**C**) Yes, I am.

    (**B**) Are you free too?   (**D**) No, I'm not free.

3. **DAVID:** Who is taller, Ken or Marty?

    LISA: _____

    (**A**) Are you taller?   (**C**) I am shorter.

    (**B**) Ken is taller.   (**D**) Both are taller.

4. **ANNIE:** Was it cold?

    MARY: _____

    (**A**) It was the coldest day of the year.   (**C**) Yes, I was sick all weekend.

    (**B**) Yes. It was cool.   (**D**) No. It was cold.

5. **BEN:** Is London larger than Paris?

    TIM: _____

    (**A**) Yes, it's the largest.   (**C**) No. New York is larger.

    (**B**) Paris is larger than New York.   (**D**) Yes, it is.

II *Compare the following movies. Write the name of the movie and the comparative or superlative form of the adjective in parentheses.*

Don't Tell Grandma	The Bees	Katie Raye
★ ★ ★ ★	★ ★ ★	★ ★ ★ ★ ★
starring Robert Nichols	starring Nicole Jolie	starring Renée Wayne
Hilarious! A laugh a minute!	Scary. Bring someone to hold on to. Good special effects.	Based on a true story. Excellent acting. Entertaining and inspiring. Don't miss it.
Time: 1 hour, 48 minutes	Time: 1 hour, 49 minutes	Time: 2 hours, 12 minutes

1. (long) _____*Katie Raye*_____ is _____*longer than*_____ *The Bees.*

2. (scary) _____ is _____ *Don't Tell Grandma.*

3. (serious) _____ is _____ *Don't Tell Grandma.*

4. (funny) _____ is _____ *Katie Raye.*

5. (long) _____ is _____ of the three movies.

6. (good) This reviewer thinks _____ is _____ of the three movies.

III *Complete these conversations. Use* **in, on,** *or* **at.**

BRIAN: Hello?

JEREMY: Hi, Brian. It's Jeremy.

BRIAN: Oh, hi, Jeremy. Listen, I'm having dinner right now. Can I call you back ___*in*___
  1.
  a few minutes?

JEREMY: Sure.

  [Ten minutes later]

JEREMY: Hello.

BRIAN: Hi, Jeremy.

JEREMY: Oh, hi. *Spider Man V* is playing at the Cineplex. Are you free _____ Saturday?
  2.

BRIAN: What time?

JEREMY: The first show is _____ noon. Is that OK?
  3.

BRIAN: Noon? No way. _____ weekends I sleep until 1:00. How about a later show?

4.

JEREMY: Well, I can't make it later. But there's a show _____ Sunday _____ 6:00.

5.   6.

BRIAN: Sounds good to me. We can meet in front of the movie theater _____ 5:45.

7.

JEREMY: OK. See you Sunday.

BRIAN: Bye.

IV *Correct the conversation. There are seven mistakes. The first mistake is already corrected.*

JUDY: How was your party?

KEN: Cool. We had lots of ~~goods~~ *good* CDs and pizzas delicious. It ended on 3:00 at the morning. Did you have a nice weekend?

JUDY: No. I just studied for my test history and watched a video bad.

KEN: What video?

JUDY: *The Bees.* It was the boring movie in the world.

KEN: You're kidding! My friends and I saw it and loved it.

▶ *To check your answers, go to the Answer Key on page RT-3.*

UNIT

31 The Future with *Be going to*: Statements

Hurry up! We're going to be late!

Grammar in Context

🎧 *Read this conversation.*

LAURA: Ken, hurry up! We**'re going to be** late!

KEN: What's the hurry? It's just a silly little soccer game!

LAURA: It's not silly, and it's not little. Sam's on the team! It's a big game. I think they**'re going to win**.

KEN: I know. That's what you told me. Is your brother a good player?

LAURA: He's really good.

KEN: Do I need an umbrella?

LAURA: No. It**'s not going to rain** . . . Come on.

[Later]

LAURA: Can't you drive any faster?

KEN: I'm already doing the speed limit. But how come you like soccer so much?

LAURA: It's a great game. A lot of people can play it. You don't have to be a giant.

KEN: But is it a real sport? Take basketball or baseball or football. Those are sports.

LAURA: Soccer is the most popular sport in the world.

KEN: Well, it's not the most popular sport in *my* world.

LAURA: Oh, no! A traffic jam! The game**'s going to start** soon.

KEN: Laura, chill out! We**'re going to make** it on time.

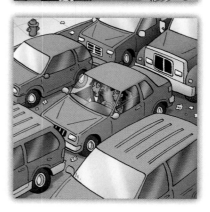

Words

🎧 *Do you know these words? Read the words. Write new ones in your notebook.*

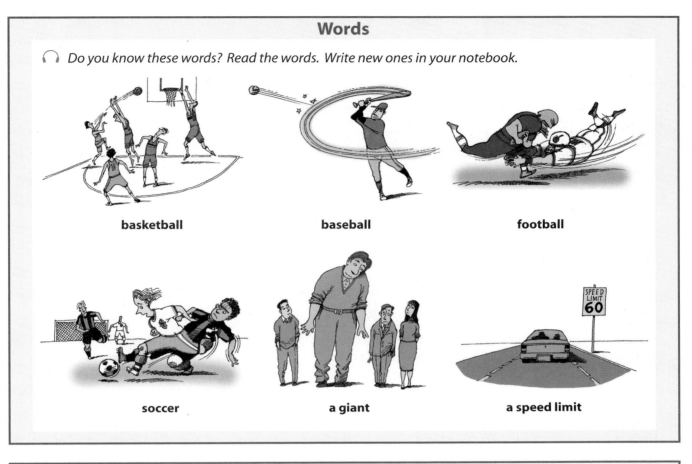

basketball   **baseball**   **football**

soccer   **a giant**   **a speed limit**

Expressions

🎧 *Do you know these expressions? Read the conversations. Write new expressions in your notebook.*

1. A: Can't you drive any faster?
   B: I'm already ***doing the speed limit***.

2. A: ***How come*** you like soccer so much?
   B: It's a great game.

   *chill out = very informal for *relax

3. A: Oh no! Look at this traffic!
   B: Laura, ***chill out***.* We're going to make it on time.

Working Together

A *Practice the conversation in the opening reading with a partner.*

B *Think of three sporting events. Tell your partner who you think is going to win.*

   Example: I think Brazil is going to win the next World Cup.

Grammar Presentation

THE FUTURE WITH *BE GOING TO*: STATEMENTS

Affirmative Statements		
am going to	*is going to*	*are going to*
I **am going to have** a party next weekend.	He **is going to graduate** in June. She **is going to be** an Olympic athlete. It **is going to rain** today.	We **are going to see** a movie tonight. You **are going to enjoy** this party. They **are going to bring** pizza to the party.

Negative Statements		
am not going to	*is not going to*	*are not going to*
I **am not going to drive** fast. I'**m not going to drive** fast.	It **is not going to rain**. It'**s not going to rain**. It **isn't going to rain**.	We **are not going to be** late. We'**re not going to be** late. We **aren't going to be** late.

Future Time Expressions		
this afternoon	*tonight*	*tomorrow*
He's going to study **this afternoon**.	He's going to play soccer **tonight**.	He's going to visit his parents **tomorrow**.

GRAMMAR NOTES	EXAMPLES
1. We can use *be going to* to talk about the **future**.	• We'**re going to be** late. • It'**s going to rain**.
2. To form the future with *be going to*, use **am**, **is**, or **are** + *going to* + the **base form** of the verb.	• They **are going to win**.
3. To make a **negative sentence**, place *not* before *going to*.	• They **are not going to lose**. • It **is not going to snow**.

4. Use **contractions** in conversation and informal writing.	• The game**'s going to start** soon. • It **isn't going to rain**. Don't worry.

🎧 Pronunciation Note

In conversation, we sometimes pronounce ***going to*** as "gonna." But we write "going to."

Reference Notes
For ***yes / no* questions with *be going to***, see Unit 32.
For ***wh- questions* with *be going to***, see Unit 33.

Focused Practice

1 | DISCOVER THE GRAMMAR

Underline the examples of **be going to** + *base form used to make statements about the future. Then match these questions and answers.*

1. Josh, do I need my heavy coat? __e__

2. Mom, what are we going to have for dinner? _____

3. Dad, where's Mom going? _____

4. Do you think Mark and Kathy are going to get married? _____

5. What's going to happen next June? _____

6. Does Jason have a serious girlfriend? _____

a. Yes, he's going to see her tonight.

b. Probably. They're a great couple.

c. Judy's going to graduate.

d. To the store. We're out of milk.

e. Yes. It's going to snow.

f. We're going to have steak.

2 | ANNIE'S VOLLEYBALL GAME   *Grammar Notes 1–2*

Complete the sentences. Use the correct form of **be going to** *and the verbs in parentheses.*

It's Saturday. Annie Olson is on a volleyball team. Her team _____*is going to play*_____

this afternoon. The weather _____ warm. Everybody in the family
                                    2. (be)

_____ the game. Ben _____ four friends, and
   3. (attend)   **4. (invite)**

Jeremy _____ his girlfriend. Tim and Jessica
                5. (take)

_____ the game. Mary and Bill Beck _____
   6. (videotape)   **7. (go)**

with their friends. Everyone thinks Annie's team _____ —everyone
                                                        8. (win)

except Annie. She doesn't think she _____ very well.
                                          9. (play)

3 | WHO'S GOING TO WIN?

Grammar Notes 1–3

Look at the pictures. Complete each sentence with affirmative or negative forms of **be going to** and the verbs in parentheses.

1. Skier 34 _____is going to win_____.
(win)

2. Skier 21 _____ second.
(finish)

3. The Porpoises _____.
(win)

4. The Dolphins _____.
(win)

5. Runner 81 _____.
(lose)

6. Runner 6 _____.
(win)

7. Magic Dancer _____.
(win)

8. Petunia _____ last.
(finish)

4 | EDITING

Correct Amanda's note. There are six mistakes. The first mistake is already corrected.

> Dear Kathy,
>
> I hope you're going ˄to be in town Sunday evening. Josh and I are have
> a little party to watch the big game on TV. We are going have pizza and
> dessert. We be going to start the meal about 5:00. I think the game are
> going to start at 6:00. Please come if you can. But can you let us know?
> We going to be out of town until Tuesday. Call after that, OK?
>
> Amanda

Communication Practice

5 | LAURA'S BROTHER'S GAME

🎧 *Read these sentences. Listen to the conversation. Then listen again and check (✓)*
True, **False**, *or* **No Information**.

	True	False	No Information
1. Ken thinks the game is boring.	☐	☐	☐
2. Ken thinks it's going to rain.	☐	☐	☐
3. Laura thinks it's going to rain.	☐	☐	☐
4. The score is 2–1.	☐	☐	☐
5. Laura thinks Sam's team is going to win.	☐	☐	☐
6. Laura has another brother besides Sam.	☐	☐	☐
7. Sam kicks a goal.	☐	☐	☐
8. Ken wants to go to another game sometime.	☐	☐	☐

6 | GAME: WE'RE GOING TO ATTEND THE NEXT OLYMPICS

*Play in groups. Your group is going to take a trip to the next Olympics. Each person says
one thing he or she is going to take on the trip. The person who can remember everything
is the winner.*

Example: **ELENA:** I'm going to take my binoculars.
AHMED: Elena is going to take her binoculars. I'm going to take my tape recorder.
ANNA: Elena is going to take her binoculars. Ahmed is going to take his tape recorder. I'm going to take my camera . . .

The Future with *Be going to*: Yes / No Questions

Are you going to have a big part?

🎧 *Read this conversation.*

JESSICA: How was work, Tim?

TIM: Not bad. How was your day?

JESSICA: Actually, I had an interesting call.

TIM: Oh?

JESSICA: You know Dan Evans, the TV producer?

TIM: Sure I do.

JESSICA: Well, he has an idea for a new show.

TIM: Really?

JESSICA: Uh-huh. It's going to be on national TV, and he wants me to be in it.

JEREMY: Awesome! **Are you going to have** a big part?

JESSICA: As a matter of fact, yes. I'm going to be the main reporter.

JEREMY: That's so cool.

TIM: Hmm . . . **Is it going to mean** a lot of travel?

JESSICA: I think so.

ANNIE: Don't take it, Mom. I don't want you to travel.

BEN: Yeah. You always help me with homework. Who's going to help me with my homework?

TIM: Hey, guys. I'm still going to be here.

JESSICA: Anyway, kids, this is all very new. The show isn't going to air for a long time.

Words

🎧 *Do you know these words? Read the words. Write new ones in your notebook.*

a producer   **national TV**   **a big part**

Expressions

🎧 *Do you know these expressions? Read the conversations. Write new expressions in your notebook.*

1. A: How was work?
   B: *Not bad*.

2. A: How was your day?
   B: Actually, I have *some interesting news*.

3. A: Are you going to have a big part?
   B: *As a matter of fact*, yes.

4. A: What does it mean?
   B: I don't know. This is *all very new*.

Working Together

A *Practice the conversation in the opening reading with four partners.*

B *Work with a partner. Is your partner going to make any of these changes this year? Ask your partner.*

get married   *graduate*   *get a job*   *move*   *become a parent*

Example: A: Are you going to graduate this year?
              B: Yes, I am. I'm going to graduate in June.

Grammar Presentation

THE FUTURE WITH *BE GOING TO*: *YES / NO* QUESTIONS

Yes / No Questions
Am I going to get the job?
Is it going to mean a lot of travel?
Are we going to move?

Short Answers	
Yes, **you are**.	No, **you're not**. OR No, **you aren't**.
Yes, **it is**.	No, **it's not**. OR No, **it isn't**.
Yes, **we are**.	No, **we're not**. OR No, **we aren't**.

GRAMMAR NOTES

1. For *yes / no* questions with *be going to*, put *am*, *is*, or *are* **before the subject**.

2. We usually use **contractions** in negative short answers.

EXAMPLES

- **Am I** going to have a part in your show?
- **Is he** going to change jobs?
- **Are they** going to buy a house?

A: Is he going to change jobs?
B: No, he**'s not**. OR No, he **isn't**.

Focused Practice

1 | DISCOVER THE GRAMMAR

Underline the yes / no questions with **be going to**. *Circle the main verb in each question.*
Then match the questions and answers.

_b_ **1.** Is it going to (rain)?

_____ **2.** Are we going to be late?

_____ **3.** Is the soccer game going to be in the park?

_____ **4.** Do they go to the movies every week?

_____ **5.** Are they going to win?

_____ **6.** Is she going to work tomorrow?

_____ **7.** Are you going to have pizza?

a. No, it's going to be at the school.

b. I think so. Those clouds are very dark.

c. No, she's off tomorrow.

d. No, I'm not. I don't like it.

e. Yes, they are.

f. Yes, they do.

g. No, it's early. We have a lot of time.

2 | NOT AGAIN!

Complete the sentences. Use the simple past, the simple present, the present progressive, or **be going to** *for the future. Use the verbs in parentheses.*

1. (rain)

    TIM: It _____*rained*_____ yesterday. It__*'s raining*_____ now. _____*Is*_____

    it ____*going to rain*____ tomorrow?

    JESSICA: I'm afraid so. That's what the weather channel says.

2. (have)

    JEREMY: I'm tired of tofu. We _____ tofu last night. We _____

    tofu now. _____ we _____ tofu tomorrow?

    TIM: Oh, no. Tomorrow we _____ veggie burgers.

3. (wear)

    JESSICA: I know you like that sweater, but you always _____ it. You

    _____ it every day last week. You _____ it now.

    _____ you _____ it tomorrow?

    JEREMY: Probably. Michelle likes the color.

    JESSICA: Oh.

4. (watch)

    JESSICA: You _____ that movie last night. Why _____ you

    _____ it again now?

    ANNIE: I love it. I _____ it tomorrow too.

5. (cook)

    JEREMY: Who _____ dinner tonight?

    JESSICA: I am.

    TIM: No, I _____ tonight. You _____ dinner last night and

    the night before. It's my turn.

    JESSICA: Oh, that's right.

    JEREMY: That's good. No tofu tonight.

3 | JESSICA'S AND TIM'S THOUGHTS
Grammar Note 1

Write yes / no *questions with* **be going to** *and the words in parentheses.*

A. Jessica's thoughts about the new job:

1. (I / get the job) *Am I going to get the job* ?

2. (it / mean a lot of work) _____?

3. (the children / be OK) _____?

4. (Tim / spend more time at home) _____?

B. Tim's thoughts about the new job:

5. (Jessica / change) _____?

6. (Jessica / work all the time) _____?

7. (we / have time together) _____?

8. (Jessica / earn more than I do) _____?

4 | EDITING

Correct Jessica's phone messages. There are four mistakes. The first mistake is already corrected.

1. Hi, Jessica. This is Maria. Are you going ~~being~~ *to be* in San Francisco for the conference? I need to know. Please call me at 931-8878.

2. Hi, honey. I forgot my date book. Is Fred and Janet going to meet us at 8:00 or 8:30? Please call.

3. This message is for Jessica Olson. This is George Selig. Is the conference going start on the 6th or the 7th?

4. Hi Mom. I'm not going to be home until 9:00. Al and I am going to study together.

Communication Practice

5 | WHAT'S THE STORY?

🎧 *Josh gets a phone call from Amanda. Listen to their conversation. Then listen to the conversation between Josh and Jason. Listen again and check (✓)* **Yes**, **No**, *or* **No Information**.

	Yes	No	No Information
1. Are Amanda and Josh going to have a baby in six months?	☐	☐	☐
2. Are Amanda and Josh going to move before the baby is born?	☐	☐	☐
3. Is Amanda going to stay home for three months?	☐	☐	☐
4. Is Josh going to change jobs?	☐	☐	☐
5. Is Josh's mother going to take care of the baby?	☐	☐	☐
6. Is it going to cost over $100,000 to raise a child?	☐	☐	☐

6 | ASK THE FORTUNE TELLER

You can ask the fortune teller three questions. Which three questions are you going to ask? Put a checkmark (✓) next to the questions. Then write one question of your own. Work in small groups. Compare your choices.

_____ **1.** Am I going to be rich?

_____ **2.** Am I going to be famous?

_____ **3.** Am I going to find true love?

_____ **4.** Am I going to make a difference in the world?

_____ **5.** Are scientists going to find a cure for AIDS? Cancer? Heart disease?

_____ **6.** Are people going to travel to the moon on vacations?

_____ **7.** Are most people going to live to be 120 years old?

_____ **8.** _____?

7 | LEADERS

Work with a partner. Student A, pretend you are the mayor of your city. Student B, pretend you are the director of your English school. Ask your partner four questions about his or her job. Use **be going to** *and the ideas in the box or your own ideas.*

Mayor	Director
build inexpensive homes	have better food in the cafeteria
build more schools	have more free clubs and activities
fight crime	have smaller classes
lower taxes	lower tuition

Example: **B:** Are you going to build inexpensive homes?
A: Yes, I am. People need more inexpensive places to live. I'm going to build 3,000 inexpensive homes.

8 | GAME: WHAT ARE THEY GOING TO DO?

Work with a partner. Look at the picture. Write as many sentences as you can with **be going to**. *The pair of partners with the most correct sentences wins.*

The Future with *Be going to*: *Wh-* Questions

What are you going to do on Sunday?

Grammar in Context

🎧 *Read these conversations.*

KATHY: Mark, what's bothering you? You seem nervous.

MARK: I *am* nervous. **How am I going to say** this?

KATHY: Say what?

MARK: Well, I have something important to say.

KATHY: Let me guess . . . You're going to give up chocolate. Or . . . maybe you're going to clean your closet.

MARK: No. This is about us . . . Will you marry me?

KATHY: Well . . . I only have one thing to say.

MARK: Oh, no. What?

KATHY: What took you so long to ask?

[*Later*]

MARK: Hello?

JOSH: Hey, Mark. This is Josh. **What are you going to do** on Sunday evening?

MARK: No plans. Why?

JOSH: A bunch of us are going to watch the big game. Do you want to come over?

MARK: Well, sure. By the way, Kathy and I have some big news.

JOSH: Oh yeah? What?

MARK: We're engaged.

JOSH: What? That's great, man! Congratulations!

MARK: Thanks. I'll tell you about it on Sunday. So **what time is the party going to start**?

Words

🎧 *Do you know these words? Read the words. Write new ones in your notebook.*

engaged

a bunch of people*

* Informal for *a group of people*

Expressions

🎧 *Do you know these expressions? Read the conversations. Write new expressions in your notebook.*

1. A: *What's bothering you?* You look nervous.
B: I *am* nervous.

2. A: *Will you marry me?*
B: Yes, *I will*.

3. A: Could you help us with the wedding?
B: Of course. *What took you so long* to ask?

4. A: *By the way*, we have some news.
B: Oh yeah? What?

5. A: Kathy and I are engaged.
B: That's great! *Congratulations!*

Working Together

A *Practice the conversations in the opening reading with two partners.*

B *Look at the pictures. Ask and answer questions with one partner. First ask a yes / no question. Then ask a question with **what**, **where**, **when**, or **why**.*

watch TV

go shopping

read a novel

go skiing

Grammar Presentation

THE FUTURE WITH *BE GOING TO*: *WH*- QUESTIONS

Wh- Questions
How am I going to say this?
When is he going to ask?
What are you going to do on Sunday?

Answers
Say what?
Probably tonight.
Watch the big game.

Wh- Questions about the Subject
Who is going to win the game?
What's going to happen?

Answers
The Titans (are).
They're going to score.

GRAMMAR NOTES

EXAMPLES

1. To ask a *wh-* **question** in the future with *be going to*, start with the *wh-* **word**. Use the correct form of *be* + a **subject** + *going to* + the **base form** of the verb.	**A: What are** you **going to do** on Sunday? **B:** Watch the game.

2. For a *wh-* **question about the subject**, use *who* or *what* + *is* + *going to* + the **base form** of the verb.	**A: Who is going to win** the game? **B:** The Titans (are).

Focused Practice

1 | DISCOVER THE GRAMMAR

Circle the wh- *questions with* **be going to**. *Underline the* **be going to** *statements. Then match the questions and answers.*

1. Mom, (what time are we going to have dinner?) _d_

2. Are they ever going to get married? _____

3. What are you going to do tonight, Steve? _____

4. Why are you going to sell your car, Judy? _____

5. Who's going to do the dishes tonight, kids? _____

6. Are you going to be away very long? _____

a. Jeremy is, Dad.

b. Yes, for about a month.

c. Yes. The wedding's going to be in June.

d. At six o'clock sharp.

e. I'm going to watch a video.

f. It's always in the shop.

2 | THE ENGAGEMENT

Complete this conversation with wh- *questions. Use the words in parentheses.*

AMANDA: This is fantastic! So _____*when are you going to have*_____ the wedding?
1. (when / you / have)

KATHY: Next summer, we think—probably in June.

JUDY: A June wedding! Perfect. _____?
2. (Where / it / be)

MARK: Right here in Seattle.

JOSH: What about your honeymoon? _____?
3. (Where / you / go)

MARK: Well, we're thinking about India.

STEVE: India? Wow! _____? Big bucks?
4. (How much / that / cost)

MARK: Well, quite a bit. But Kathy works at a travel agency, you know. It doesn't cost

her much to travel. And our parents are going to help—as a wedding present.

JOSH: _____ in India?
5. (How long / you / be)

KATHY: At least two weeks.

STEVE: _____?
6. (What places / you / visit)

MARK: Well, the Taj Mahal, Mumbai, and Calcutta for sure. And we have to see the

Ganges River. Hope we can go to some other places too.

AMANDA: Awesome. And what about when you come back?

_____?
7. (Where / you / live)

KATHY: In an apartment, at first. Eventually we're going to look for a house.

MARK: OK, enough questions about us. Now *I've* got a question.

_____ this game?
8. (Who / win)

3 | EDITING

Correct these conversations. There are seven mistakes. The first mistake is already corrected.

1. A: Who ^is^ going to do the dishes tonight, kids?

    B: Jeremy going to do them, Mom. I did them last night.

2. A: Amanda, how many people we are going to invite?

    B: I think about eight.

3. A: Where Mark and Kathy are going to go on their honeymoon?

    B: They're going to go to India.

4. A: What time is going to start the party?

    B: It's going to start at about 5:30.

5. A: How the weather is going to be on Saturday?

    B: The weatherman says is going to be sunny and warm.

Communication Practice

4 | WHAT ARE WE GOING TO EAT?

🎧 *Listen to Josh and Amanda's conversation before their party. Listen again and write the five* wh- *questions with* **be going to***.*

1. _____?

2. _____?

3. _____?

4. _____?

5. _____?

5 | CONSIDER THE FUTURE

Work in small groups. Ask questions. Use the words in the box. Then tell the class about your answers.

what / important thing / buy soon	where / live / in 10 years
what / job / have in five years	who / next leader

Example: **A:** Who's going to be the next leader of your country?
B: I think _____ is going to be the next leader.
C: She thinks _____ is going to be the next leader.

6 | GAME: VACATION TIME FOR THE GRANDPARENTS AND THE GRANDCHILDREN

*Work in small groups. Discuss the picture. Each group makes as many wh- questions as possible with **be going to**. Use **where**, **who**, **how long**, **what**, **what time**, and **when**. The team with the most questions wins.*

Example: **A:** Where are Mary and Bill going to take their grandchildren?
B: Orlando, Florida.

Review Test X

I *Complete these conversations. Circle the correct letter.*

1. JOSH: What are you going to do tonight?

   MARK: _____

   (**A**) We're going out tomorrow night.

   (**B**) We're going to watch a video.

   (**C**) What are you doing tonight at 9:30?

   (**D**) Are you going to stay home tonight?

2. FELIX: Is it going to rain?

   TIM: _____

   (**A**) Why is it always raining?

   (**B**) It isn't raining.

   (**C**) It's not snowing.

   (**D**) I think so.

3. KATHY: What's bothering you?

   MARK: _____

   (**A**) I'm here.

   (**B**) We're late.

   (**C**) We're happy.

   (**D**) I'm interested.

4. BILL: When are we going to go shopping?

   MARY: _____

   (**A**) We're out of food.

   (**B**) We're going to go shopping.

   (**C**) At two o'clock.

   (**D**) Rose is going to come with us.

5. KEN: _____

   LAURA: It's a really exciting game.

   (**A**) How come you like soccer?

   (**B**) Where does your brother play soccer?

   (**C**) When is the soccer game?

   (**D**) How do you play soccer?

II Look at these pictures. Write sentences about what is going to happen. Use the verbs in the box.

| go | cook | get | watch |

1. _____ TV.

2. _____ a rock concert.

3. _____ dinner.

4. _____ married.

III Write a question for each answer. Use **be going to** in each question.

1. **ROSE:** _____ *When is Jeremy going to graduate* _____?

   MARY: Jeremy's going to graduate a year from now.

2. **FELIX:** _____?

   TIM: Yes, it is. Actually, it's going to snow a lot.

3. **BILL:** _____?

   AMANDA: Mark and Kathy are going to go to India on their honeymoon.

4. **MARK:** _____?

   JUDY: Yes, Ken's going to go to college.

5. **MARY:** _____?

   ROSE: Don't you remember? *You're* going to drive us to the airport.

IV *Correct this letter. There are five mistakes. The first mistake is already corrected.*

Dear Mary,

Thanks for driving us to the airport. We arrived in Acapulco at 1:00 P.M. and went right to the hotel. The weather is beautiful so far, but it looks like ^it^ is going to rain. Tomorrow we going to go swimming in the morning. In the afternoon are we going to go fishing out in the ocean.

When you and Bill are going to come with us on a trip? We always have such a good time when we travel.

The only thing I miss about Seattle is baseball. Our team is going to win?

I'll write again soon.

Love,

Rose

► *To check your answers, go to the Answer Key on page RT-3.*

From **Grammar** to **Writing**

PART I   Using Imperatives

E-mail a friend. Give directions from your school to your party.

First, look at the map below. Your school is on Pine Street between First and Second Streets. The party is at Bella Vista Restaurant. Bella Vista Restaurant is on Fourth Street between Pine and Maple Streets. Draw a line from your school to the restaurant. Then write your e-mail. Follow the model.

(continued)

Model

Bill's school is on Maple Street between Fourth and Fifth Streets. The party is at Star Restaurant. Star Restaurant is on Maple Street between Fifth and Sixth Streets.

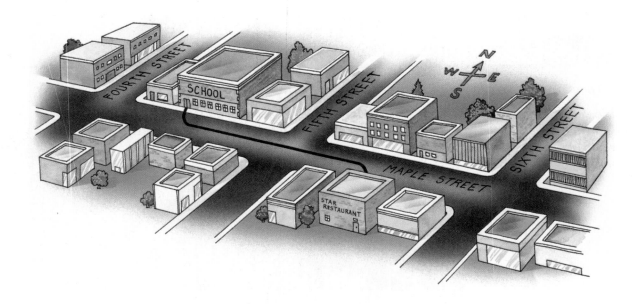

Dear Joe,

I'm glad you can come to my party.

Here are the directions from school.

Walk one block east. The party is at Star Restaurant. It's on Maple Street between Fifth and Sixth Streets.

See you Saturday at eight o'clock.

Bill

1 *Draw a picture or bring in photos of three friends.*

2 *Fill out these charts for your friends. Choose from the list of qualities in the box.*

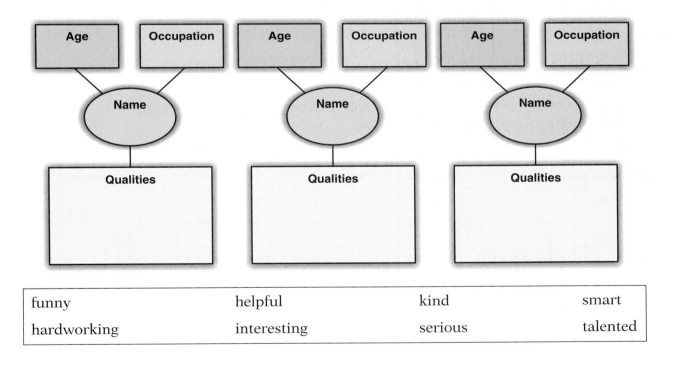

| funny | helpful | kind | smart |
| hardworking | interesting | serious | talented |

(continued)

3 *Now write about your friends. Follow the model.*

These are my good friends _____, _____, and _____. _____ is on the left. He's / She's _____ years old. He's / She's a / an _____. He's / She's _____ and _____. _____ is next to _____. He's / She's _____ years old. He's / She's a / an _____. He's / She's _____ and _____. _____ is on the right. He's / She's _____ years old. He's / She's a / an _____. He's / She's _____ and _____.

Model

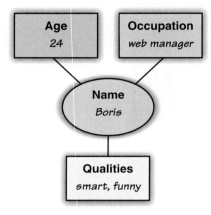

This is my good friend Boris. Boris is on the left. He's twenty-four years old. He's a web manager. He's smart and funny.

PART III Using the Present of *Be* (*Wh-* Questions)

E-mail a friend. Ask your friend four questions about his or her first day in English class. Choose from the question words in the box. Follow the model.

Who	Where	What	How	Is	Are	Was	Were

Model

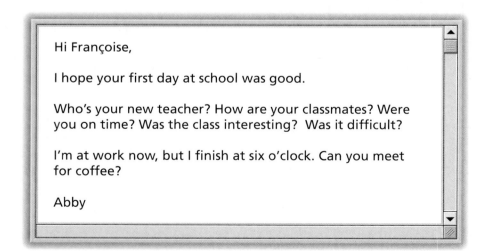

Hi Françoise,

I hope your first day at school was good.

Who's your new teacher? How are your classmates? Were you on time? Was the class interesting? Was it difficult?

I'm at work now, but I finish at six o'clock. Can you meet for coffee?

Abby

You and a good friend are in different cities. Answer your friend's letter. Follow the model.

Dear _____ ,

    I often think about you. How is everything in _____? Are you busy? What are your days like? What do you usually do on weekends? Do you ever ski?

    Please write.

_____

Model

Dear Marta,

    I was so happy to hear from you.

    My life here is different. Sometimes it's busy and exciting. Sometimes it's lonely. It's hard to speak a second language all the time.

    I enjoy my job. I'm a graphic artist for a small publisher. I love to design CD and book covers, but I don't love to work on very long books.

    I start work at 9:00 and finish at 5:00. I get to work by train. My co-workers are friendly and helpful, but I don't have any good friends yet.

    In the evening I usually watch videos. On weekends I go to the movies. I still love movies. I never ski. It's too expensive here.

    I miss our trips to the museum and the stores. I also miss our skiing trips.

    Please tell me about yourself. Perhaps you can visit me this summer.

Best wishes,

Alfredo

PART V   Using the Present Progressive

1 *Bring in a photo with four or more people in it. Answer these questions.*

Where are the people? _____

Who are the people?

     Person A: _____

     Person B: _____

     Person C: _____

     Person D: _____

What are they doing? _____

2 *Describe the photo. Follow the model.*

Model

A Train Station in Italy

    This is a photo of people at a train station in Italy. On the left, a young man is looking up at a sign. It shows train departures. Behind him, several people are standing near a snack bar. In the center of the picture, three young men are waiting for a train. One is wearing a red shirt and shorts. The young man sitting next to him is also wearing shorts. He is looking to the right. Their backpacks are sitting on the station floor. Everyone is enjoying the warm weather.

PART VI Using Nouns and Articles; *Can* and *Can't*

You and a friend are planning to go to a movie. E-mail your friend and say when you can and can't go. Use **can**, **can't**, **let's**, *and* **the** *in your e-mail. Follow the model.*

Before you write: *Fill out this chart.*

	Example	**You**
Can't go	Any time on Saturday	
Can go	Sunday afternoon or evening	
Don't want to see	*Batman Begins*	
Want to see	*Cinderella Man*	
Meet at	3:15 or 6:45	

Model

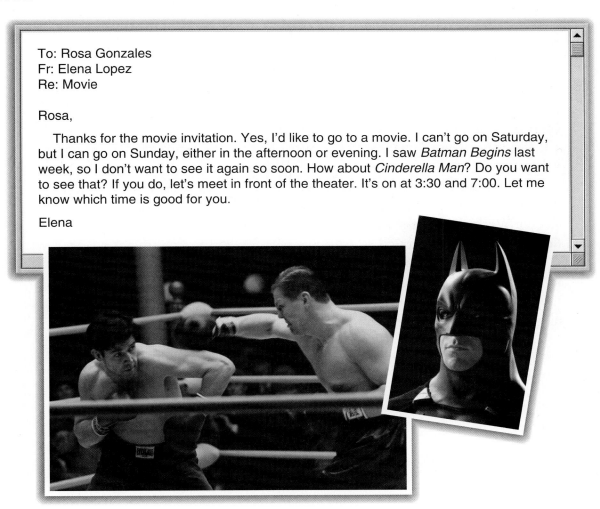

To: Rosa Gonzales
Fr: Elena Lopez
Re: Movie

Rosa,

    Thanks for the movie invitation. Yes, I'd like to go to a movie. I can't go on Saturday, but I can go on Sunday, either in the afternoon or evening. I saw *Batman Begins* last week, so I don't want to see it again so soon. How about *Cinderella Man*? Do you want to see that? If you do, let's meet in front of the theater. It's on at 3:30 and 7:00. Let me know which time is good for you.

Elena

You are on vacation. Write a letter to your parents or to a friend. Tell them about your vacation. Use regular and irregular simple past verb forms in your letter. Follow the model.

Before you write: *Note things that you did in this chart.*

Example	You
Arrived at 10:00 P.M.	
Took a taxi to the hotel	
Spent the day at the beach	
Swam in the Caribbean	
Got a sunburn	
Went to a folk festival	
Ate at a great restaurant; had delicious seafood	
Went shopping	

Model

Dear Mom and Dad,

Greetings from Jamaica! It's beautiful here. The weather is warm and sunny.

Mary and I arrived on Tuesday evening about 10:00 P.M. It was very late, so we took a taxi to the hotel. Our room is small but comfortable.

On Wednesday we spent the day at the beach. We both swam in the Caribbean. I got a sunburn.

On Wednesday evening we went to a folk festival. It was fun and interesting. There were some good singers.

On Thursday we went shopping in Kingston. I bought you both something nice. In the evening we ate at a restaurant. I had some delicious seafood.

I'll write again soon.

Love,
Amy

*You and a friend are preparing for a picnic. Write an e-mail message to your friend. Say what you have and don't have. Ask your friend what he or she can bring. Use quantifiers and **there is / there are**. Follow the model.*

Before you write: *Complete the chart. Say what you have and what you need.*

Have	Need

Model

To: Jerry Williams
Fr: Linda Hurst
Re: Our picnic

Hi, Jerry,

  Let's have the picnic at Washington Park. There are a lot of picnic tables. There's a volleyball net. There's also a nice swimming pool, so people can play volleyball or go swimming.

  I have enough hamburgers for 12 people, but I don't have any hot dogs. Can you bring three packages of them? And can you also bring three packages of hot dog buns? I have several bottles of juice, but I don't have any other drinks. Can you bring about 4 liters of soda? Oh, one more thing: I'll bring a large salad. Can you bring something for dessert, maybe some cookies? Or maybe a couple of pies?

  Let me know if this is OK. See you soon.

Linda

Write a description of two places you know well. Say how they are similar and how they are different. Follow the model.

Before you write: Draw two circles. In one circle, put the name of one place and write adjectives describing that place. In the other circle, put the name of the other place and write adjectives describing that place. In the middle, write adjectives showing how the two places are similar.

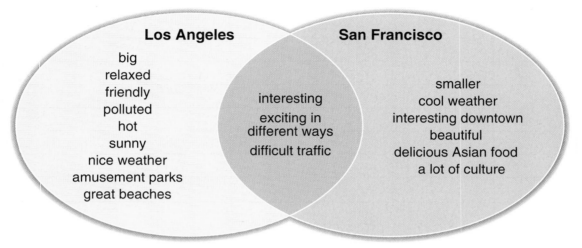

Los Angeles — big, relaxed, friendly, polluted, hot, sunny, nice weather, amusement parks, great beaches

interesting, exciting in different ways, difficult traffic

San Francisco — smaller, cool weather, interesting downtown, beautiful, delicious Asian food, a lot of culture

Model

Los Angeles and San Francisco are two of my favorite cities. They're different in many ways. Los Angeles is a lot bigger than San Francisco, and it's friendlier and more relaxed. It has great amusement parks and beaches. The weather is nicer than the weather in San Francisco. It's hotter and sunnier. But it's also more polluted. San Francisco is cooler. It's more beautiful than Los Angeles. It's more exciting too. It has an interesting downtown and a lot of culture. There's a lot of good food in San Francisco, especially Asian food.

San Francisco and Los Angeles are similar in some ways. They're both very nice, and they're both interesting in their own ways. It's hard to drive in both places because there's so much traffic. But it's worse in Los Angeles.

I like both cities a lot, but I love the weather, the beaches, and the amusement parks in Los Angeles. For me it's a better place.

PART X Using the Future with *Be going to*

*You are going to be in a friend's city next month. Write a note to your friend. Ask if you can get together Use the future with **be going to** in your note. Follow the model.*

Before you write: *Complete this chart.*

	Example	**You**
Who	You and your husband	
Where	Los Angeles, California	
When	July 15 to 19	
Why	Attend a conference; visit cousins	
Free on	Tuesday, July 16, and Thursday, July 18, evenings	

Model

Dear Jean,

   Mark and I are going to be in Los Angeles from July 15 to 19. I'm going to attend a conference, and Mark is going to visit his cousins. Are you going to be in town then? If you are, can we get together? We're free on Tuesday, July 16, and Thursday, July 18, in the evening. We're going to stay at the Best Western Hotel in Venice. Is that near you?

   Please let me know. I hope we can see each other.

Best,

Gina

APPENDICES

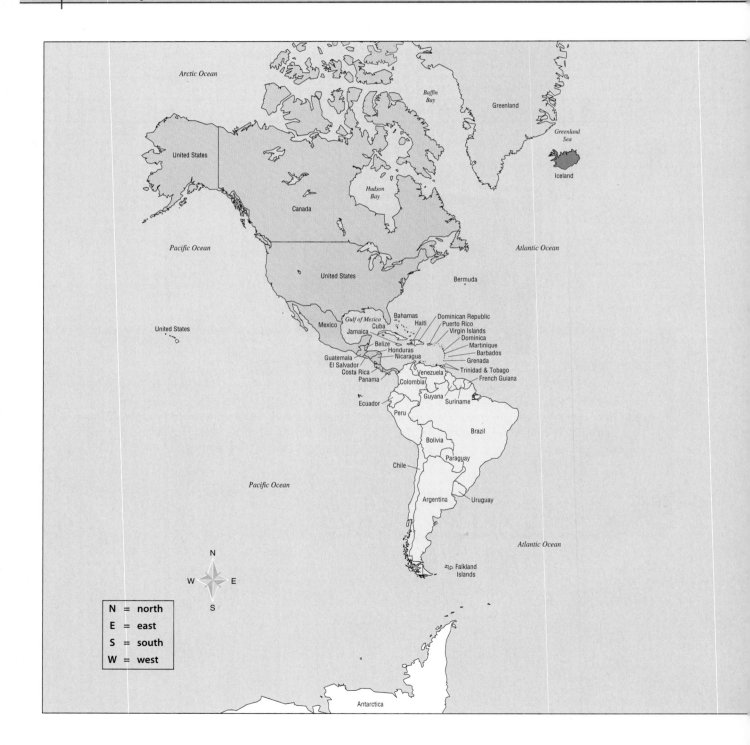

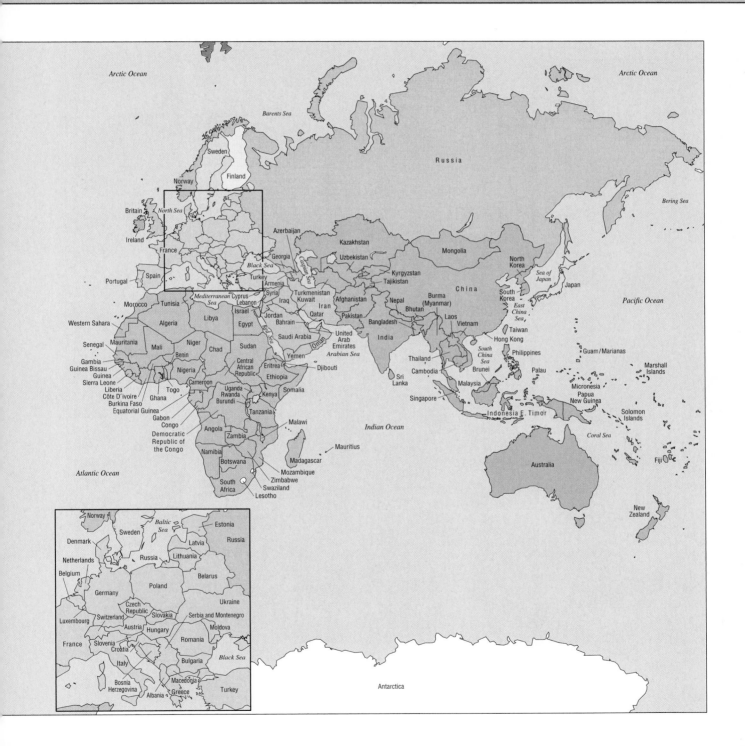

Arctic Ocean

Arctic Ocean

Barents Sea

Bering Sea

Russia

Sweden

Norway

Finland

North Sea

Britain

Ireland

France

Azerbaijan

Kazakhstan

Mongolia

North Korea

Sea of Japan

Japan

Portugal

Spain

Georgia

Black Sea

Uzbekistan

Kyrgyzstan

Tajikistan

China

South Korea

East China Sea

Pacific Ocean

Morocco

Tunisia

Turkey

Armenia

Syria

Iraq

Turkmenistan

Kuwait

Afghanistan

Nepal

Burma (Myanmar)

Laos

Taiwan

Cyprus

Mediterranean Sea

Lebanon

Israel

Jordan

Bahrain

Iran

Qatar

Pakistan

Bhutan

Vietnam

Hong Kong

Western Sahara

Algeria

Libya

Egypt

Bangladesh

India

Senegal

Mauritania

Mali

Niger

Chad

Sudan

Saudi Arabia

Yemen

United Arab Emirates

Oman

Arabian Sea

Thailand

South China Sea

Philippines

Guam / Marianas

Marshall Islands

Gambia

Guinea Bissau

Guinea

Sierra Leone

Liberia

Côte D´ivoire

Burkina Faso

Equatorial Guinea

Benin

Nigeria

Central African Republic

Eritrea

Djibouti

Cambodia

Brunei

Micronesia

Togo

Ghana

Cameroon

Ethiopia

Sri Lanka

Malaysia

Papua New Guinea

Gabon

Congo

Uganda

Rwanda

Burundi

Kenya

Somalia

Singapore

Indonesia E. Timor

Solomon Islands

Democratic Republic of the Congo

Angola

Zambia

Tanzania

Malawi

Indian Ocean

Coral Sea

Fiji

Namibia

Botswana

Madagascar

Mauritius

Atlantic Ocean

South Africa

Zimbabwe

Swaziland

Lesotho

Mozambique

Australia

New Zealand

Antarctica

Norway

Baltic Sea

Estonia

Denmark

Sweden

Russia

Latvia

Russia

Netherlands

Lithuania

Belgium

Belarus

Germany

Poland

Luxembourg

Ukraine

Czech Republic

Switzerland

Slovakia

Serbia and Montenegro

France

Austria

Hungary

Moldova

Slovenia

Croatia

Romania

Italy

Bulgaria

Black Sea

Bosnia Herzegovina

Macedonia

Albania

Greece

Turkey

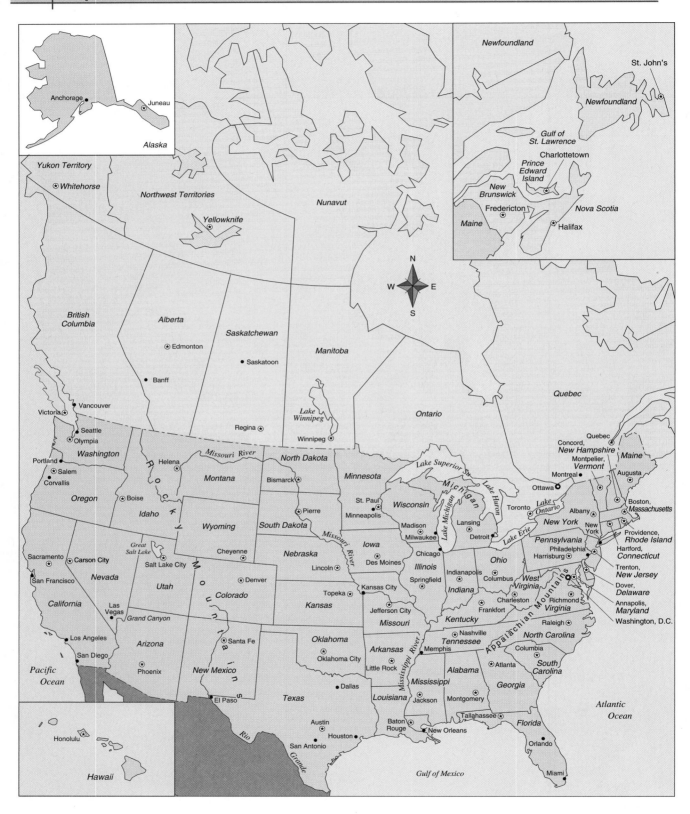

CARDINAL NUMBERS

1 = one	11 = eleven	21 = twenty-one
2 = two	12 = twelve	30 = thirty
3 = three	13 = thirteen	40 = forty
4 = four	14 = fourteen	50 = fifty
5 = five	15 = fifteen	60 = sixty
6 = six	16 = sixteen	70 = seventy
7 = seven	17 = seventeen	80 = eighty
8 = eight	18 = eighteen	90 = ninety
9 = nine	19 = nineteen	100 = one hundred
10 = ten	20 = twenty	101 = one hundred and one
		200 = two hundred
		1,000 = one thousand
		1,000,000 = one million
		10,000,000 = ten million

EXAMPLES

That book has **eighty-nine** pages.
There are **thirty** days in September.
There are **five** rows in the room.
She is **eleven** years old.
He has **three** children.

ORDINAL NUMBERS

1st = first	11th = eleventh	21st = twenty-first
2nd = second	12th = twelfth	30th = thirtieth
3rd = third	13th = thirteenth	40th = fortieth
4th = fourth	14th = fourteenth	50th = fiftieth
5th = fifth	15th = fifteenth	60th = sixtieth
6th = sixth	16th = sixteenth	70th = seventieth
7th = seventh	17th = seventeenth	80th = eightieth
8th = eighth	18th = eighteenth	90th = ninetieth
9th = ninth	19th = nineteenth	100th = one hundredth
10th = tenth	20th = twentieth	101st = one hundred and first
		200th = two hundredth
		1,000th = one thousandth
		1,000,000th = one millionth
		10,000,000th = ten millionth

EXAMPLES

It's his **fifty-first** birthday.
It's September **thirtieth**.
He's in the **fourth** row.
It's her **eleventh** birthday.
Jeremy is their **first** child.
Annie is their **second** child.
Ben is their **third** child.

TEMPERATURE

We measure the temperature in degrees (°).

Changing from degrees Fahrenheit to degrees Celsius:

$$(°F - 32) \times 5/9 = °C$$

Changing from degrees Celsius to degrees Fahrenheit:

$$(9/5 \times °C) + 32 = °F$$

DAYS OF THE WEEK

WEEKDAYS	WEEKEND
Monday	Saturday
Tuesday	Sunday
Wednesday	
Thursday	
Friday	

MONTHS OF THE YEAR

MONTH	ABBREVIATION	NUMBER OF DAYS
January	Jan.	31
February	Feb.	28*
March	Mar.	31
April	Apr.	30
May	May	31
June	Jun.	30
July	Jul.	31
August	Aug.	31
September	Sept.	30
October	Oct.	31
November	Nov.	30
December	Dec.	31

*February has 29 days in a leap year, every four years.

(continued)

THE SEASONS

NORTHERN HEMISPHERE

Spring: March 21–June 20

Summer: June 21–September 20

Autumn or Fall: September 21–December 20

Winter: December 21–March 20

SOUTHERN HEMISPHERE

Spring: September 21–December 20

Summer: December 21–March 20

Autumn or Fall: March 21–June 20

Winter: June 21–September 20

TITLES

Mr. (Mister) /mɪstər/	unmarried or married man
Ms./mɪz/	unmarried or married woman
Miss/mɪs/	unmarried woman
Mrs./mɪsɪz/	married woman
Dr. (Doctor)/daktər/	doctor (medical doctor or Ph.D.)

4 | Time

It's one o'clock.
(It's 1:00.)

It's five after one.
(It's 1:05.)

It's one-ten.
It's ten after one.
(It's 1:10.)

It's one-fifteen.
It's a quarter after one.
(It's 1:15.)

It's one twenty-five.
It's twenty-five after one.
(It's 1:25.)

It's one-thirty.
It's half past one.
(It's 1:30.)

It's one forty-five.
It's a quarter to two.
(It's 1:45.)

It's one-fifty.
It's ten to two.
(It's 1:50.)

TALKING ABOUT TIME

1. You can ask about time this way:

A: What time is it?

B: It's one o'clock.

It's 10:00 **a.m.**

2. A.M. means before noon
(the hours between midnight and noon).

P.M. means after noon
(the hours between noon and midnight).

It's 10:00 **p.m.**

▶ **BE CAREFUL!** When people say 12:00 A.M.,
they mean midnight. When people say 12:00 P.M.,
they mean noon.

3. We often write time with numbers.

It's one o'clock. = It's **1:00**.

It's two-twenty. = It's **2:20**.

5 | Parts of the Body

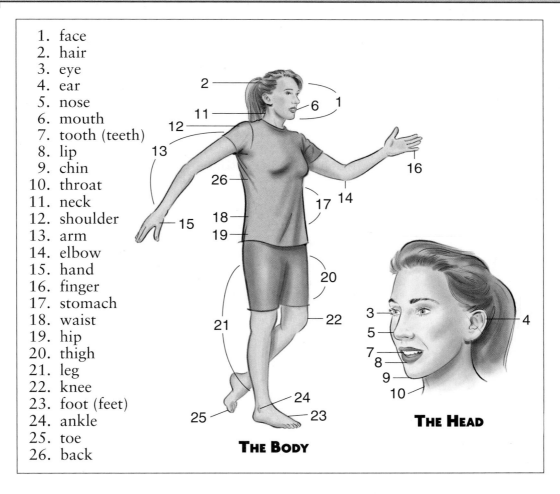

1. face
2. hair
3. eye
4. ear
5. nose
6. mouth
7. tooth (teeth)
8. lip
9. chin
10. throat
11. neck
12. shoulder
13. arm
14. elbow
15. hand
16. finger
17. stomach
18. waist
19. hip
20. thigh
21. leg
22. knee
23. foot (feet)
24. ankle
25. toe
26. back

THE BODY

THE HEAD

SPELLING RULES

1. Add **-s** to form the plural of most nouns.	book car video photograph	book**s** car**s** video**s** photograph**s**
2. Add **-es** to form the plural of nouns that end in **ss**, **ch**, **sh**, and **x**. (This ending adds another syllable.)	class sandwich dish box	class**es** sandwich**es** dish**es** box**es**
3. To form the plural of nouns that end in a **consonant** + **y**, change the **y** to **i** and add **-es**.	party strawberry	part**ies** strawber**ries**
4. To form the plural of nouns that end in a **vowel** + **y**, add **-s**.	boy key	boy**s** key**s**
5. Some plural nouns are **irregular**.	man woman child	**men** **women** **children**
6. Some nouns **do not have a singular form**.	person	**people** **clothes** **(eye)glasses** **pants**

⌒ PRONUNCIATION RULES

1. The **final sounds** for regular plural nouns are /**s**/, /**z**/, and /**ɪz**/.		
2. The plural is pronounced /**s**/ **after** the **voiceless sounds** /**p**/, /**t**/, /**k**/, /**f**/, and /**θ**/.	cup**s** cat**s** book**s**	puff**s** brea**ths**
3. The plural is pronounced /**z**/ **after** the **voiced sounds** /**b**/, /**d**/, /**g**/, /**v**/, /**m**/, /**n**/, /**ŋ**/, /**l**/, /**r**/, and /**ð**/.	cab**s** card**s** dog**s** wi**ves** room**s**	pan**s** song**s** ball**s** car**s** pa**ths**
4. The plural is pronounced /**z**/ **after** all **vowel sounds**. Vowels are voiced.	key**s** tomat**oes**	mov**ies**
5. The plural is pronounced /**ɪz**/ **after** the sounds /**s**/, /**z**/, /**ʃ**/, /**ʒ**/, /**tʃ**/, and /**dʒ**/. (This adds another syllable to the word.)	kiss**es** buzz**es** dish**es**	gara**ges** mat**ches** a**ges**

1. Add **'s** to form the possessive of singular nouns.

   Lulu**'s** last name is Winston.

2. To form the possessive of plural nouns ending in **s**, add only an **apostrophe (')**.

   The girl**s'** gym is on this floor.
   The boy**s'** locker room is across the hall.

3. In phrases showing joint possession, only the last word is possessive in form.

   Elenore and Pete**'s** apartment is comfortable.

4. To form the possessive of plural nouns that do not end in **s**, add **'s**.

   The men**'s** room is next to the water fountain.

5. To form the possessive of one-syllable singular nouns that end in **s**, add **'s**.

   James's apartment is beautiful.

   To form the possessive of words of more than one syllable that end in **s**, add an **'** or an **'s**.

   McCullers's novels are interesting.
   OR
   McCullers' novels are interesting.

6. **BE CAREFUL!** Don't confuse possessive nouns with the contraction of the verb *be*.

   Carol's a student. = **Carol** *is* a student.
   Carol's book is open. = **Her** book is open.

COMMON NON-COUNT NOUNS*

Food
bread
broccoli
butter
cake
cauliflower
cheese
chicken
dessert
fish
ice cream
meat
pasta
pepper
pie
pizza
rice
salsa
salt
soup
spaghetti
sugar
yogurt

Liquids
coffee
juice
lemonade
milk
soda
tea
water

Weather
fog
ice
rain
snow

School Subjects
algebra
biology
chemistry
Chinese
English
geography
history
music
psychology
science
Spanish

Sports
baseball
basketball
football
soccer
swimming
tennis
volleyball

Abstract Ideas
advice
beauty
energy
existence
happiness
help
noise
stress

Others
furniture
homework
information
mail
medicine
money
news
paper
sleep
time
work

*Some nouns can be either count or non-count nouns.

Do you want some pizza? (*non-count*)
Let's order a pizza. (*count—an entire pizza*)

I don't want salad tonight. (*non-count*)
Mom is making a salad. (*count*)

QUANTIFIERS

a bottle of (*juice, milk, soda, water*)
a bowl of (*cereal, soup*)
a can of (*soda, tuna*)
a cup of (*coffee, hot chocolate, tea*)
a foot of (*snow, water*)
a gallon of (*gasoline, juice, milk*)
a glass of (*juice, milk, water*)

a liter of (*juice, milk, soda, water*)
a loaf of (*bread*)
a meter of (*snow, water*)
a pair of (*gloves, pants, shoes, skis, socks*)
a piece of (*cake, meat, paper, pie*)
a quart of (*milk, oil*)
a slice of (*cake, cheese, pie, pizza, toast*)

1. *A* and *an* are the **indefinite articles**. We use them before **singular count nouns**.

- My sister has **a truck**.
- She has **an old car** too.

2. Use *a* before a word that begins with a **consonant sound**.
   Use *an* before a word that begins with a **vowel sound**.

- I ate **a sandwich** for lunch.
- My brother drives **an orange car**.
- Sally is attending **a university** in Montreal. (*The word* university *begins with the consonant sound* /y/—*not with a vowel sound.*)

3. *The* is the **definite article**. You can use *the* before singular count nouns, plural count nouns, and non-count nouns.

- **The cat** is sleeping. (*singular count noun*)
- **The students** are studying. (*plural count noun*)
- **The coffee** is delicious. (*non-count noun*)

4. Use *the* for **specific things** that the listener and speaker know about.

A: How was **the movie**?
B: It was really exciting.

5. Use *the* when the speaker and listener know there is **only one** of the item.

A: **The weather** is beautiful.
B: Yes. **The sun** is really bright.

6. Use *the* when you are talking about **part of a group**.

- There are a lot of houses in my neighborhood. **The houses on Elm Street** are all beautiful. **The houses on Maple Street** are all ugly.

7. Use *the* when you talking about something for the **second time**.

A: Do you have any pets?
B: Yes, I have a parrot and a cat. **The parrot** can talk. **The cat** just sleeps all the time.

8. Use *the* before the **plural name** of a whole family.

- **The Becks** live in Seattle.
- **The Olsons** live in Redmond.

9. Use *the* with **phrases with *of*** when there is only one of the item that follows *the*.

- Ankara is **the capital of Turkey**.
- Sally attends **the University of Montreal**.
  BUT   I'd like **a cup of coffee**.

10. Use *the* with the names of a few countries.

- We live in **the United States**.
  BUT   We live in America.
- Colin is from **the United Kingdom**.
  BUT   Colin is from Britain.
- Jan is from **the Netherlands**.
  BUT   Jan is from Holland.

The Simple Present of *Be*: Statements

Subject	*Be*	(*Not*)	
I	am		
You	are		
He She It	is	(not)	from the United States.
We You They	are		

The Simple Present of *Be*: *Yes / No* Questions

Be	Subject	
Am	I	
Are	you	
Is	he she it	from the United States?
Are	we you they	

The Simple Past of *Be*: Statements

Subject	*Be*	(*Not*)		Time Marker
I	was			
You	were			
He She It	was	(not)	In Canada	last month.
We You They	were			

The Simple Past of *Be*: *Yes / No* Questions

Be	Subject		Time Marker
Was	I		
Were	you		
Was	he she it	in Canada	last month?
Were	we you they		

The Present Progressive: Statements

Subject	*Be*	(*Not*)	Base Form of Verb + *-ing*
I	**am**		
You	**are**		
He She It	**is**	**(not)**	**working**.
We You They	**are**		

The Present Progressive: *Yes / No* Questions

Be	Subject	Base Form of Verb + *-ing*
Am	I	
Are	you	
Is	he she it	**working**?
Are	we you they	

(continued)

The Simple Present of Regular Verbs: Statements

Affirmative		Negative		
Subject	**Verb**	**Subject**	*Don't / Doesn't*	**Verb**
I You	**work.**	I You	**don't**	
He She It	**works.**	He She It	**doesn't**	**work.**
We You They	**work.**	We You They	**don't**	

The Simple Present of Regular Verbs: *Yes / No* Questions

Do / Does	**Subject**	**Verb**
Do	I you	
Does	he she it	**work?**
Do	we you they	

The Simple Past of Regular Verbs: Statements

Affirmative		Negative		
Subject	**Base Form of Verb + *-ed / -d / -ied***	**Subject**	*Didn't*	**Verb**
I You		I You		
He She It	**worked.** **arrived.** **cried.**	He She It	**didn't**	**work.**
We You They		We You They		

The Simple Past of Verbs: *Yes / No* Questions

Did	Subject	Verb
Did	I you	
	he she it	**go**?
	we you they	

Be going to **Future: Statements**

Subject	*Be*	(*Not*)	*Going to*	Base Form of Verb	Time Marker
I	**am**				
You	**are**				
He She It	**is**	(**not**)	**going to**	**run**	tomorrow.
We You They	**are**				

Be going to **Future: *Yes / No* Questions**

Be	Subject	*Going to*	Base Form of Verb	Time Marker
Am	I			
Are	you			
Is	he she it	**going to**	**run**	tomorrow?
Are	we you they			

BASE FORM	PAST FORM	BASE FORM	PAST FORM	BASE FORM	PAST FORM
be	was, were	go	went	see	saw
begin	began	grow	grew	sing	sang
break	broke	have	had	sit	sat
bring	brought	hear	heard	sleep	slept
build	built	hit	hit	speak	spoke
buy	bought	know	knew	spend	spent
come	came	leave	left	stand	stood
do	did	lose	lost	swim	swam
drink	drank	make	made	take	took
drive	drove	mean	meant	tell	told
eat	ate	meet	met	think	thought
fall	fell	put	put	understand	understood
find	found	read /rid/	read /rɛd/	wake	woke
fly	flew	ride	rode	wear	wore
forget	forgot	run	ran	win	won
get	got	say	said	write	wrote
give	gave				

1. Add *-ing* to the **base form** of the verb.	bring cook see	bring**ing** cook**ing** see**ing**
2. If a verb **ends in a silent *e***, drop the final *e* and add *-ing*.	writ**e**	writ**ing**
3. If the last three letters of a **one-syllable verb** are a consonant, a vowel, and a consonant (**CVC**), double the last consonant before adding *-ing*. However, do not double the last consonant if it is a **w**, **x**, or **y**.	CVC run clap grow fix play	CVC run**n**ing cla**pp**ing growing fixing playing
4. In **longer verbs** (two or more syllables) that end in a consonant, a vowel, and a consonant (**CVC**), double the last consonant only if the last syllable is stressed.	permít (The last syllable is stressed.) devélop (The last syllable is not stressed.)	permi**tt**ing developing

SPELLING RULES FOR THE THIRD-PERSON SINGULAR AFFIRMATIVE

1. **Add -s** to form the third-person singular form of most verbs.	• Jessica works. I work too. • Jeremy wears T-shirts. I wear blouses.
Add -es to words that end in *ch*, *s*, *sh*, *x*, or *z*.	• I teach Chinese. Steve teaches journalism. • I fix my mountain bike. Tim fixes his own car.
2. If the verb ends in a **consonant** + **y**, change the *y* to *i* and add **-es**. If the verb ends in a **vowel** + **y**, do not change the *y* to *i*. Add **-s**.	• I study in the library. Judy studies at home. • I play volleyball. Annie plays soccer.
3. Some verbs have **irregular forms** for the third-person singular.	• I have. He **has**. • I do. She **does**. • I go. It **goes**.

∩ PRONUNCIATION RULES FOR THE THIRD-PERSON SINGULAR AFFIRMATIVE

1. The **final sound** for the third-person singular form of the simple present is pronounced /s/, /z/, or /ɪz/. The final sounds of the third-person singular are the same as the final sounds of plural nouns. See Appendix 6 on page A-6.	/s/ walks	/z/ rides	/ɪz/ dances
2. **Do** and **say** have a change in vowel sound.	I do. /du/ I say. /seɪ/	She does. /dʌz/ He says. /sɛz/	

SPELLING RULES

1. If the verb **ends in an** *e*, add *-d*.	move	move**d**
2. If the verb **ends in a consonant**, add *-ed*.	cover	cover**ed**
	seem	seem**ed**
3. If the last three letters in a **one-syllable verb** are a consonant, a vowel, and a consonant (**CVC**), double the last consonant and add *-ed*.	CVC	
	hu**g**	hu**gg**ed
	ru**b**	ru**bb**ed
However, do not double the last consonant if it is a *w*, *x*, or *y*.	ro**w**	ro**w**ed
	mi**x**	mi**x**ed
	sta**y**	sta**y**ed
4. If a **two-syllable verb** ends in a consonant, a vowel, and a consonant (**CVC**), double the last consonant only if the last syllable is stressed.	CVC	
	refér	refe**rr**ed (stressed)
	énter	enter**ed** (not stressed)
5. If the verb ends in a **consonant** + *y*, change the *y* to *i* and add *-ed*.	marr**y**	marr**ied**
	stud**y**	stud**ied**
6. If the verb ends in a **vowel** + *y*, do not change the *y* to *i*. Add *-ed*.	enj**oy**	enjo**yed**
	pl**ay**	pla**yed**
There are **exceptions** to this rule. These verbs are **irregular verbs**.	pay	**paid**
	lay	**laid**
	say	**said**

1. The **final sounds** for regular verbs in the simple past are **/t/**, **/d/**, and **/ɪd/**.			
2. The final sound is pronounced **/t/** after the **voiceless sounds /f/, /k/, /p/, /s/, /ʃ/, and /tʃ/.**	laughed liked	developed crossed	washed watched
3. The final sound is pronounced **/ d /** after the **voiced sounds /b/, /g/, /dʒ/, /l/, /m/, /n/, /r/, /ŋ/, /ð/, /ʒ/, /v/, and /z/.**	rubbed hugged judged called	hummed cleaned hired banged	bathed massaged moved used
4. The final sound is pronounced **/d/** after vowel **sounds.**	stayed agreed	died argued	snowed
5. The final sound is pronounced **/ɪd/** after **/t/** and **/d/. /ɪd/** adds a syllable.	act end	acted ended	

15 | Comparisons with Adjectives

Comparative Form				
(To Compare Two People, Places, or Things)				
Seattle	is	older **busier** **more exciting**	**than**	Redmond.
Redmond	is	**smaller** **prettier** **more peaceful**	**than**	Seattle.

Superlative Form				
(To Compare Three or More People, Places, or Things)				
Jim	is	**the**	oldest **happiest** **most successful**	of my three brothers.
Nancy	is	**the**	**youngest** **prettiest** **most interesting**	of my four sisters.

These are the pronunciation symbols used in this text. Listen to the pronunciation of the key words.

VOWELS		CONSONANTS			
Symbol	**Key Word**	**Symbol**	**Key Word**	**Symbol**	**Key Word**
i	beat, feed	p	pack, happy	ʃ	ship, machine, station, special, discussion
ɪ	bit, did	b	back, rubber		
eɪ	date, paid	t	tie	ʒ	measure, vision
ɛ	bet, bed	d	die	h	hot, who
æ	bat, bad	k	came, key, quick	m	men
ɑ	box, odd, father	g	game, guest	n	sun, know, pneumonia
ɔ	bought, dog	tʃ	church, nature, watch	ŋ	sung, ringing
oʊ	boat, road	dʒ	judge, general, major	w	wet, white
ʊ	book, good	f	fan, photograph	l	light, long
u	boot, food, student	v	van	r	right, wrong
ʌ	but, mud, mother	θ	thing, breath	y	yes, use, music
ə	banana, among	ð	then, breathe		
ɚ	shirt, murder	s	sip, city, psychology		
aɪ	bite, cry, buy, eye	z	zip, please, goes		
aʊ	about, how				
ɔɪ	voice, boy				
ɪr	deer				
ɛr	bare				
ɑr	bar				
ɔr	door				
ʊr	tour				

GLOSSARY OF GRAMMAR TERMS

action verb   A verb that describes an action.
- *Jeremy and Yoshio **are studying** at the library.*
- *Tim **drives** to work every day.*

adjective   A word that describes a noun or pronoun.
- *Redmond is a **small, peaceful** city.*

adverb   A word that describes an action verb, an adverb, an adjective, or a sentence.
- *We're leaving on vacation **tomorrow**.*

adverb of frequency   A word that tells the frequency of something.
- *We **usually** eat lunch at noon.*

affirmative statement   A sentence that does not use a negative verb form (not).
- ***I have two brothers.***

apostrophe   A punctuation mark used to show possession and to write a contraction.
- *He's in my father's car.*

base form   The simple form of a verb without any ending, such as -ing, -ed, or -s.
- *Arnold is going to **come** at 8:00. We can **eat** then.*

be going to future   A verb form used to make predictions, express general facts in the future, or to talk about definite plans that were made before now.
- *Amanda says it**'s going to be** cold, so she**'s going to take** a coat.*

capital letter   The large form of a letter of the alphabet. Sentences start with a capital letter.
- ***A, B, C**, and so on.*

comma   A punctuation mark (,) used to separate items in a list or parts of a sentence.
- *We went to a restaurant**,** and we ate chicken**,** potatoes**,** and broccoli.*

common noun   A noun for a person, place, or thing. It is not capitalized.
- *The **man** got a **book** at the **library**.*

comparative form   An adjective or adverb ending in -er or following *more*. It is used in comparing two things or people.
- *My sister is **older** and **more intelligent** than my brother.*

consonants   The letters **b, c, d, f, g, h, j, k, l, m, n, p, q, r, s, t, v, x, z**, and sometimes **w** and **y**.

contraction   A short form of two words. An apostrophe (') replaces the missing letter(s).
- ***it's** = it is*
- ***I'm** = I am*
- ***can't** = cannot*

count noun   A noun you can count. It usually has a singular and a plural form.
- *The **man** has one big **dog** and two small **dogs**.*

definite article *the*   It makes a noun specific.
- *We saw a movie. **The** movie starred Jackie Chan.*

exclamation point   An end punctuation mark (**!**). It shows strong emotion.
- *Help**!** Call the police**!***

formal language   Language we usually use for business settings, academic settings, or with people we don't know.
- ***Good morning, ladies** and **gentlemen. May** we begin?*

imperative   A sentence used to give instructions, directions, commands, and suggestions. It uses the base form of the verb. The subject (*you*) is not a part of the sentence.
- ***Turn** right at the corner. **Drive** to the end of the street. **Stop!***

indefinite article *a* or *an*   It is used before singular non-count nouns.

- *Josh brought **a** sandwich and **an** apple for lunch.*

informal language   The language we usually use with family and friends, in e-mail messages, and in other informal settings.

- ***Hey**, Jeremy, **what's up**?*

irregular verb   A verb that does not form the simple past by adding *-d* or *-ed*.

- *They **ate** a fancy meal last night. Jessica's boss **came** to dinner.*

negative statement   A statement with a negative verb form.

- *Ben **didn't** study. He **wasn't** ready for the test.*

non-action (stative) verb   A verb that does not describe an action. It can describe an emotion, a state, a sense, or a thought. We usually don't use non-action verbs in the progressive.

- *I **like** that actor. He **is** very famous, and I **believe** he won an award.*

non-count noun   A noun we usually do not count. We don't put *a*, *an*, or a number before a non-count noun.

- *All we need is **rice**, **water**, **salt**, and **butter**.*

noun   A word that refers to a person, animal, place, thing, or idea.

- ***Annie** has a **friend** at the **library**. She gave her a **book** about **birds**.*

noun modifier   A noun that describes another noun.

- *Samantha is a **chemistry** professor. She loves **spy** movies.*

object   A noun or pronoun that receives the action of the verb.

- *Jason sold the **car**. Mark bought **it**.*

object pronoun   A pronoun following a verb or a preposition.

- *We asked **him** to show the photos to **them**.*

ordinal number   The form of a number that shows the order or sequence of something.

- *The team scored 21 points in the **first** quarter and 33 in the **fourth** quarter.*

period   A punctuation mark (**.**) used at the end of a statement or to show an abbreviation.

- *Mr**.** Mendoza, please call on Saturday**.***

plural   The form that means more than one.

- ***We** sat in **our chairs** reading **our books**.*

possessive   An adjective, noun, or pronoun that shows possession.

- ***Her** book is in **John's** car. **Mine** is at the office.*

preposition   A word that goes before a noun or pronoun object. A preposition often shows time or place.

- *Maria saw it **on** the table **at** two o'clock.*

present progressive   A verb form that shows an action happening now or planned for the future.

- *I**'m working** hard now, but I**'m taking** a vacation soon.*

pronoun   A word that replaces a noun or a noun phrase.

- ***He** is a friend. I know **him** well.*

proper noun   The actual name of a person, place, or thing. A proper noun begins with a capital letter.

- ***Helen** is living in **St. Louis**. She is studying **Spanish** at **Washington University**.*

quantifier   A word or phrase that comes before a noun and expresses an amount or number of that noun.

- *Jeannette used **a little** sugar, **some** flour, **four** eggs, and **a liter** of milk.*

question mark   A punctuation mark (**?**) used at the end of a question.

- *Where are you going**?** How long are you going to be out**?***

regular verb   A verb that forms the simple past by adding *-d* or *-ed*.

- *We **lived** in Kenya. My mother **visited** us there.*

sentence   A group of words with a subject and a verb. It can stand alone.

- ***We opened the window.***
- ***Did they paint the house?***

simple past   A verb form used to show a completed action or idea in the past.

- *The plane **landed** at 9:00. We **took** a bus to the hotel.*

simple present   A verb form used to show habitual actions or states, general facts, or conditions that are true now.

- *Yoshio **loves** to ski, and it **snows** a lot in his area, so he**'s** very happy.*

singular   The form that means only one.

- *I put on **my hat** and **coat** and closed the **door**.*

small letter   The small form of a letter of the alphabet. We use small letters for most words except for proper nouns and the first word of a sentence.

- ***a, b, c**, and so on.*

subject   The person, place, or thing that a sentence is about.

- ***The children** ate at the mall.*

subject pronoun   A pronoun used to replace a subject noun.

- *Kathy works hard. **She** loves her work.*

superlative form   An adjective or adverb ending in *-est* or following *most*. It is used in comparing three or more things or people.

- *We climbed the **highest** mountain by the **most dangerous** route.*

syllable   A group of letters with one vowel sound. Words are made up of one or more syllables.

- *One syllable—**win***
- *Two syllables—**ta ble***
- *Three syllables—**im por tant***

third-person singular   The verb form used with *he, she*, and *it*.

- *Jessica **is** a reporter. She **works** for a TV station.*

verb   A word used to describe an action, a fact, or a state.

- *Ken **drives** to work now. He **has** a new car, and he **is** a careful driver.*

vowels   The letters *a, e, i, o, u*, and sometimes *w* and *y*.

wh- question   A question that asks for information. It begins with *how, what, when, where, why, which, who*, or *whose*.

- ***What**'s your name?*
- ***Where** are you from?*
- ***How** do you feel?*

yes / no question   A question that has a *yes* or a *no* answer.

- ***Did you arrive on time?** Yes, I did.*
- ***Are you from Uruguay?** No, I'm not.*
- ***Can you swim well?** Yes, I can.*

INFORMATION GAPS

Unit 6, Exercise 7

Student B, answer your partner's questions about business cards 1 and 2. Then look at cards 3 and 4. Ask your partner questions and complete the cards.

1.

China Palace

30 Main Street

Ann Arbor, Michigan 48104

U.S.A.

2.

Turkish Delights

213 East 79th Street

New York, New York 10021

U.S.A.

3.

The Fitness Club

80 _____ Street

_____, Ontario

Canada

4.

Jim's Gym

_____

Vancouver, British Columbia

_____

Unit 8, Exercise 7

Student B, answer your partner's questions about the weather in Tokyo. Then complete this chart. Ask your partner questions about the weather in Rio.

Example: **B:** How was the weather in Rio last Sunday?
A: It was sunny and warm.

	Tokyo	Rio de Janeiro
Sunday	warm	
Monday	cool	
Tuesday	cool	

Unit 11, Exercise 7

Student B, answer Student A's questions. Choose an answer from your list below. Then ask Student A about the meaning of a word from your list. Write the answer. Take turns.

> **Example:** **B:** *Tiny* means "very small." What does *large* mean?
> **A:** *Large* means "big."

Student B's Words

1. large _big_

2. relatives _____

3. opposite _____

4. smart _____

5. cousins _____

6. cute _____

7. single _____

8. second _____

Student B's Answers

12:00 A.M.	not interesting
12:00 P.M.	very bad
great	good
very small	sad

▶ *To check your answers, go to the Answer Key on p. P-1.*

INFORMATION GAP FOR STUDENT B

Unit 16, Exercise 7

Student B, listen to Student A. Look at the pictures and name the places.

Niagara Falls

Sugar Loaf Mountain, Rio de Janeiro

The Great Pyramid, Giza

Now read your sentences to Student A. Student A names the places.

1. People are speaking Swahili. I'm visiting Tanzania. I'm climbing a mountain. (*Kilimanjaro*)

2. People are speaking Spanish. I'm visiting Mexico. I'm swimming. (*Acapulco Beach, Acapulco*)

3. I'm speaking English. I'm visiting the United States. I'm taking an elevator to the top of a building. (*the Empire State Building, New York City*)

Unit 30, Exercise 7

Student B, first answer Student A's questions. Use the phrases in the box. Use **in**, **on**, *or* **at** *in each answer. Then ask questions with* **when** *or* **what time.**

Example: **A:** When do Americans vote?
B: Americans usually vote on a Tuesday. When do the French vote?
A: The French usually vote on a Sunday.

Student B's answers		
December 21	February or March	March
a Tuesday	12:00 noon	

Student B's questions

1. the French / vote / ?

2. winter normally begin / in the Northern Hemisphere / ?

3. each day / begin / ?

4. Canadians / celebrate / Canada Day / ?

5. fall normally begin / in the Northern Hemisphere / ?

▶ *To check your answers, go to the Answer Key on p. P-2.*

PUZZLES, GAMES, AND INFORMATION GAPS ANSWER KEY

UNIT 4

Working Together

B. the Space needle

UNIT 8

Working Together

B. a museum

UNIT 9

9. True or False?

1. Antonio Banderas comes from Spain. True
2. Most people in Thailand eat with chopsticks. False. Most people in Thailand don't eat with chopsticks.
3. People in Japan drive on the left. True.
4. People in Great Britain drive on the right. False. People in Great Britain don't drive on the right. OR People in Great Britain drive on the left.
5. People live at the North Pole. False. People don't live at the North Pole.
6. Penguins live in deserts. False. Penguins don't live in deserts.
7. It snows in Chile in July. True.

UNIT 11

Working Together

C. drive a bus

7. Information Gap

Student A's Answers

2. relatives: your parents, brothers, sisters, grandparents, and so on
3. opposite: totally different
4. smart: intelligent
5. cousins: the children of your aunt of uncle
6. cute: good-looking
7. single: not married
8. second: between first and third

Student B's Answers

2. boring: not interesting
3. noon: 12 P.M.
4. midnight: 12 A.M.
5. super: great
6. unhappy: sad
7. terrible: very bad
8. nice: good

UNIT 12

Working Together

B. Wolfgang Amadeus Mozart

UNIT 18

Working Together

C. a salad

UNIT 30

7. Information Gap

Student A's Questions / Student B's Answers

2. When does summer normally begin in the Southern Hemisphere? / Summer normally begins in the Southern Hemisphere on December 21.
3. When OR What time does afternoon begin? / Afternoon begins at 12:00 noon.
4. When do Brazilians celebrate Carnaval? / Brazilians celebrate Carnaval in February or March.
5. When does fall normally begin in the Southern Hemisphere? / Fall normally begins in the Southern Hemisphere in March.

Student B's Questions / Student A's Answers

2. When does winter normally begin in the Northern Hemisphere? / Winter normally begins in the Northern Hemisphere on December 21.
3. When OR What time does each day begin? / Each day begins at 12:00 midnight.
4. When do Canadians celebrate Canada Day? / Canadians celebrate Canada Day on July 1.
5. When does fall normally begin in the Northern Hemisphere? / Fall normally begins in the Northern Hemisphere in September.

REVIEW TESTS ANSWER KEY

Note: In this answer key, where a short or contracted form is given, the full or long form is also correct (unless the purpose of the exercise is to practice the short or contracted forms).

PART I

I (Unit 2)
2. B   **5.** D
3. D   **6.** C
4. A

II (Unit 2)
2. These are   **5.** These are
3. This is   **6.** This is
4. This is

III (Unit 2)
2. They   **5.** She
3. It   **6.** We
4. They

IV (Units 1 and 2)
Don't
2. ~~Dont~~ write your name.
Turn
3. ~~Turns~~ left.
are
4. These ∧ my new notebooks.
These
5. ~~This~~ are my parents.
Don't
6. ~~No~~ listen to the CD.

V (Unit 1)
1. Close your books.
2. Listen to the CD.
3. Write the homework in your notebook.
4. Practice with a partner.

PART II

I (Units 3, 5, and 6)
2. D   **4.** D
3. A   **5.** B

II (Unit 4)
1. Is that   **3.** Are those
2. Is this   **4.** Are these

III (Unit 4)
2. their   **5.** her
3. their   **6.** their
4. their

IV (Units 3 and 6)
2. is on
3. is on . . . across from
4. is on . . . between
5. is next to
6. are across from
7. is on . . . across from
8. are on
9. is next to

PART III

I (Units 7 and 8)
2. B   **5.** A
3. A   **6.** C
4. D   **7.** C

II (Unit 7)
2. it wasn't   **5.** he was
3. they weren't   **6.** she was
4. I was OR we were

III (Unit 8)
2. Where   **5.** How long
3. What   **6.** How
4. When

IV (Unit 7)
2. was   **7.** 'm
3. were   **8.** 's OR is
4. 're   **9.** 's
5. 's OR is **10.** is OR 's
6. are   **11.** are

PART IV

I (Units 9–11)
2. D   **5.** B
3. A   **6.** D
4. C

II (Unit 13)
2. He never arrives at 9:00.
3. He usually arrives at 9:15.
4. Where do you usually eat?
5. Do you always have lunch at noon?

III (Unit 12)

2. is	6. have
3. is	7. is
4. have	8. is
5. has	

IV (Unit 11)
A. 2. Where does she work?
   3. What time does she start?
   4. How long does she stay?
B. 1. Who lives in that house?
   2. What do they do?
   3. Do they have children?
   4. Is the boy on the bike their son?

PART V

I (Units 14–16)

2. B	4. B
3. D	5. C

II (Unit 14)

2. is making	6. 's reading
3. are singing	7. 's watching
4. is playing	8. are sleeping
5. are sitting	

III (Units 14–16)
1. B. She's playing a game
2. A. Is Ben playing too
2. B. No, he's playing with the cat
3. A. Why are you laughing
3. B. The cat is wearing a hat
4. A. Where's Jessica going
4. B. She's going to the supermarket

IV (Unit 16)
2. What are they playing
3. Why is he making dinner
4. What's he making
5. Who's singing
6. Who's playing the guitar

PART VI

I (Units 17–20)

2. D	4. C
3. A	5. D

II (Units 17–19)
2. How does it look
3. Do you like the black shoes
4. Yes, but I can't understand his message
5. Can Jeremy play the guitar

III (Unit 18)
2. They don't have any coffee
3. They don't have any juice
4. They don't have any fruit
5. They have some bagels
6. They have some milk

IV (Unit 19)

2. a	9. an
3. ones	10. a
4. ones	11. the
5. an	12. one
6. a	13. the
7. one	14. one
8. the	

V (Unit 17)
2. It's Annie's cat.
3. It's the men's department.
4. It's the women's department.
5. It's Jessica's parents' house.

PART VII

I (Units 21–23)

2. A	4. C
3. A	5. D

II (Units 21 and 22)

2. didn't like	6. didn't get
3. completed	7. made
4. received	8. went
5. wanted	9. got

III (Units 21 and 22)

2. did	9. didn't open
3. was	10. did / give
4. missed	11. gave
5. Did / miss	12. was
6. did	13. Did / get
7. did / serve	14. bought
8. Did / get	

IV (Unit 23)
2. When did you leave? OR What time did you leave?
3. Why did it take five hours?
4. Who changed the tire?
5. When did you get home? OR What time did you get home?

PART VIII

I **(Units 24–26)**

2. C 4. B
3. A

II **(Unit 25)**

2. How many miles did you drive?
3. How many people went on the trip?
4. How much did the trip cost?

III **(Unit 25)**

2. A few 5. much
3. Some 6. a little
4. many

IV **(Unit 26)**

2. They are 8. It is
3. There is 9. there are
4. There are OR It has 10. They are
5. There are 11. There are
6. there are 12. There are
7. There is 13. There is

PART IX

I **(Units 28–30)**

2. A 4. A
3. B 5. D

II **(Unit 28)**

2. *The Bees* / scarier than
3. *Katie Raye* / more serious than
4. *Don't Tell Grandma* / funnier than
5. *Katie Raye* / the longest
6. *Katie Raye* / the best

III **(Unit 30)**

2. on 5. on
3. at 6. at
4. On 7. at

IV **(Unit 27)**

JUDY: How was your party?

KEN: Cool. We had lots of ~~goods~~ *good* CDs and ^*delicious* pizzas
~~delicious~~. It ended ~~on~~ *at* 3:00 ~~at~~ *in* the morning.
Did you have a nice weekend?

JUDY: No. I just studied for my ^*history* test ~~history~~ and
watched a ^*bad* video ~~bad~~.

KEN: What video?

JUDY: *The Bees*. It was the ^*most* boring movie in the
world.

KEN: You're kidding! My friends and I saw it and
loved it.

PART X

I **(Units 31–33)**

2. D 4. C
3. B 5. A

II **(Unit 31)**

1. He's going to watch.
2. They're going to attend a rock concert.
3. She's going to cook dinner
4. They're going to get married.

III **(Units 32 and 33)**

2. Is it going to snow
3. Where are Mark and Kathy going to go
on their honeymoon
4. Is Ken going to go to college
5. Who's going to drive you to the airport

IV **(Units 31–33)**

Dear Mary,

Thanks for driving us to the airport. We

arrived in Acapulco at 1:00 P.M. and went

right to the hotel. The weather is beautiful so

far, but it looks like ^*it* is going to rain.

Tomorrow we ^*'re* going to go swimming in the

morning. In the afternoon ~~are we~~ *we're* going to go

fishing out in the ocean.

When ~~you and Bill are~~ *are you and Bill* going to come with

us on a trip? We always have such a good time

when we travel.

The only thing I miss about Seattle is

baseball. ~~Our team is~~ *Is our team* going to win?

I'll write again soon.

Love,

Rose

INDEX